SUPPLY and DEMAND

MASCOT BOOKS
an imprint of Amplify Publishing Group

www.mascotbooks.com

Supply and Demand: The Development of Arlington and Fairfax Counties, 1649–1960

For more information, please contact:
Mascot Books, an imprint of Amplify Publishing Group
620 Herndon Parkway, Suite 220
Herndon, VA 20170
info@mascotbooks.com

Library of Congress Control Number: 2024917077
CPSIA Code: PRV1124A
ISBN-13: 978-1-63755-580-4

Printed in the United States

For David Reynolds, with thanks for the opportunity to write for Elan.

SUPPLY and DEMAND

The Development *of* Arlington *and* Fairfax Counties, 1649–1960

KAREN WASHBURN

MASCOT BOOKS
an imprint of Amplify Publishing Group

CONTENTS

PREFACE

This is the story of the development of Northern Virginia and its transformation from a remote frontier to an agrarian economy, and finally to a suburb of the nation's capital. It is about successes, failures, and the ideas of our predecessors, both good and bad. It is also about their rationale for all of the above, their habits and customs, many of which still have influences and ramifications on daily life in this area.

I first wrote this history as a series of magazine articles for *Elan*, published between 2010 and 2012. It was a downtime for Northern Virginia real estate sales, caused by the subprime mortgage crises and the Great Recession of 2008. Every social conversation seemed to be dominated by the subject of local real estate sales. That was not unusual, because for decades real estate sales have been a primary spectator activity in Northern Virginia. But this time the tone was different.

People were very nervous about the market, especially those who had purchased property at the inflated prices that prevailed during the first years of the twenty-first century. For too many, the American dream of homeownership had just turned into a nightmare. There was no way that homes purchased for the stratospheric prices commanded from 2000 to 2006 could be sold without a loss.

It was a very depressing time. Not just for homeowners who saw their largest financial asset decline in market value but also for the many people who based their livelihood on property sales. Real estate agents, mortgage brokers, and title companies were all suffering.

In the spirit of transparency, I must confess that I sell real estate for a living, but I am also a trained historian. I have researched and studied the history of Northern Virginia for the last thirty-five years. My primary focus has been on the day-to-day lives of the people who lived here and how different events affected them personally.

As a historian, I knew this economic downturn and fall in real estate prices was nothing new. And I wanted to deliver a positive message. It had happened in the area many times during the previous three centuries. And the good news was that while the economy could fall into the ditch, somehow it always recovered, albeit sometimes the recovery was long and slow. The time frames were never predictable. Ultimately, real estate prices would go up again and eventually surpass the top prices paid in the previous hot market.

At the time the history of the repeated rise, fall, and recovery of Northern Virginia real estate prices seemed to be a good subject for my articles. As I started this series, I thought I would just describe the high and low points of different eras. It was never intended to be an in-depth study of the local economy. Nor is it now.

It is a synopsis of the economic situations and real estate values from 1649 to 1960 and a more detailed description of how the population dealt with the different phases. I have added many facts and a few more eras in order to fill in some gaps in the original work. And while the area officially recognized as Northern Virginia includes four counties, for the purpose of this work, I use the term to define only the counties of Fairfax and Arlington and the city of Alexandria. My apologies to Loudoun and

Prince William, but to correctly research and add those histories would take me another lifetime.

In the course of my years studying local history, I have spent hundreds of hours in the archives of courthouses reading through many legal records. Those include deeds, wills, birth and death registers, tax records, and road order books. I needed to know who the players were before I could possibly attempt to interpret their lives and the times they lived in.

Chancery suits, cases filed with the Southern Claims Commission after the Civil War, diaries, letters, and historic photographs also provided an enormous amount of information on lifestyles and sometimes very valuable clues to peoples' inner thoughts and personalities. Various surviving company accounting records yielded many interesting facts. Newspaper and magazine articles and advertisements published during the times of the events covered were another valuable source of information, as were the copious works published by other historians on specific subjects.

In addition to the official and written records, I have used the great treasure of many people's personal memories gathered through oral history interviews. During the years I have been researching local history, I have had the privilege of interviewing many people. Their generosity and willingness to share personal experiences made history come alive. And I have very much appreciated access to the fine oral history collections of various libraries and historical societies.

Last, I must acknowledge the contributions of Edith Sprouse, Connie Ring, and Beth Mitchell. These ladies were the organizers, interpreters, and guardians of the Fairfax County Court Archives. I was extremely fortunate to have them as my mentors. They allowed me to have firsthand access to many fragile records. Many times I was permitted to untie the red tape binding a chancery suit that had been unopened since it was bound up a century or two ago. They taught me a great deal, encouraged me to publish, and never ran out of patience with my many questions.

During the course of my studies, I have learned several valuable lessons. First, history does repeat itself more often than we realize. It would be beneficial to society if more people would learn from the successes and failures of the past. And while circumstances and times are very different from those of the past, the one thing that has not changed is human nature.

Chapter 1

THE NORTHERN NECK PROPRIETARY

Northern Virginia has held an interest for many since it was first seen by John Smith in 1608. Having survived their first winter in Virginia, Smith, with fourteen colonists, sailed from Jamestown to explore the Chesapeake Bay. Along the way, they discovered the Potomac River and sailed up it as far as the Little Falls.

Unlike those who came later, their quest was not to acquire real estate but to seek a source for precious metals, furs, and other valuable commodities. On their return to Jamestown, in spite of finding no sources for gold or silver, Smith was very enthusiastic about the region's other riches. The forests were full of game, the river was full of fish, and furs were readily available to trappers and hunters. Even with this glowing report, it would be many years before any English settlers came to live on the land.[1]

In the beginning, the value of the land was questionable. The first group of nonnative landowners lived in England and France. They never visited the land nor did they reap any financial benefit from it. Through the centuries, the value of the land rose and fell according to the influence of many different factors, such as soil fertility, location, war, population, and individual financial stability. During this same time of changing property values, credit crises and major alterations in farming techniques propelled the region's economy through a series of peaks and valleys. Although the situations then were quite different from those of the modern era, a brief look at some of the historical highs and lows provides some interesting facts.

The story of Northern Virginia real estate began in 1649, when the exiled English king Charles II gave all the land between the Rappahannock and Potomac rivers to seven of his loyal followers. The gift was his way of expressing gratitude for his followers' loyalty during the English Civil War. The grant, known as the Northern Neck Proprietary, encompassed more than five million acres. Under the terms of the proprietary, the proprietors had the right to grant patents for acreage to others, who might want to own parcels of land, and to collect the quitrents, which were similar to modern-day real estate taxes.

No one really knew exactly how large the tract was or what resources it contained, so there was little basis for valuation. Only a few intrepid explorers had actually ventured into parts of the territory, and most of it had not been mapped. It was a lot of land without any European settlements.[2]

According to the economic law of supply and demand, this scenario fell into the category of large supply, little demand. Furthermore, one could even have questioned the right of the king to bestow title to the property since, at the time, he was dethroned. In today's world, the question of clear title would certainly be raised.

The granting of the Northern Neck Proprietary was one of those real estate deals that looked good on paper. For the deposed monarch, it had the advantage of appearing generous in magnitude while not costing him anything from his bankrupt treasury. No doubt the seven recipients of the gift hoped it had some value beyond bragging rights. And one does

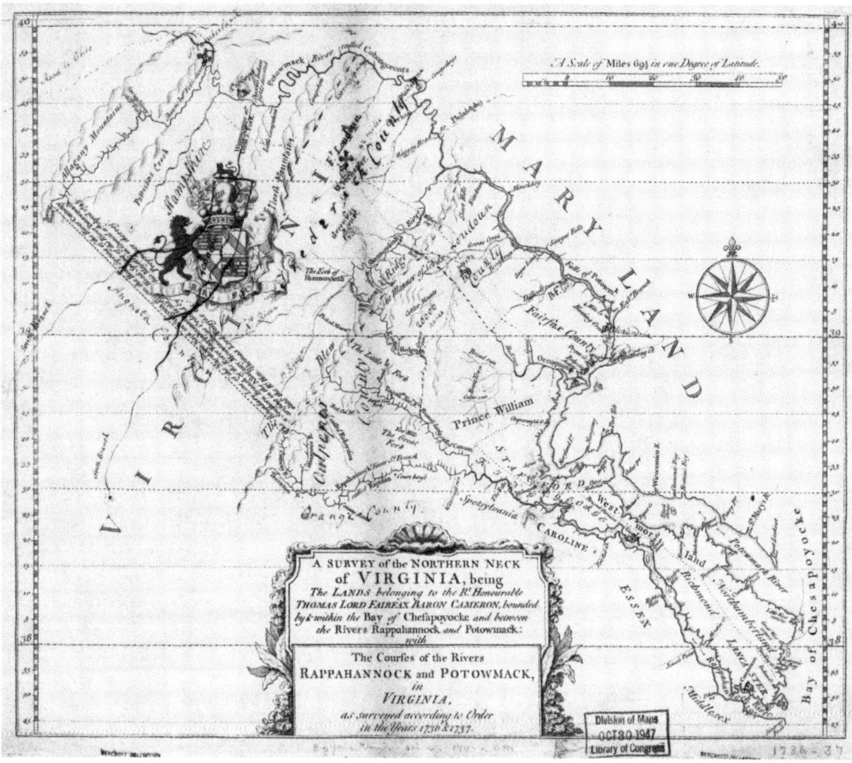

John Warner map created for Lord Thomas Fairfax, 1737

have to wonder whose idea this was because the king was only nineteen years old at the time.

One thing was certain: these absentee landlords would have to try to make a profit from afar. Most of them chose not to brave an arduous sail across the Atlantic Ocean and then live far from civilization in a place filled with unknown dangers. There was also the issue of the Native American inhabitants. Since they had inhabited the land for thousands of years, they claimed it. Meanwhile, the English colonial government of Virginia ignored any claims by either of the other "owners" and handed out land grants within the Northern Neck to the few people who applied for them.[3]

The first patent in the area that would eventually become Fairfax County was awarded in 1651 to Robert Turney for 2,109 acres. Other patents followed, usually for tracts bordering on the riverfront or deep creeks. About half of those claims were for parcels of 1,000 acres or more. The other half were more modest in size, around 500 acres. The largest patent was William Fitzhugh's Ravensworth tract, which was 21,996 acres. The sizes of the different patents were probably influenced by the patentee's ability to pay the quitrents of two shillings per each hundred acres.[4]

Only one of the original proprietors was brave enough to come to Virginia. Sir Dudley Wyatt arrived in Jamestown with his family in 1650 and died in 1651. It is doubtful that he ever visited the Northern Neck Proprietary. For the next twenty years, through different machinations of the English colonial government, the rights of the proprietors were infringed upon, and they did not collect quitrents. Ultimately, the government renewed the terms of the proprietary. By then the original seven recipients had died, leaving just six heirs as proprietors.

The land that comprised the Northern Neck Proprietary finally achieved a cash value in 1673. The colonial government was greatly concerned that such a vast amount of land was under the control of a private company. In an attempt to correct that situation, the government offered to buy the land from the proprietors for £400 per share. The government was not successful, but it set the stage for one proprietor—Thomas, second Lord Culpeper—to purchase all but one share. Finally, the heirs of the original proprietors made a little money. After a quarter century of ownership, it was not what one would call a quick return. On the other hand, there were no carrying costs associated with the land.

Upon the death of Lord Culpeper in 1689, his daughter Catherine inherited five-sixths of the Northern Neck shares. The remaining share went to his widow. Catherine married Thomas, fifth Lord Fairfax, who immediately took over management of the property and set out to make a profit. Recognizing that the land would gain in value only if it was settled, Fairfax appointed Robert "King" Carter as his land agent in 1702. An astute businessman, Carter was one of the richest men in

Virginia. He owned multiple plantations on the Northern Neck and made a huge profit from his tobacco exports to England.[5]

Robert "King" Carter

Carter's task was to promote the area within the proprietary and grant patents for parcels of land to those who were prepared to pay the quitrents. The owners of the patents were required to settle and develop the land. If they failed to meet the settlement criteria, the land reverted to the proprietor. Carter fulfilled his job well. In 1708, he forwarded to Fairfax £684 for one year's quitrents. He also was able to patent an additional 83,000 acres for himself. Included in those claims was the 762-acre Frying Pan tract (modern-day Herndon), where he established a copper mine.[6]

Ultimately, ownership of the proprietary was consolidated in 1719 through inheritance by Catherine's son, Thomas, sixth Lord Fairfax. By then the value of the land had appreciated as a result of settlement and the granting of patents; however, it was still almost impossible to assign a monetary value per acre or even per parcel. Added to that issue were numerous boundary survey problems—a true appraiser's nightmare.

In the early days of the proprietary, surveyors used ships' compasses to measure the metes and bounds of a property. And because most of the early patents were claimed along waterways, the surveyors would visit the property by boat. Unfortunately, due to fears of the unknown and attacks by the native inhabitants, the surveyors frequently did not get out of their boat. They conducted the entire survey from the safety of the water. A boundary line along a creek or ravine would be clearly defined; however, those

Lord Thomas Fairfax, sixth Baron Cameron

without fixed natural landmarks were very problematic. A survey might read that the line ran along the creek until it got to a corner marked by a certain tree. Since the surveyors were viewing said tree from a boat, there were often later debates as to which tree marked the boundary. In time, surveys became more sophisticated. The surveyors actually walked on the land, and the tree's bark was marked with slashes.[7]

Thomas, sixth Lord Fairfax, was the first of the proprietors to actually visit his holdings in Virginia. When Carter died in 1732, Lord Fairfax appointed his cousin William Fairfax to be his land agent. William claimed land on the Potomac River next to Mount Vernon and established Belvoir Plantation. Thomas arrived for his first look at Virginia in 1735. He stayed until 1737 at Belvoir. During that time, he explored the proprietary. By then settlement had spread into the hinterland as far as the Shenandoah Valley and he realized he should reserve some of the land for himself. He ordered different parcels to be surveyed and reserved about 162,000 acres for his own use.

Lord Fairfax returned to England in 1737 to settle his business affairs there, with the idea that he would soon return to Virginia. But one of his concerns was having his claim to the Northern Neck Proprietary confirmed by the English government. That took much longer than he had anticipated. It was not until 1747 that he was able to return to Virginia. During his absence, Fairfax County had been created in 1742 and named for his family.[8]

Chapter 2

TOBACCO AS LEGAL TENDER

While the various owners of the Northern Neck Proprietary were trying to find ways to reap rewards from their land, the population and the economy of colonial Virginia were growing. During the development of the seventeenth century, new business practices were established, some of which would ultimately exact a huge penalty from subsequent generations. A lack of currency eventually led to an economy based on credit secured by annual tobacco production.

English colonist John Rolfe introduced tobacco cultivation to the Jamestown settlers. Through experimentation, he learned to successfully cultivate the plant and harvested his first crop in 1613. He sent that crop to London, where it was very favorably received. The product, which had recently been introduced in various European countries, was in high demand and quickly became the cash crop of the Virginia colony. Once supply ships began returning to England filled with the precious weed, tobacco quickly surpassed currency as a medium of trade. Cultivation increased rapidly as Virginians raced to plant "money." In nine years, from

1618 to 1627, the quantity exported annually grew from twenty thousand to five hundred thousand pounds.[1]

Tobacco processing, curing, storing, barreling, and selling

Using tobacco as money had its drawbacks and led to numerous credit issues. Until the product was sold at auction in Europe, no one knew what it was worth. In a good year, the prices were high; in a year when the market was saturated, prices were lower. European countries imported tobacco from multiple locations, which made it hard for Virginians to know the market conditions. Although the purchaser and seller of any item might agree on how much tobacco was required to close the sale, neither could assign a monetary value to the transaction until the tobacco was actually sold. In the meantime, tobacco growers used credit notes against the crop to pay their debts.

Tobacco cultivation was a labor-intensive process that quickly debilitated the soil. Innovations such as fertilizers and crop rotation were still far in the future. Once the land was used up, more uncultivated land was required to produce a successful crop, a solution viewed as a bonus for the Northern Neck Proprietary. As the demand for land increased, settlers migrated from the Tidewater area, moving north along the Potomac and Rappahannock rivers. Still, settlement of remote Northern Virginia was impeded by the settlers' fears of the native inhabitants. This situation slowly began to change after the English colonial government convinced the Iroquois to accept the Treaty of Albany in 1722.

The Iroquois were a confederacy of six fierce, combative tribes from what is now Upstate New York. They annually raided through Northern

Virginia, pillaging, plundering, and killing those in their path, both native peoples and white settlers. The Treaty of Albany required the Iroquois to restrict their raids to the west side of the Blue Ridge Mountains; however, settlement in Northern Virginia was still hampered by lingering doubts that the Iroquois would honor the treaty.[2]

Another problem affecting tobacco cultivation was the lack of a labor force. To profit from the crop, landowners needed many strong hands to clear land, plow, plant, and protect crops from parasite damage. Once tobacco plants were ready to be harvested, they had to be cut, hung to dry, packed in large wooden barrels called hogsheads, and hauled to the docks for shipment to England.

Moving the hogsheads was a labor-intensive chore that required strong men to wrestle with a very heavy and unwieldy cargo. Hogsheads measured four feet tall and four feet across and weighed about one thousand pounds when fully packed. After a hogshead was packed, it was tipped on its side, and a pole was inserted end to end through the center as an axle. Horses, mules, or oxen could then be hitched to the hogshead to roll it to the shipping area. Landowners eventually resolved the labor shortage, but the solution came with long-term social consequences. In 1619, an English privateer ship landed in Virginia and introduced the colonists to its cargo of captured African tribesmen, whom it offered for sale as slaves. These unwilling immigrants, and many others delivered in the following years, helped solve the labor conundrum and were used to settle remote areas of the Northern Neck.[3]

Most patent holders of land in the Northern Neck Proprietary never moved to their property. Indeed, it is doubtful that many of them ever laid eyes on it. Eventually, these investors found ways to satisfy the requirements of settlement and seek profit without risking their own lives. For example, a landowner might send enslaved workers under the supervision of an overseer to clear and plant the land. Or he might farm-lease it to a family who was brave or desperate enough to move to the wilderness.

Rolling a tobacco hogshead to market

The lessee was required to inhabit the property, build a modest home, clear land for crops, and get the land planted within three years. The lease was in effect for the lives of three people listed on the document. It expired with the death of the "longest liver." Generally, the lessees were a husband and wife and one of their children. Such leases did not net landowners much income; annual rents varied from as much as twenty shillings—payable in money, tobacco, or some other commodities—to as little as one peppercorn plus labor provided to the landlord. What the landowner—or, in many cases, his heirs—ultimately gained was a piece of cleared, albeit worn-out, land when the lease expired.

At the close of the seventeenth century, tobacco reigned supreme in Virginia. There was very little money in circulation, and the economy was based largely on the barter system or on tobacco, which was considered legal tender. All manner of debts, including taxes, could be paid in tobacco, and the government used it to pay the wages of its officials. The dependence on tobacco as tender created a volatile and precarious economy. While many landowners worked hard to grow their own "money," they contended with fluctuating European markets and spotty tobacco quality. Bad growing seasons, bad land management practices, and bad processing produced some crops that were little more than trash weeds.

In an effort to gain tighter control over the colony's output, the Virginia colonial government enacted a control system for tobacco in 1730. Growers could no longer trade directly with purchasers. Official tobacco warehouses were established at key locations on navigable rivers. Growers were required to deliver crops packed in wooden hogsheads to warehouses where government inspectors assessed its quality. Once the tobacco was graded, it was stored in the warehouse to await shipping. The landowner was given a receipt, known as a tobacco note, for the quantity delivered. The tobacco note system certainly simplified the ability to make major purchases. On the downside, though, commerce was conducted with notes for which the cash value had yet to be determined.[4]

Throughout most of the eighteenth century, the net worth of a Virginian was calculated in land, slaves, crops in the field, tobacco notes, and various and sundry other personal possessions. It is surprising that an economy based on a commodity of such fluctuating value could work as well as it did for more than a century and a half. Perhaps it was because most of the population lived on self-sufficient plantations or farms, and even in a bad tobacco market people still had food, clothing, and shelter. To many Northern Virginians, actual money just wasn't that important. There were very few commercial centers, and individuals acquired what they needed from the land or through barter.[5]

During the second half of the eighteenth century, settlement expanded throughout the region, and commercial centers were established in numerous locations, including the deepwater port city of Alexandria, and Georgetown across the Potomac River. In spite of the growth, most of the area was still farmland, and the economy was based on agriculture. Although many farmers still used the barter system and tobacco notes to trade for goods, some transactions required actual money. Officially, values were expressed in British pounds sterling. In reality, money in circulation consisted of coins from many different sources, predominantly Spanish, French, and English. Because the coins were made of precious metal, it appears they were accepted for their weight, and no one got too excited about an exchange rate. But money was still rare in the region. Many people probably never handled more than a few coins during their lifetimes.[6]

In the third quarter of the eighteenth century, Northern Virginia's economy began shifting away from tobacco. The crop had depleted the soil to such an extent that it was becoming difficult to produce a product that would pass inspection at the warehouses. A century earlier, when there was still plenty of new land available, worn-out fields did not deter the planters. Now, with increased settlement, it was time for a change.

As the landowners took stock of their properties, they began experimenting with salable grain crops that did not deplete the soil as rapidly. Newly cleared fields were planted with wheat, corn, rye, or oats. Old fields were allowed to grow back into woodlands that would eventually provide timber. By the close of the eighteenth century, tobacco was no longer used as a medium of trade.

Chapter 3

TOBACCO SALES CREATE NEW TOWNS

One positive result of the tobacco trade was the development of towns along the upper Potomac. As the quest for fresh ground for tobacco cultivation enticed more settlers to push deeper into the Northern Virginia wilderness, the demand for local towns and commercial centers grew. Fredericksburg, established in 1728, was the northernmost town, which was a long way from the upper Potomac plantations. It was a lengthy journey for those who had to travel by horseback, wagon, or cart over rough roads that were adapted from Native American and wildlife trails.

In response to the increased settlement, several Scottish merchant firms competed with each other to establish trading centers in the region. These centers started as primitive trading posts located near the Potomac River, where settlers could obtain some of the necessities for life on their wilderness farms. As time passed and the population grew, the trading posts evolved into stores owned and operated by large Scottish tobacco trading companies. Those merchants also promoted the development of towns along the river to conduct their import-export trade. The Scots had their sights fixed on not only the local trade but also opportunities from as far west as the Shenandoah Valley.[1]

The location of official tobacco inspection warehouses played a major role in where citizens believed the towns should be established. The planters had to take their tobacco to the warehouse to be inspected and shipped. The first of these warehouses was in Alexandria. Plantation owners in the areas that would become Arlington, Fairfax, and Loudoun counties had been hauling their tobacco to the inspection warehouse there since about 1732.[2]

Owned by Hugh West, the Alexandria warehouse was sited where Hunting Creek met the Potomac. A ferry, a tavern, and several houses belonging to Scottish tobacco factors were also there. So why not a whole town? To that end, in 1748, local plantation owners sent a petition to the House of Burgesses in Williamsburg, stating that "inhabitants of Fairfax

A plan of Alexandria, 1749, George Washington

[are] praying that a town may be established at Hunting Creek Warehouse on Potowmack River."[3]

Lawrence Washington, from Mount Vernon, delivered the petition. It included a sketch drawn by his younger half brother, George, to demonstrate the advantages of the site. The fact that the landowners—cousins John and Phillip Alexander—were not initially enthusiastic about the proposed site doesn't seem to have caused too much worry to the petitioners. Ultimately, the Alexanders were persuaded to participate in the plan. The town was chartered on May 2, 1749. Next, a public auction was advertised for the sale of the town lots. Fairfax County surveyor John West had to scramble fast to get the sixty acres subdivided into lots bounded by streets and alleys by the auction date of July 13, 1749. Approximately fifty of the lots were sold at the auction. Many of the purchasers were those who had signed the petition. Alexandria was launched.[4]

The politically influential citizens who had petitioned for Alexandria lost no time in petitioning to move the Fairfax County Courthouse to their new environs. Much business was conducted at the county court, and many found its remote location near present-day Tysons to be very inconvenient. Moving the court was also a way to guarantee traffic into the new town. The petitioners were successful. The county court was moved to Alexandria in 1752.[5]

Tradesmen, shopkeepers, wealthy plantation owners, and merchants such as John Carlyle built family homes in the new town. Carlyle, one of the original petitioners, bought two lots at the auction. He started building a grand Georgian-style mansion for his family in 1751. The Carlyle family took up residence in 1753, and others followed suit.[6]

Over the next twenty years, docks, warehouses, shops, stores, taverns, offices, and other business buildings were erected in the town. Churches and schools were added as the population increased. Ships from Great Britain arrived regularly with cargoes of manufactured goods, tea, coffee, spices, and fabrics of all types. Ships from the West Indies brought sugar,

Carlyle House, Alexandria

salt, and rum. They left carrying tobacco and grain bound for England and Europe. At the same time, an intercoastal trade with other colonies was established. Among other commodities, wheat was shipped to Baltimore and Philadelphia to be ground into flour.[7]

The commercial success of Alexandria caused a rise in real estate prices not only in town but also in the surrounding countryside. It was deemed very advantageous to live near the town. Although the location of Alexandria suited many upriver farmers and planters, it was not very convenient for those from the southwestern part of Fairfax County. The latter watched the ships employed in the lucrative import-export trade sail right past their area without having a place to do business. Since they did not want to be left behind, these citizens applied for a charter for the town of Colchester in 1753.

The new town was to be located on the Occoquan River, a tributary of the Potomac. It would be near the intersection of two main thoroughfares: the Potomac Path and Ox Road. The Potomac Path, originally a Native American trail, was the main north-south route along the river. It eventually became Kings Highway. Ox Road was created by Robert "King" Carter to bring copper ore from his Frying Pan mines to the Occoquan River for shipping. When the mines failed, the road became a rolling road for tobacco hogsheads.

As early as 1690, a ferry to cross the Occoquan had been established about two miles upriver. A blacksmith's shop and tavern were built there shortly afterward. In that area, the Occoquan was deep enough for ocean-going vessels to safely navigate, so in 1734, a tobacco inspection warehouse was built just below the fall line and some distance upstream from the ferry. Ox Road connected with other rolling roads to provide access to the warehouse for farmers as far distant as what is now western Loudoun County. Because of the intersection of the two main roads, it was deemed that a site two miles downstream from the tobacco warehouse was a more strategic location for the new town. Alternatively, the choice for the town site may have been at the encouragement of the landowner, Peter Wagener, who was also the clerk of the Fairfax County Court.

The area dedicated to Colchester was much smaller than that of Alexandria. It had only twenty-five acres to be divided into forty-two lots. Unlike the popularity of Alexandria, only fourteen lots sold at the initial public auction. Perhaps that was an indication that it might have been more advantageous to locate the town at the site of the tobacco

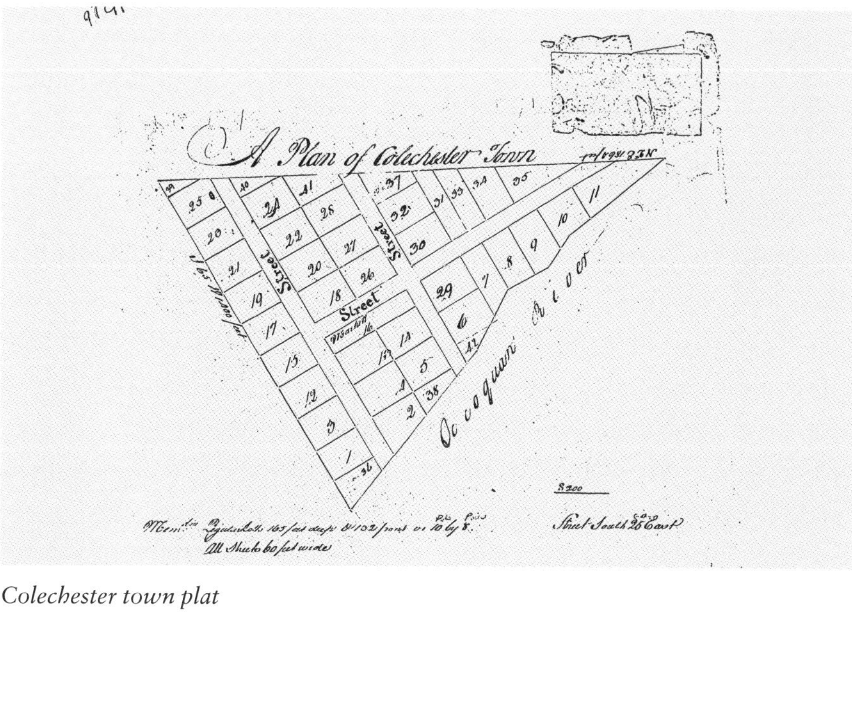

Colechester town plat

warehouse. Nonetheless, new taverns and houses were built on the lots that sold.[8]

The Scottish tobacco trading firm of John Glassford and Company established a store in Colchester in 1758. This company, based in Glasgow, Scotland, did business on both sides of the upper Potomac and had trading centers in numerous locations in Virginia and Maryland. As trade increased, so too did the quantity and quality of the products traded. When the town was only a decade old, the company's ships would arrive from England loaded with fabrics, rugs, blankets, clothes, wines, spices, coffee, tea, sugar, salt, dyes, tropical fruits, window glass, tools, locks, and other hardware. The ships departed with cargoes of tobacco, corn, wheat, flour, pork, hemp, lumber, iron, and furs. To facilitate loading, the tobacco inspection warehouse moved to the town in 1763.[9]

In spite of the commercial success of John Glassford and Company, Colchester did not create much competition for the merchants in Alexandria. The latter town was much bigger in area, had a much larger population, and served a wealthier clientele. It was also about sixteen miles upriver from Colchester. Alexandria's real competition was the Maryland settlement of Georgetown, eight miles upriver.

Located along the Potomac, just below the Little Falls, Georgetown had started in 1738 as a Maryland tobacco inspection warehouse and wharf. A deepwater port, it also had a ferry to cross the river. In less than a decade from its inception, the site had become very popular. Private warehouses, wharves, and a tavern had been built on the riverfront. The Maryland Assembly authorized the town in 1751. It was to be composed of sixty acres divided into eighty lots with intervening streets, lanes, and alleys. Like Alexandria, it was much sought-after. Sixty-nine lots were sold at the initial public auction. Merchants immediately began the construction of more wharves, warehouses, and stores. Houses were built, but at times settlement faltered. By the end of its first decade as a town, Georgetown was a fairly busy commercial center, but it developed more slowly than Alexandria.[10]

The Potomac River between Georgetown and Alexandria was a wide and formidable barrier. In the western countryside above the Great Falls, however, the Potomac was not nearly as wide or deep. There were fords and ferries in many locations. At times it was much easier for the Virginia planters and farmers above the falls to access Georgetown than it was to make the trip to Alexandria eight miles farther south. The almost simultaneous founding of these two towns created a mercantile competition that would continue for the next 150 years. Some of the results of this competition were great innovations and improvements in transportation for Northern Virginians.

Georgetown waterfront, c. 1820

Chapter 4

CREDIT-BASED ECONOMY

During the first two decades after their founding, the towns of Alexandria and Colchester had grown. Both had become busy trading ports for oceangoing ships and intercoastal trade with the other colonies. Colchester attracted most of its business from the southern parts of Fairfax and Loudoun counties, whereas most of Alexandria's trade came from central and northern Fairfax and Loudoun counties and the upper Shenandoah Valley.

Alexandria had far outdistanced Colchester in size and was a major regional port by the beginning of the 1770s. The town's population had increased dramatically as the original lots were subdivided several times to make room for new businesses, and real estate prices rose with the demand. On the river, new docks and warehouses had been added, and there was a very active shipyard for both new construction and repairs. There were more than twenty mercantile firms, eleven taverns, a commercial brewery, and a distillery.

Alexandria colonial buildings, Mason's Ordinary and Coffee House

It was a very prosperous time for the towns because the farms and plantations that were being established in the backcountry were doing well. The development of the towns seems to have encouraged more people to brave living in the areas farther inland from the Potomac. Fairfax County's population grew from 6,949 in 1768 to 8,310 in 1773.[1]

Along with the population growth came a change in farm crops. New settlers were turning away from tobacco and planting grain crops instead. There were several reasons for this change. Landowners were finally taking notice of how debilitating tobacco was to the soil. Also, many new settlers were leasing their land, and the leases at times forbade the cultivation of tobacco. Due to differences in the soil composition, tobacco grown in Northern Virginia was often not as good as that grown in the tidewater areas and didn't sell for top prices. There was also the fact that it took a very long time for planters to potentially realize a profit from a tobacco crop. They would plant it in the spring, harvest it in August, and hang it to dry. It was not until summer of the following year that it could be packed in hogsheads and taken to market.[2]

By the 1770s, there was a huge demand in Europe for North American wheat and flour. Wheat loaded on ships at Alexandria often went to Baltimore or Philadelphia to be ground into flour. From there, traditionally it had gone to the West Indies to be traded for rum, sugar, molasses, and salt. Now the European market for flour made wheat a very viable sales crop. In spite of the market for grain, the shift of cash crops from tobacco was fairly gradual. The large plantations were still growing substantial quantities of tobacco for export, and tobacco remained legal tender.[3]

All the business in both Colchester and Alexandria was run on a credit-based economy operated mainly by British trading companies primarily from London and Glasgow; however, the mercantile systems practiced by the traders from these two cities differed greatly in style. Traders from the English ports of Whitehaven, Liverpool, and Bristol also competed for tobacco, but they did not match the great quantities imported by London and Glasgow traders.

The London companies had served the import-export needs of Virginians from the founding of the colony. As time passed, many of the large-plantation owners still continued to conduct business in the same time-honored way with the London merchants, shipping them their tobacco and financing their lifestyles with tobacco credits. It sounds fairly straightforward, but there was nothing simple about the complex business systems employed in this trading style.

A tobacco planter with a large plantation would contract with a consignment agent in London, who would sell his tobacco and also fill and ship his orders for goods and supplies. It was a relationship that had to be built on complete trust by both parties. The planter was sending his main source of income to a stranger who he had never met in person and with whom he only communicated in letters, which could take two to six months to be received. The agents worked on commission and usually had to invest large sums of their own money to complete the tasks required to get the tobacco sold. They also had to guess how much it would sell for and to spend carefully to fill the planter's orders for goods. Because of the time lag involved and fluctuating market prices, the entire business was a gambling game.[4]

Planters would take their tobacco hogsheads to the warehouse, where after inspection the tobacco would be stored until it could be shipped. Since most planters did not harvest enough to fill a ship, it might be necessary to wait until other planters delivered their tobacco. The planter would then pay the freight charges and, if he chose, insure his shipment. At times the rates were so high due to wars or privateer activity that planters would risk shipping without insurance.

Once the tobacco reached England, the agent met the cargo at the dock, paid the import duties, arranged for warehouse storage, paid for the hauling and storage, and then set about arranging a sale. At times the import duties on the product were more than half of what it would eventually sell for. If there was a high demand, the tobacco might sell very quickly. But during slower periods, it might stay in the warehouse for months while the agent waited for market prices to rise.[5]

Meanwhile, the agent would set about filling the planter's orders for goods. Those orders encompassed everything imaginable to support life on a large plantation. Surviving records from George Washington and Robert Carter provide a glimpse into how dependent they were on England to provide them with not only luxury goods but some of life's necessities as well. It was the beginning of the mail-order business without the benefit of catalogs, photographs, or prices. The whole matter of quality, cost, and style was entrusted to the agent as a personal shopper.

Planters ordered clothing for their families, slaves, and indentured servants. Measurements might be sent for the family members, but the descriptions were somewhat vague—for example, "a suit in the current style out of the best cloth in a dark color." Or they might order hose or shoes "larger rather than smaller" and a lady's "fashionable hat or bonnet." Children's clothes were to be sized and styled suitably for their sex and age. No measurements were provided. The order might also include age-appropriate toys and books.

Fabric was also ordered, as were sewing notions such as pins, needles, different threads, multiple styles of buttons, and scissors. Luxuries for the ladies of the house were not confined to clothes, silk hose, kid gloves, hankies, and lace. The orders included different perfumes and many pounds of talcum powder, which ladies also used in their hair.

In addition to clothing, planters ordered hardware, window glass, nails, tools, horse tack and equipment, farm equipment, writing paper, seeds, drugs, and herbal medicines. Housekeeping necessities such as laundry supplies of starch, bluing, and soap were on the list, and so were candles and whale oil for lighting.[6]

Household furniture was also included. Washington ordered a tester bed of a certain length and specified that the bed draperies and coverlet were to be in a blue-and-white fabric, and window curtains to match with cornices. No other specifics, such as window sizes, were mentioned.

To complete their decorating needs, planters asked for paint supplies of turpentine, oil, pigment, and paintbrushes. One of Washington's orders included eight statues, for which he specified busts of famous historic leaders, such as Julius Caesar, Alexander the Great, and the Duke of Marlborough, among others. In this order, he was very specific as to sizes, except when he asked for "sundry small ornaments" for the chimneypiece and pictures for the walls.

Members of the planter class were also particular about how they set their tables. Silver serving dishes, cutlery, and candelabra, some with monograms, were requested in the latest style. Fine china and glassware for wine, dessert dishes, and servers were a requirement. And although the plantations provided the bulk of the food for the table, items that were not grown or made locally were ordered.

Those items included anchovies, capers, olives, salad oil, Indian mangoes, almonds, raisins, cheeses, candy, tea, and coffee. Multiple wines were purchased in large quantities, and Washington included a hogshead of the "Best Porter" in his order. Staples purchased for food preparation included white sugar, salt, mustard, and various spices.[7]

After receiving these lists of hundreds of vaguely described items, the consignment agent had to fulfill his role as personal shopper and set out to purchase the items. At times this involved dealing with more than forty different shopkeepers, tailors, and other artisans. There were no department stores at that time.

Once the items were purchased, they had to be packed in barrels for shipping. Export duties had to be paid, and the agent then had to find a ship sailing to the correct destination. Because of the sparse amount of settlement on the upper Potomac, this could require a long wait because the area was not a popular destination for ship captains. They much preferred the tidewater locations with larger populations.[8]

The cost of all this shopping, duties, and shipping was then deducted on the planter's balance sheet against the profit from selling his tobacco. Many times the bottom line reflected a large debt incurred by the planter, which was increased by the interest the agent charged. But no one seemed to get too excited about this debt because the agent and the planter shared the optimistic view that the next tobacco shipment would even things out. And if the debt got too large, the planter could always find a new agent. If the account remained in good standing, the planter could also withdraw his sale profits in sterling certificates, which he could use in place of money for large purchases, such as land or slaves.

Relationships between planters and their agents were frequently contentious. Because it often took ten to twelve months for planters to receive their orders, it was almost impossible for them to return any items that were not what they ordered or were broken in shipment, or items they didn't like. Planters complained bitterly about poor-quality merchandise or the price paid for it. On top of all the other chores assigned to their agent, planters expected the agent to seek out the best prices for their orders and bargain shop for them. They also complained about the price received for their tobacco and were free with their criticism of the methods used to secure the sale. On top of that, there were accusations of price-fixing and of usury for the interest charged on their accounts.[9]

Additionally, delivery to the wrong address was a major irritant to planters. If their orders were sent on a ship going to a different river, their merchandise could be left far from their home plantation. Then the planter would have to wait even longer to receive the order, plus pay high freight fees to have it delivered cross-country by wagon. Nonetheless, they continued doing business with their agents until the American Revolution halted the practice.[10]

The alternative to the English consignment agent for tobacco sales was the Scottish trading companies from Glasgow. While the English consignment agents remained in England, it was the shrewd Scots traders from firms in Glasgow who had the courage to penetrate the wilderness when Northern Virginia was first being settled. And the Scots traders' business model was quite different from that of the London agents. The traders' target market was the small planter or farmer who could sell crops outright to them for tobacco notes or sell for store credit. The traders paid higher prices on store credit sales.[11]

Scottish firms were willing to extend credit to the owners and tenants of small farms. They understood that new settlers would not have a crop to trade until they established their farm and got a crop planted, harvested, hung, and dried. The Glasgow firms extended credit to the settlers with no payment required for four years. That was the same policy every time a new debt was incurred. Settlers could purchase all the tools and items necessary to build and plant their new homesteads before their first crop was planted. And credit was an absolute necessity because no one had very much actual money.[12]

In order to force the colonists to keep their trade limited to British companies, English law forbade the export of English coins in bulk to the colonies. It also forbade the construction of colonial mints. So while the British monetary system of pounds, shillings, and pence was used for accounting purposes, many of the actual coins that were used in Virginia came from several different European countries brought in by sailors and other travelers. Therefore, even the wealthiest planters had very little real money. Everyone's lives were financed on credit to some degree.[13]

In the beginning, the Scots started with crude trading posts that carried only the bare essentials and were staffed by a company representative sent out from Scotland. These men negotiated the purchase of tobacco and retrieved their expenditures at profit when they sold the farmer the supplies he needed. As demand grew, these posts evolved into shops that carried a much larger selection of goods. Those included many luxury items, tools, firearms, all types of housewares, furniture, clothing, exotic foods, dyes, spices, tea, and coffee. The shop staffs also expanded to a supervisor, one or two clerks, and several slaves to move and unpack merchandise.[14]

As the population increased, so too did the traders' business, and more shops were opened in the towns. These shops accepted cash or would barter for salable items or services, but the bulk of their trade was done on credit.

Scottish traders were remarkably successful, and by the mid-eighteenth century controlled much of the mercantile business along both sides of the Potomac River. More company employees were sent from Scotland to work as tobacco factors, separate from storekeepers. The factors' sole mission was to negotiate crop purchases. In years of high demand, the competition was so stiff that sometimes tobacco was purchased before it was harvested.

As part of their jobs, these company representatives were required to send back detailed reports about weather, projected crop harvest, current tobacco prices, and orders for merchandise, along with a commentary on what the local lifestyle required. The representatives also passed along complaints about the quality and quantity of the merchandise the company had sent.

Alexander Henderson, who managed the Colchester store for John Glassford & Company, did not hesitate to express his complaints to the home office in Scotland when he sent letters with orders for new goods. His frustration at being supplied with poor stock is evident in his statement: "The ribbons sent are ill chosen, particularly the figured ones which are too broad and most despicable patterns. It is therefore hoped that this will be prevented." He also wrote, "The inhabitants of this country have large feet and must have large shoes—those sent out this year are much too small."

In another letter, he complained about the length of time it took to receive his orders and the condition in which they arrived: "Sundry packages have sustained damage; it has been a few days of five months from the time these goods were shipped at London until their arrival at Colchester . . ." Obviously, store management was not an easy job. And his irritation was well founded given the size and location of the company he worked for. In fact, it is surprising that the goods he received were shipped from London.[15]

John Glassford & Company, the largest of the Scottish firms, had stores established in every upper Potomac town. The stores were served by a fleet of at least twenty-five company-owned ships. The Scots even lured some of the great tobacco planters away from the London traders. There were good reasons for their success.[16]

Glasgow, the home port of the traders' companies, is located on the river Clyde in western Scotland. Not only is that location where the trade winds first hit Europe; it is also one hundred nautical miles closer to North America than any other British or European port and two hundred nautical miles closer than London. This location gave the Scots a tremendous advantage. With good winds, they could make the Atlantic crossing on average in five weeks or less, which was two or three weeks less sailing time than those leaving from other British or European ports.

Scottish trading companies' ships also had a very quick turnaround once they reached the Potomac ports. Because the tobacco was already purchased and stored, it was not difficult to accumulate a complete shipload. And because the company owned the ships, there was no need for protracted freight-fee negotiations. For the planters, there was the advantage of having an immediate sale and not having to wait for months to learn how much the crop sold for. The disadvantage for the planter was that the merchandise stocked by the shops was not as extensive or luxurious as that from London. But that does not seem to have prevented some of the owners of large plantations from using the Scottish companies for at least a part of their crop.[17]

Not surprisingly, by 1760, Glasgow was the premier tobacco port in Britain and far surpassed London in that trade. But that came with risks.

Colchester Inn

Chapter 5

REVOLUTION CAUSES ECONOMIC TRIALS

The American Revolution was many years in the making. It was not a plan hatched overnight by a few political hotheads. And while there are a few firebrands included in its history, the actual series of events that lead to the final act of revolt spanned more than a decade.

The American conflict with England began with colonists requesting their rights as Englishmen. What started as objections to high taxes levied on them by the mother county culminated in a full-scale war of rebellion. Ultimately, the colonists created a new country, and Britain lost one of its primary financial assets. The economic cost during the war years and the postwar period was suffered on both sides of the Atlantic.

In the period leading up to and during the war, most of Northern Virginia was still sparsely populated and fairly remote. British military forces did not occupy the region nor were any battles fought there; however, its remote location did not prevent local citizens from contributing to the fight for independence. Some men joined militias and became soldiers. There were others who agreed with the cause in principle but

George Mason of Gunston Hall plantation

did not necessarily feel the call to serve in the army. They felt they needed to continue working on their farms and plantations.

Fairfax County farmers provided food for the American army and pasturage for its cattle. Without a doubt, the most important local contributions to the revolution were the services of George Washington and George Mason. Nevertheless, no matter what role they pursued, Northern Virginians were not exempt from the economic impact of the war.

Virginia's economy was deeply entangled with that of Britain. The English had financed the founding of Virginia, hoping to make a profit from the colony. With the rise of the tobacco culture, many British merchants had indeed become very wealthy. The English government jealously guarded this source of wealth by severely restricting Virginia's colonial trade with other nations.

Virginians who could afford to enjoyed many imports, such as tea, coffee, silk fabrics, spices, and fine porcelain dishes brought from the Far East. All these items had to pass through British ports first. The same was true of other items, such as wine imported from various European countries. Only after the government collected import taxes could these items be shipped on to the American colonies through British merchant houses. Those merchants in turn received tobacco and other commodities from Virginia to sell on the European market. Those commodities were also taxed. This monopolistic arrangement was fairly well accepted by Virginians, with minor complaints until the mid-1760s.

New taxes imposed by England on the colonies were the catalyst that began a serious change in attitude toward the government. The English government had spent a fortune fighting a protracted war with France from 1757 to 1763 in both North America and in Europe. Britain won the war but found that conducting hostilities on multiple fronts had proved to be very expensive. Known as the Seven Years' War in Europe, in America the conflict was called the French and Indian War.

Northern Virginians were quite familiar with the French and Indian War because British troops had arrived in the area, ostensibly to protect the settlers on the colony's western frontier. Conversely, a major part of the British mission was to secure the Ohio country and Canada from the French. As frontier settlement pushed farther west, both the English and the colonists were anxious to obtain the rich commodities from those regions. Ultimately, England was victorious, and its chief goals were met, although it does not appear that the frontier settlements were any safer from the native tribes than they had been before.

Virginians had long had their eyes on the Ohio country. In 1748, Thomas Lee—with a group of investors that included John Carlyle, William Fairfax, George Mason, Philip Ludwell Lee, and brothers Lawrence and Augustine Washington—formed the Ohio Company, hoping to profit from the trade benefits of the region. In 1749, they received a grant from King George II for five hundred thousand acres. In order to retain the grant, they were required to populate the land with at least one hundred families, build a fort, and pay for a garrison to protect the settlers from the native tribes within seven years. For various reasons, that had not worked, but the investors still hoped to come up with a viable plan.[1]

At the time, furs, which were richly prized in Europe, were the main commodity from the Ohio country. For long-range investment, the land looked promising for grain cultivation. Surprisingly, this group of investors, who were mainly Northern Virginians, planned to use the port of Georgetown instead of Alexandria for their export-shipping location.

With the successful end of the French and Indian War, the investors had renewed hope of pursuing their Ohio plans. That was not to be. As part of the peace negotiations, the English government signed the Treaty of Paris with the French in 1763. The treaty appeared to be a benefit to the Virginians; however, also negotiated was a peace treaty with the multiple native tribes in the Ohio country that forbade English settlement in the area west of the Appalachian Mountains.

Once again the efforts of investors were blocked. To add insult to injury, the British Parliament began to impose new taxes on the American colonies to help pay for the war with France.

The first tax to be enacted was the Sugar Act in 1764. This law listed specific goods that could be exported only to Britain, including lumber. It also put high tariffs on items widely consumed in the American colonies. After much public outcry on both sides of the Atlantic, the act was repealed in 1765. It was replaced by the Stamp Act.

Perhaps best remembered as a cause of the revolution, the Stamp Act required a duty to be paid on every type of paper used in the colonies. Legal documents, newspapers, ships' papers to enter and leave ports, bills of lading, receipts for purchases, and bills for accounts due were all subject to the tax. The latter caused many shopkeepers to resort to barter to avoid taxation. Although it was not an expensive tax, colonists resolved to avoid paying it on the general principle of taxation without representation. The royal governor of Virginia even found a way to circumvent charging the tax.[2]

The Stamp Act was repealed in 1766—only to be followed by the Townshend Acts in 1767–1768, which levied taxes on glass, paper, paint, lead, and tea. While all these tax laws were short-lived, with the exception of the tax on tea, they did create some economic hardship on the residents of the thirteen colonies. More importantly, they instilled a deep anger in many citizens at the British government and gave birth to ideas of revolt.[3]

Northern Virginians stayed informed of the growing unrest in the northern colonies through news carried on ships that plied the intercoastal trade. In response to the Townshend Acts, Virginians instituted a nonimportation agreement for all British imports. It was hoped that this would cause the British merchants to lobby for a repeal of the taxes. Unfortunately, that was not a success. One Scottish factor reported to his company that all its stores on the Virginia side of the Potomac had the usual goods, and no notice was taken by purchasers of the nonimportation agreement. However, that situation was not to last for long. Much more severe economic limitations would soon be implemented.

In the decade preceding the revolution, the Scots did have some concern over the Americans'—particularly Virginians'—dissatisfaction with the British government. But things were much quieter in Virginia, especially in the backcountry of Northern Virginia, than in the northern colonies. To keep abreast of the political climate, the Scots required their factors and storekeepers to include news of the current conditions in their regular reports.

The men in the Scottish home offices were not overly concerned about an actual rebellion until it was almost upon them. They had become accustomed to reports of political unrest and firmly believed that if in reality it accelerated into open warfare, the British army would soon subdue the revolt. After all, it had not been too many years since they had experienced the British army at work in Scotland. So they believed the entire conflict would be short-lived and "normal relations" would soon be reestablished. In the meantime, it would be business as usual.

As Virginians were attempting to conduct business as usual, reports from Massachusetts told of growing problems. News of the Boston Tea Party in December 1773 was received in Virginia with mixed opinions. But it was the reaction of the English government to those activities that finally drove Virginia to take a stand. For various reasons, Boston had long been a hotbed of rebellion against the English government. When England closed the port of Boston and inflicted other punishments on its citizens, Virginians realized the same could happen to them. They had been complaining and arguing for some years about the denial of their constitutional rights as Englishmen to no avail.[4]

It was time to show support for the citizens of their sister colony. Virginians resolved to take more stringent actions to secure their rights as Englishmen.

This idea did not sit well with Lord Dunmore, the royal governor of Virginia. He retaliated by disbanding Virginia's local government, the House of Burgesses, in May 1774. But the burgesses refused to be disbanded. They met at the Raleigh Tavern in Williamsburg to continue their discussions. They decided to hold a special convention in August with representatives from each Virginia county to determine a course of action.

George Washington and Charles Broadwater were elected by the citizens of Fairfax County to represent them at the convention. A committee was formed and met in Alexandria to draft a document that would, in Washington's words, "define our constitutional rights."

George Mason served on that committee. He and Washington met at Mount Vernon on July 17 to complete the draft of the document that became known at the Fairfax Resolves. In addition to addressing the issues of abuse of constitutional rights and avowing support for the citizens of Boston, the document also called for no importation of British goods and no exportation of Virginia produce to Britain. The latter certainly got the attention of the Scottish mercantile houses.[5]

The embargo was not due to go into effect until September 1775. The time lag was caused partly by the mechanics of the meeting of the convention but also probably by forward planning. Virginia was an agrarian society, and the livelihood of most of the delegates to the convention was dependent on having a market for the crops they raised. They were also well aware of their dependence on British manufactures. So the delay gave everyone time to plan for hardships.[6]

Scottish traders instructed their storekeepers to sell off their inventory, to close credit to all except customers who would post bond, and to collect the debts owed. The last was easier said than done. With so little cash available, most customers could not pay their debts. Because the county courts had closed in 1774, there was no way to get judgments against debtors.[7]

Those attempts to collect on accounts due and the Scottish storekeepers' denial of further credit caused much ill will among their customers, who responded with varying degrees of violence. Merchants in Fairfax County were spared the worst of that which occurred in other Virginia counties. No stores were looted or burned, and no storekeepers were tarred and feathered as they were elsewhere. Nonetheless, the merchants feared for their safety.

Some had purchased land away from towns and decided to relocate to their own farms. Others had married native Virginia women, which gave them some measure of safety because they were accepted as permanent residents. A few hoped to continue with operating their businesses as usual. Still others closed up their stores and fled back to Scotland when the Virginia Convention ordered: "All natives of Great Britain who are partners, agents, factors, storekeepers for merchants of Great Britain to leave within forty days."[8]

Scottish storekeepers and tobacco factors were not the only ones who left. As the prospect of war became more of a reality, there were others who could not agree to a permanent break with the mother country. Branded as Tories, some of those people moved to Canada and others to England, where they were determined to wait out the rebellion. Among them were George Washington's neighbors, George William Fairfax and Sally Fairfax from Belvoir. They had gone to England on family business and were never to return to their Virginia plantation. George William's brother, Bryan Fairfax, remained in Northern Virginia but was a Tory.

Those citizens who stayed began to worry and take stock of how vulnerable they might be to different hardships. Most were not worried about starvation because they raised their own food, hunted, and fished. But they were worried about their economic well-being and their personal safety. This was especially true of the residents of Colchester and

John Carlyle, builder and owner of Carlyle House in Alexandria

Alexandria, who feared the British navy might come into the ports and take everything they had.

Many remembered the experience of having General Braddock's troops camped in Alexandria during the French and Indian War. Braddock had stayed in the Carlyle house for some time, planning his campaign against the French while his sixteen hundred soldiers ran wild over the town. Braddock's troops complicated things by assuming the role of a conquering army. John Carlyle tells the story well in a letter to his brother George:

> They differed, us & them, & by sum means or another came in so prejudiced against us & our country, so that they used us like an enemy country & took everything they wanted & paid nothing, or very little for it, & when complaints was made to the Comdg officers, they curst the country & inhabitants, calling us the spawn of convicts, the sweeping of the Gaols, etc which made their company very disagreeable—[The General and his party] lodged with me, he took everything he wanted, abused my home, & furniture, & made me little or no satisfaction.[9]

And they were supposedly there to protect the Virginians. What would happen if British troops came as the enemy?

Alexandrians were well aware of the violence that had occurred in Boston. Some residents moved farther inland from the port. Due to their lack of currency and the political instability, however, no one was buying property, and real estate sales were at a standstill. The exception was the

British merchants' property. It was taken as forfeiture to the state, which presented a good opportunity for local merchants to acquire it cheaply.[10]

For protection, a company of militias was raised. George Washington took on the task of drilling the members and attempted to make them into soldiers. A new local tax was levied on the landowners to pay for uniforms, arms, and ammunition for the company. To some who had opposed the British taxes, this might have been a case of "out of the frying pan and into the fire." They took little consolation that this tax was imposed by their own local government.

Among their other problems, the date for the embargo loomed large in the minds of the merchants and the planters alike. Many had hoped that the situation would be resolved before it was necessary to implement it. But the English government was not making any effort to ease the political tension. By the spring of 1775, it appeared the embargo would go into effect. The Scottish mercantile houses still believed the rebellion would be put down in short order, but they thought they should prepare for a year or two with no tobacco imports. So they were determined to purchase as much as possible before the supply was shut off.

On the other side, all the major tobacco growers were anxious to sell one last crop before their ready market was closed. This included both George Mason and George Washington, the authors of the very document that would close the market. Because of a late frost, the wheat crop was reduced in volume, but there were bumper crops of corn and tobacco. Neither boded well for the earnings from the produce. At least the Scots were buying.[11]

The Scottish firms put sail to every vessel they owned and leased all the others they could find. In Alexandria, there were soon no available ships because all vessels were leased. Ship decks that were normally used to carry other types of export cargoes were packed tightly with tobacco hogsheads. Due to the enormous quantity, the planters got greatly reduced prices for the crop, but it was better than nothing.[12]

Meanwhile, in Glasgow and London, the merchants had to contend with the glut they were causing on the European market. Prices bottomed out. Since this was the only way they had to attempt to collect on the huge amount of debt incurred by the Virginians, they had to get it right, especially the London consignment agents. All that uncollected store credit was estimated to amount to more than £1 million owed to the Glasgow tobacco traders by Virginians alone. And that did not include what was owed to the London merchants. It was a very large sum of money at the time—money they would never see except for the sale of the 1775 tobacco crop.

Because of the low sale prices in Europe, the savvy merchants decided to store the tobacco and dole it out when the prices rose. But storage was a major problem. Every warehouse in Glasgow was full. Every other building that could be rented for storage was full. There were ships in the harbor lying at anchor because there was nowhere to unload. The lack of storage forced some merchant houses to sell at rock-bottom prices. The result was a very depressed tobacco market and bankruptcy for some companies. Added to that was the extreme drop in Scottish exports from £260,033 in 1774 to only £46,637 in 1775.[13]

Some even came to believe that one of the primary causes of the revolution was to free the Virginians from their enormous debt to the British merchants.

In Virginia, the first effects of British retaliation were being felt. Lord Dunmore declared martial law in November 1775. This declaration had little immediate effect on Northern Virginia because the British army and navy were in the far-off tidewater. But Dunmore's second proclamation had a much bigger impact.

That proclamation offered freedom to any slaves who belonged to revolutionary citizens if they would serve with the British forces. This offer caused great consternation among Virginians in general, even those who did not own slaves. People feared a slave uprising that would result in the general killing of the white population. For the slave owners, even without a bloody uprising, the loss of the slaves would have a very negative economic effect. Enslaved workers were a major part of the planters'

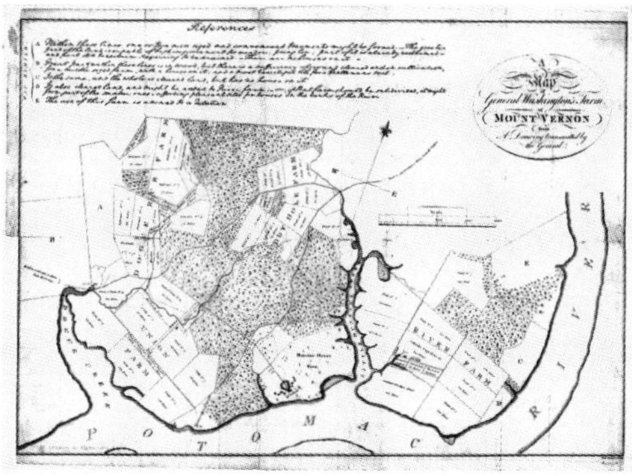

Map of George Washington's farms at Mount Vernon

labor force, and their monetary value represented a large portion of their owners' net worth. A small number of slaves did escape, but there was no general uprising, and few left Northern Virginia.

Lord Dunmore's acts continued to cause concern to the residents of Northern Virginia. Rumors in October 1775 that he was advancing up the Potomac with a large raiding force caused more inhabitants from Colchester and Alexandria to flee inland. He did not make it up the Potomac that time.

The following year, a British fleet stopped at Aquia and burned a plantation. They then sailed up the Occoquan and burned a flour mill and a few dwellings. They were repelled by the Prince William County militia before much more damage was done. Nonetheless, all throughout the war years, the residents of Colchester and Alexandria were never free from the fear of invasion.

The last time invasion was a threat was in 1781. George Mason reported that the British came within two miles of Alexandria, burning houses, plundering, and stealing slaves. On that same trip, they stopped at George Washington's Mount Vernon. The British had just landed a raiding party across the Potomac, which was burning houses in Maryland. They demanded supplies from Washington's caretaker and said they would burn Mount Vernon if he refused. Supplies were provided, and the plantation was saved, but seventeen slaves departed with the British.[14]

The largest impact of the British retaliation was the prevention of shipping into the Potomac River. British naval ships patrolled the waters of the Chesapeake Bay and the Atlantic specifically to stop trade with other nations. Virginians had voluntarily agreed to live without imports and had given up drinking tea because doing so was viewed as an unpatriotic act. They thought that with advanced planning they could survive the conflict without great hardship; however, there were two imports that they had neglected to stockpile or really take notice of: salt and sugar. Both of these items were important to their food supply.

Sugar was necessary for the production of alcoholic beverages, which were widely used in everyday life. Because water sources were often contaminated, most people drank small beer for their daily hydration. This beer, brewed in most homes, had a low volume of alcohol and did not easily cause inebriation. Even children and servants were supplied with it to replace drinking water. But it required sugar or molasses to brew it.

Salt was even more crucial. It was not merely a condiment used to make food taste better; it was the critical substance for meat preservation. Most of the salt Virginians used was imported from the British West Indies or Europe. Because it was cheap, little effort had been made to develop salt production in the colony. Now, with the normal supply route cut off, people resorted to harsh measures to get what they could. Those who had any salt began to hoard it. Salt became the target for armed robberies. In one year, the price for a bushel rose from two shillings to thirteen shillings or more. Blockade runners brought in some salt and sugar, but the British navy captured many of those who tried. If any did get through, the Virginia government purchased most of their cargo and distributed it in small quantities among the counties.

The scarcity of salt and sugar was finally eased in 1778, when the French entered the war to aid the Americans. Their navy ships helped to stave off British warships, which allowed more trading vessels to successfully run the blockade. Even with this help, however, key commodities, while no longer scarce, still remained in short supply, and prices remained high. With limited cash and useless tobacco credits, even the wealthy suffered.[15]

Despite having no local battles or occupation by the enemy troops, residents of Northern Virginia did suffer from the effects of the war. Their import-export economy was halted, and much business stopped. Gunpowder, shot, firearms in general, and many other manufactured items for comfortable living became very scarce. Farmers had very limited markets in which to sell crops. They could now deal with merchants from European countries but had to rely on those ships that could run the British blockade. Many farmers retreated into survival mode, especially since there were some bad crop years during the war.

A serious lack of coin money added to the economic woes of the region. The American government began to print paper money to fill the void for legal tender. Without a real treasury to back it, that money fell dramatically in value. By 1780, it was not worth the value of the paper it was printed on.

Northern Virginia may not have suffered from enemy occupation, but its towns and countryside did suffer from the occupation of the American army and that of their French allies. Large groups of soldiers, even those who were not the enemy, tended to be very hard on the area and its inhabitants when they passed through or were quartered there. Often, crops were trampled, fences broken, food items taken, and water sources contaminated or depleted. Added to that was the damage to the roads from the large volume of traffic. Although few records remain, it stands to reason that both Alexandria and Colchester suffered over and over from the armies passing through.

The war finally ended with the Treaty of Paris in 1783. The end of the war ushered in a new age for Northern Virginia. It was the start of a time of many changes for the region and its citizens.

Chapter 6

POST-REVOLUTION ECONOMICS

The success of the American Revolution caused many Virginians to anticipate a return to prewar prosperity. The British naval blockade was gone, and they were now free to trade with any countries that chose to send ships into the Potomac ports. Even better, they no longer would have to pay English duties on imports or exports. The wartime shortages were over.

Despite these benefits, the hopes of a surge in economic growth were not generally realized. While there were periods of prosperity in some sections, the next half century was one of much economic turmoil for the residents of Northern Virginia.

Alexandria rebounded from the ill effects of the war very quickly. In 1799, Congress awarded it the status of being an official port of entry for the upper Potomac. This status was viewed as a large advantage over other Potomac ports in Virginia because it meant that ships arriving from foreign countries could sail straight to Alexandria. They were not required to stop elsewhere to register or pay duties on the imports they carried. It also removed the temptation to sell those goods in other ports instead of making the long journey upriver. Unfortunately for Alexandria merchants, Congress had also conveyed the same status on their archrival, Georgetown.[1]

Business in Alexandria grew at a rapid rate for the next two decades but remained based predominantly on the import and export trades. Ships arrived there from many European countries, the West Indies, and other American ports.

Cargoes from Britain consisted of all types of household goods, furniture, tools, hardware, and sewing supplies. Ships from other European countries brought hats, shoes, umbrellas, and leather goods. Imports also included many luxury items previously only available to planters who dealt with London consignment agents. Now French wines, Italian olive oil, jewelry, and elegant European fabrics were available to everyone who could afford them. So were tea, coffee, liquor, cigars, exotic fruits, sugar, salt, and spices imported from the West Indies. Ships left Alexandria loaded with wheat, corn, flour, tobacco, and lumber for the West Indies and Europe.[2]

Tobacco production had diminished considerably in the postwar years. Prices had fallen from a prewar high of twenty-five shillings per hundred weight in 1770 to only thirteen shillings in 1788. The lack of production caused Alexandria to close two of its three inspection warehouses in 1793. The third, with a capacity of twenty-five hundred hogsheads, contained only three hundred ready for shipping.

Grain products and lumber were now Northern Virginia's primary exports. An increasing demand for flour in Europe and the Caribbean islands soon made it the top export. It rose in price from ten shillings a barrel in 1770 to thirty-one shillings a barrel in 1784. It also had to be inspected, and Alexandria gained a flour inspector in 1772.

Not all Potomac communities benefited from the postwar trade. The town of Colchester did not regain its prewar prosperity. While Alexandria attracted more businesses and residents, postwar Colchester consisted of only twenty houses and four mercantile establishments.[3] With the decline of the tobacco culture, local farmers no longer felt compelled to access the nearest town with an inspection warehouse, and Colchester did not get a flour inspector until 1819. Wagons loaded with grain, flour, or lumber were much more maneuverable than unwieldy tobacco hogsheads. As a result, many farmers preferred to go to Alexandria or Georgetown—both of which had much more to offer in the way of shops, commodity brokers, taverns, and entertainment.

Alexandria had turned into a boomtown. The population—estimated at 2,000 in 1785—continued to grow. In the next five years, the town's boundaries were enlarged. Its streets were paved with cobblestones, and there was much new construction. Buildings of frame or brick, some as tall as three stories, gave the town a substantial air of prosperity. The population grew to 2,748, and there were four hundred houses by 1790. In addition to the import and export companies, there were numerous artisan businesses that provided local goods and services for residents and visiting farmers. Many of these craftsmen had migrated south from Philadelphia and other northern communities when they fled from the British occupation during the revolution.[4]

New businesses included bakers, tailors, dressmakers, shoemakers, painters, rope makers, cabinet and chair manufacturers, and potters. There were also metalworkers engaged in gold- and silversmithing, engraving, and a factory making copper- and tinware. The shift in farm produce from tobacco to grain had also led to the establishment of numerous distilleries and a brewery. All this commercial expansion was certainly good for real estate prices in the town.[5]

In the last decade of the eighteenth century, the Potomac River shipyards had more marine artisans than any other river on the East Coast. In spite of the great influx of new businesses and residents, however, the town's economic base was still precarious. All the new businesses existed only to serve the residents of the area. No goods were being manufactured for export to other sections of the country or overseas. The town and its surrounding farm communities were totally dependent on the export of their crops and lumber as their sole source of income.[6]

In Fairfax County, many farmers were not doing well. Crop production was often low and of a poor quality. There were a number of reasons for this. Primarily, the tobacco culture had reigned for too long, and people were having trouble shifting their plantings to grain. While wheat was not as labor intensive as tobacco, it was more difficult to grow a good grain-producing crop. Some of the more progressive farmers had started that shift in the late 1760s.

In the decade before the revolution, George Washington had concluded that it was a bad idea to base his income on the success of only one crop, tobacco, and he had begun to diversify his plantations. He experimented with soil amendments and fertilizers and planted many different types of grain to determine which variety grew best. There were others who did the same, but they were the exceptions. Most farms were still suffering from worn-out tobacco fields.

With this lack of local production, the only way for Alexandria merchants to expand their economy was to attract more exports from the western counties of Virginia and, hopefully, the Ohio country. Alexandria was a very busy international port, but it lagged behind its two major competitors: Baltimore and Philadelphia.

The sought-after western grain trade started in northwestern Loudoun County and stretched westward into the Shenandoah Valley. Both of those areas had been settled by the Scotch-Irish, Germans, and Quakers who farmed tracts of two hundred to five hundred acres, did not practice the one-crop plantation economy, and were quite used to diversified farming. During the time that tobacco was a profitable commodity, farmers in the west country did plant tobacco, but for the most part those in the northwestern sector never dedicated their whole efforts to that one crop. By the 1760s, flour was the area's main export. Alexandria and Georgetown were the closest markets for the Loudoun County farmers.

Both vied for their trade, but Philadelphia and Baltimore were in direct competition with the Potomac towns for the Shenandoah Valley trade.[7]

The main commercial center of the northern Shenandoah was the town of Winchester, founded in 1744. Strategically located on the Great Wagon Road that ran from Philadelphia down the Shenandoah Valley, the town was situated to become a major trading center for the valley's farmers. And because many of these settlers had migrated from Pennsylvania, they had an affinity for Philadelphia. But because the road had evolved from an Indian trail, it was not an easy route to travel, and it was a very long journey to Philadelphia from the Shenandoah Valley. Baltimore merchants who were competing to attract that trade had the same problem of bad roads. The roads to Alexandria were also in very primitive condition, but the town was closer to Winchester.[8]

The Alexandria flour merchants aggressively set out to win the trade competition. Most flour was shipped to commission agents in town, who charged 2 percent of the sales price to sell it for the farmer. In the beginning, these agents sent out representatives to meet wagons on the road coming into the town to garner farmers' business. That quickly evolved to sending representatives to Winchester to make advance arrangements. The commission agents also advertised in the Winchester newspapers. And although prices paid for flour in Alexandria were not as high as those offered in the other cities, the freight costs to ship it to that port were about half as much as to the others.[9]

Their methods were successful. The amount of flour exported from Alexandria rose dramatically from five thousand barrels in 1783 to one hundred thousand barrels in 1803. But Alexandria still lagged behind Philadelphia and Baltimore. And while the valley farmers might ship their flour to Alexandria, Winchester's merchants ordered all their imported stock from Philadelphia and Baltimore. The Alexandria merchants believed that if they could only find a way to improve their access from the west, they could win both the flour and import trades.[10]

Farmers in the northern regions of Fairfax and Loudoun counties often opted to go to Georgetown instead of Alexandria. Aside from the fact that Georgetown was closer to their farms and therefore easier to access, the tariffs charged on salt, coffee, sugar, and distilled spirits were cheaper in Georgetown. Alexandria merchants constantly protested to the Virginia state government about those high tariffs. They complained that lower tariffs gave Georgetown merchants a great advantage; however, probably due to the large amount of port traffic at the Alexandria docks, the legislature did not feel any need to heed those pleas for lower rates.[11]

Nonetheless, citizens of Alexandria were hoping for a great economic boost when the town was included within the boundaries of the newly formed District of Columbia in 1791. On the recommendation of George Washington, Congress approved a site ten miles square on the Potomac as the location for the capital city of the United States. The new federal district was drawn from land ceded by both Maryland and Virginia and also included Georgetown. The federal district was divided into two counties: Alexandria and Washington.

Alexandrians were hoping that future residents of the new city would want to shop for all their furnishings, clothing, and daily needs in

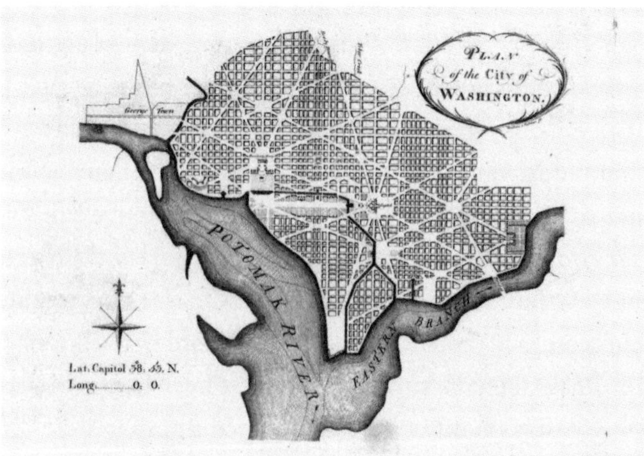

Plan of the city of Washington by Pierre L'Enfant and Thackara & Vallance

Alexandria. They didn't believe that the wide-open expanse of the Potomac River might discourage these potential shoppers. They certainly knew that Georgetown, as usual, presented competition, but it was some distance away from the area designated for the new city. Plus, it required travel over rough cart tracks that were often so muddy they were impassable. Hopefully people would prefer a boat ride over the river to do their shopping.[12]

But the new federal city would take some years to build. In the meantime, the merchants of Alexandria turned their attention to the ongoing problem of attracting western trade to their town.

Chapter 7

THE PATOWMACK CANAL

From the beginning of Virginia's colonial settlement, people had much preferred water travel to that on the primitive roads. That worked well in the tidewater areas of the rivers, but not above the fall lines. This is certainly true for the Potomac River. Owing to natural conditions, the river becomes unnavigable a short distance above Alexandria; therefore, it was not a viable route to bring western trade into the town.

Upriver from Alexandria, the first obstacle is the Little Falls, about three miles above Georgetown. A few miles above that, the Great Falls presents an even more formidable barrier. There the river falls more than seventy feet in the course of one and a quarter miles, with its swift current shooting through and over a wide and jagged rock formation. Further upstream, travel is impeded by other areas of smaller falls, white water rapids, sand and gravel bars, and shallow areas over solid rocks in the riverbed. But there are long stretches of calm water between the barriers. These navigable sections encouraged some to dream of finding a way to open the Potomac as a transportation corridor.

George Washington was one of the main proponents of opening the Potomac as a water route to the Ohio country. He started his quest in 1754 while serving in the Virginia militia during the French and Indian War. Seeking a practical way to move military supplies to the upper Potomac region, Washington set out in a canoe from Cumberland, Maryland, to explore that possibility.[1]

On his way downriver, he encountered and recorded the many obstructions that would prevent continuous river navigation. Since he and his party were traveling by canoe, they were able to go ashore and carry the canoes when their progress was blocked. After they circumvented the obstacle, the canoes were relaunched. They paddled on; however, this method of travel was not practical for boats loaded with cargo. But the trip did start Washington thinking about how to bypass the obstructions and open the river to boat traffic.

After the close of the French and Indian War, Washington's focus shifted to moving cargo downriver and bringing valuable produce from the Ohio country into Potomac River ports. For the next twenty years, Washington researched and collected much information on how to accomplish this goal. Working with others, he studied methods used to build canals in Europe. He also realized that both Maryland and Virginia would have to agree to legislation to build any type of river navigation project. He spent time negotiating fairly successfully with their governments. Just when the project was ready to launch, the Revolutionary War started, and he had to turn his attention and energies elsewhere.[2]

When the revolution ended, Washington returned to the project with great enthusiasm. With the economic shift in the region from tobacco production to grain, it seemed more important than ever to draw the produce from the west into the Potomac River ports.

Other entrepreneurs from Maryland and Virginia had various schemes to open the river. After consulting with them, Washington set up complicated negotiations with the governments of both states. Fortunately, they were united in the fear that if they couldn't provide reasonable

Potomac Canal lock in Great Falls National Park before restoration

access to the ports of Georgetown and Alexandria they would lose the valuable western trade to Philadelphia. That fear carried the vote in favor of Washington's plan.

The Patowmack Canal Company, with Washington as its president, was chartered in 1785 to provide a river navigation route from Cumberland, Maryland, to Georgetown. This endeavor would involve the construction of dams and five skirting canals, as well as the deepening of river channels. The canals at Great Falls and Little Falls would require locks. This very ambitious enterprise was plagued by a great many problems during its construction. Ultimately, it took seventeen years to complete, which was years longer than its founder had envisioned.[3]

The entire project was built with human labor using picks, shovels, and black powder for rock blasting. Deepening river channels often required blasting through solid rock. The work was difficult and dangerous. Progress was often slowed by a lack of able-bodied laborers. Workers included slaves hired from their owners, new immigrants purchased as indentured servants, and freemen, some—such as stonemasons—with construction expertise. Laborers were promised rations of one pound of salt pork, one and a quarter pounds of salt beef or one and a half pounds of fresh beef or mutton, one and a half pounds of flour or bread, and three gills (twelve ounces) of rum or whiskey per day.[4]

Poor management led to many lost workdays, as did problems with runaway indentured servants and slaves. Freemen frequently deserted due to low wages and poor living conditions. The promised rations were often not delivered. Workers were expected to carry on their backbreaking physical labor without anything to eat. At times their living quarters consisted of nothing more than shelters built out of tree branches, with leaves to shelter them from rain and snow.[5]

Injury and death also depleted the workforce. Many of the laborers were unskilled at the jobs that they were required to do, at times with disastrous results. When the canal company superintendent, James Rumsey, made a request to the company treasurer for a new supply of blasting powder in July 1786, he glumly reported the following:

> Sir We have Been much Imposed upon the last Two weeks in the powder way (we had our Blowers, One Run off the other Blown up) we therefore was Obliged to have two new hands put to Blowing and there was much attention gave to them least Axedents *[sic]* should happen yet they used the powder Rather too Extravagant.[6]

While this message seems to convey that getting the job done was more important than the safety of the laborers, he did add an explanation of sorts to clarify his problems with the workforce:

> But that was not all they have certainly stolen a Considerable Quantity as we have not more by us than will last until tomorrow noon. Our hole troop is Such Villians *(sic)* that we must for the future give the powder into Charge of a person appointed for that purpose to measure it to them on the ground by a Charger.[7]

Added to these labor problems and continual theft of supplies was a constant lack of adequate funding.

Throughout the years it took to build the canal, Washington was often on-site to check on the progress of the work up and down the river. He was very hands-on in his inspections. Occasionally, when traveling by horseback, he would ride up to the falls of the Shenandoah or Harpers Ferry and arrange to have canoes available so he could personally test the deepened channels. Because he had lifelong experience, he was able to handle a canoe skillfully and did not hesitate to shoot through white water and rapids.

More frequently, Washington visited the canal construction at Seneca and Great Falls. Those projects were only a half-day's ride from his home at Mount Vernon. Having spent much of his life in the saddle, he didn't seem to mind riding in all types of weather. His compulsion was so great to view and supervise the project that he rode to these areas in blistering heat, rain, sleet, and once in snow that was a foot deep. He usually stayed at Towlston Grange, the home of Bryan Fairfax, but occasionally he had to stay in one of the workers' huts at the falls. At times, while he was at the construction site, he had only laborers' rations to eat.[8]

After many struggles and much hard work, the river route was opened in 1797—except for the locks at the Great Falls canal. Among other problems, those locks had to be blasted sixty feet down out of solid rock. To speed up the work, the superintendent decreed that the men boring holes for the black powder charges should accomplish a minimum of six feet per day, or their whiskey ration would be withheld.[9]

Anxious to open the waterway, the canal company constructed an inclined plane parallel to the river to accommodate horse carts. Riverboats could then stop at the Great Falls basin and unload their cargo, which could then be carted down the incline and loaded onto another boat below the falls. This process was not ideal, but it did allow for a much quicker trip to market than struggling over the roads. The locks finally opened in 1802. Canal business tripled. Sadly, Washington did not live to see the completion of his project.[10]

As Washington had predicted, shipping by water was the fastest and cheapest way to move western commodities to the ports. By boat, shipping only cost about half as much as shipping by road, and it was much faster.

Three main types of riverboats were used to haul cargo. The most popular were flat-bottom boats that only drew about twelve to fourteen inches of water. These boats were generally between sixty and seventy feet long and seven to eight feet wide. They were usually staffed by a crew of four: a point man, two men on the sides with oars or poles, and one man in the stern with a long steering oar. Log rafts were also favored for their shallow draft. Some keel boats that drew more water were also used. Those craft were propelled by the current and by men using poles.[11]

All three types of riverboats could carry approximately eight to twenty tons of cargo, depending on their type. In later years, some boatmen tried larger craft—both longer and wider—that drew twenty-four inches of water and could accommodate larger cargoes. In comparison, the wagons in use had a maximum capacity of about six tons. The boats could go from Cumberland to Georgetown in three to five days, while the wagons would take about ten days. And the horses or mules pulling the wagons had to be cared for and fed, which incurred an additional expense, especially when they got to a town where stabling fees had to be paid.

Flour was the primary cargo carried on the riverboats, along with whiskey, wheat, corn, pig iron, furs, and eventually coal. Flat-bottomed boats and log rafts were constructed with wooden pegs and bolts and were built to last only for the downriver trip. When they reached Georgetown or Alexandria, they were broken up and sold as lumber.[12]

The keel boats took on manufactured goods, guns, fabrics, sugar, salt, and various groceries to make the return trip upriver. It was a difficult trip. The boats were mainly propelled by men pushing them forward with poles stuck into the river bottom or side banks. In some areas, iron rings were anchored to large rocks on the shore, and the boatmen could run a rope through the rings to pull the boat forward. James Dickey, a lifelong river man from Great Falls, later recalled that poling a boat upriver "was the hardest work ever done by man." If all went well, the trip upriver took ten to twelve days of constant struggle against a powerful current.

The opening of the canal had a positive economic impact on some areas, starting with the employment of the riverboat men. They were paid more than any other laborers for doing this skilled and dangerous job.[13] If a boat was not steered properly, it could easily go aground, collide with rocks, or get into a rough current and capsize. All those hazards could cost human life and the loss of or damage to the cargo. Even if the boat remained upright, there were still risks. Flour had to be inspected and would not pass if wet.

Other new employment opportunities created another economic benefit. The canal company required lockkeepers, traffic managers, and toll collectors. Because the canals and river channels needed constant maintenance to stay open, there were jobs for masons, blacksmiths, carpenters, teamsters, cooks, washerwomen, and general laborers.

Some riverfront locations also benefited greatly from the influx of travelers the canal brought. New riverfront warehouses were built for farmers to store their produce until it could be shipped. At the Great Falls, a new town was established. Because of the complex lock system, it was necessary to construct a large holding basin for boats waiting their turn. During peak season, they had to wait long hours to pass through the locks.[14]

Henry "Light Horse Harry" Lee, of Revolutionary War fame, saw the potential real estate opportunity this constricted location provided. He believed that once the canal opened, boatmen would need food, shelter, and perhaps entertainment while they waited to go downriver. Canal company supervisors and employees would also need a place to live. To that end, Lee leased a forty-acre tract of land beside the canal from Bryan Fairfax. Lee called the town he established Matildaville.[15]

During the construction of the canal and locks, the area was used for workers' huts and toolsheds. But by the time the town was officially chartered in 1790, it was a very busy commercial center with a gristmill, sawmill, forge, and warehouses along the riverbank. In the actual town, there were taverns, an inn, stores, a few houses, barracks for canal laborers, and the canal superintendent's house and office.[16]

The residents of and visitors to the new town also brought some new income to the surrounding countryside. Local farmers were able to sell food supplies to the canal company to feed its workers, and to the inn and taverns in Matildaville. They also benefited from the canal because they could very easily ship their produce to Georgetown without making a long wagon trip.

In the broader economic picture, the canal accomplished its original primary purpose of bringing western produce into the Potomac ports. Alexandria's grain exports almost doubled after the canal opened; however, records do not reveal how all the grain arrived in Alexandria, so all of that business was probably not solely based on canal traffic. There were multiple methods to ship to that town. And although its volume of exports was far less than Alexandria's, it does appear that Georgetown may have derived a greater benefit from the canal than Alexandria did.[17]

One of the main reasons for Georgetown's benefit was that the skirting canal at the Little Falls was very close to Georgetown. Alexandria was a further eight miles downriver. Along the way, the river got much broader and deeper. Canal boats designed to last for only one trip down the river through shallow water were not well suited for the tidewater Potomac. Many boatmen were unwilling to risk their cargoes—or maybe their lives—to go to Alexandria.

In spite of its early success, the Patowmack Canal system was plagued with recurrent problems from the beginning. Floods caused the channels, canals, and locks to constantly fill with silt, gravel, boulders, and tree trunks that had to be removed. Lock gates were subject to wood rot and frequently required repair or replacement. Keeping the river channels and canals open became a huge problem for the canal company. The tolls collected were not sufficient to pay for all the labor necessary to do the required maintenance work.[18]

When the route first opened, boats could use it nine or ten months a year. By the 1820s, the channels had become so shallow that only those boats that drew ten to twelve inches of water could navigate the entire route. This became particularly significant in extended periods of drought when, in many places, the depth lowered to less than one foot. Eventually, boating days were reduced to only twenty-five to thirty-five days in the spring and eight to ten in the fall. The limited travel days combined with the necessity of using smaller riverboats caused a large drop in tolls collected.

To make matters worse, advanced engineering techniques and successful canals built elsewhere led potential investors to favor the construction of a new still-water canal that would parallel the Potomac from Georgetown to Cumberland. All these factors caused the Patowmack Canal to close in 1828.[19] The town of Matildaville slowly faded away. The Virginia side of the Great Falls once again became a remote and obscure region.

Dickey's Tavern, early Matildaville building

Chapter 8

THE ROADS TO ALEXANDRIA

When the Patowmack Canal closed, Alexandria's biggest obstacle to attracting western trade was the lack of good road access. Roads into the interior of Northern Virginia had long been a point of major concern and contention. When settlers first penetrated the wilderness, they used trails that had been developed by Native Americans. Over time, and with increased settlement, more roads were required and established.[1]

These roads were not constructed in a true sense. In most places, they were no more than dirt trails where trees had been removed. They were widened where necessary to accommodate the width of a tobacco hogshead or a wagon. There was no surface treatment, except at times in low, boggy places, where small trees were cut to lay across the muddy surface. While this corduroy method prevented wagons from being mired in the mud, it made for a rough ride. And due to wood rot, these areas required constant repair. Bridges were built over some creeks. Several of the larger ones had ferries, but most had to be crossed at fords.

Georgetown Pike near Scott's Run, a typical Virginia muddy road, c. 1915

All these factors made overland travel slow, difficult, and at times dangerous. At best, traveling in any type of animal-drawn conveyance was extremely uncomfortable and very hard on the human body. Mrs. Browne, an Englishwoman who traveled from Alexandria to Leesburg in 1755, recorded the following comment in her diary: "The Roads are so Bad that I am almost disjointed." The following day she remarked that she "was so stiff that I was at a loss to tell whether I had any Limbs."[2]

Originally, the colonial government had been in charge of opening new roads; however, it had not given much attention to the transportation needs of the more remote areas of Northern Virginia. The area was too far from the capital in Williamsburg, it had a limited population, and the colonial government had no practical way to enforce road laws. To solve that problem, a road act was passed in 1748. It delegated all responsibilities for roads to the county governments. And because the counties did not have a workforce or the money to hire one, they passed along road maintenance work to local residents.[3]

The new law required every able-bodied man who lived within two to three miles of a public road to provide labor to work on the road for a certain number of days every year. And workers had to bring their own tools. An overseer of the road was appointed in each area to make sure residents complied. Those who did not were fined. No able-bodied man was exempt.

Those who could afford to do so could hire someone to do their work or send their slave labor. Even George Washington sent his farmhands to work on the road. While this plan may have seemed expedient to the county, it didn't work particularly well. Roads were often barely usable or completely impassable. The county court dockets were crowded with cases of failure to do the required roadwork. No one liked to work on the roads. Residents complained constantly to the government about the requirement.

In the decade before the revolution, Scots merchants in Alexandria and Colchester were actively working to attract trade from the grain farmers in the western counties. This additional traffic caused the roads to deteriorate badly. Large, heavily loaded wagons with narrow wheels cut deep ruts in the dirt roads. In dry weather, the roads were thick with dust. When the roads were wet, they were a morass of mud, at times more than a foot deep.

The Virginia government finally acknowledged the residents' complaints. A new road act was passed in 1772. County residents were still required to put in their roadwork time, but larger and more difficult construction projects, such as bridge building or creek ford maintenance, could be outsourced. To pay for those jobs, a new tax was levied. This did not please any of the county residents. Not only were they required to work on the roads, but now they had to pay a tax for them too.[4]

After the revolution, Alexandria merchants petitioned the state government for better roads leading into town. While the counties still retained responsibility for the roads, it was obvious that they were not going to be able to get any of the main routes improved. The Virginia

Assembly passed new road acts in 1785 and 1787. These acts provided for the widening and straightening of the two main east-west roads from Vestals Gap (now Route 7) and Williams Gap (now Route 50), from Winchester to Alexandria. To finance the project, they put up gates and charged tolls to use these roads.[5]

Citizens who lived along the road were outraged. They were already being taxed at a special rate to maintain the roads. They were required to work on the roads. And now they had to pay to use the roads? All this effort appeared to be only for the benefit of commuter traffic passing through on the way to Alexandria and ultimately for the profit of the merchants. Residents made their voices heard by refusing to provide the necessary labor for the roads. The impact of their revolt was so great that the road act was amended to allow local traffic to use the roads for free if the distance traveled was a quarter mile or less—a very small concession. Residents in some areas became adept at avoiding toll gates while using the main roads.

While the Alexandria merchants were struggling to get their road access improved, so too were those in Georgetown. A group of private investors formed the Georgetown Bridge Company to build a bridge across the Potomac River. Incorporated in 1791, the company was chartered to build a bridge just below the Little Falls in the location of the current Chain Bridge. After delays for several years to accumulate the necessary funding, the company was successful. The Falls Bridge opened as a toll bridge in July 1797.

As the bridge was under construction, a toll road was also being built along the Maryland shore to connect the bridge to Georgetown. When the bridge opened, the way was clear for farmers from the northwestern section of Virginia to reach Georgetown without having to depend on a ferry. But there was still the issue of the terrible condition of the road to the bridge on the Virginia side.[6]

Not to be outdone by its rival, Alexandria took proactive steps to compete. The county and state governments were frustrated because no amount of additional requirements for local citizens to maintain roads had improved their condition. The resolution to the problem was privatization of the highways. The Virginia General Assembly granted its first private road charter in 1796. Company shares were sold to raise construction capital. Income for maintenance and shareholders was to be provided by tolls. With that began the era of Northern Virginia turnpikes, which lasted for more than a century.[7]

Turnpike companies usually acquired a fifty- to sixty-foot-wide right of way. It often included an old established road. These routes were then widened and straightened to allow for a twenty-foot width of pavement and an untreated summer road next to it. As the name implies, summer roads were only to be used in dry weather, but they did allow faster traffic to pass that was traveling at a slower rate.

New methods were employed to reconstruct the old surfaces. The roadbeds were excavated, stone foundations were laid, and the top of the road was paved with gravel or water-bound macadam. The latter process involved laying stone dust on top of the foundation stones and rolling it while it was wet to bind the stone dust with the underlying stones. Road building was very labor intensive. All the work was done by men with shovels, picks, and some blasting powder. Mules and horses were used to drag large rocks and trees out of the way and to pull rollers.[8]

The first of these private roads to be completed was the Little River Turnpike in 1806. It connected Aldie in Loudoun County to Alexandria. A few years later, the old roads over the mountains via Ashby Gap and Snickers Gap were also chartered as private turnpikes to connect with the Little River Turnpike. The new roads provided access for western trade to Alexandria Williams Gap (now Route 50) from Winchester to Alexandria.[9]

Two more road companies were chartered in 1813. Alexandria merchants and others founded and financed the Alexandria and Leesburg Turnpike Company. They hoped to secure the trade from the northwest by building a new road from Alexandria to Leesburg using parts of the old Vestals Gap road, later the Middle Turnpike Road. This road had been the main east-west route from Alexandria through Leesburg to Winchester. It had been in use since the beginning of European settlement but was not a particularly direct route. Due to natural obstacles, it tended to meander to provide the easiest way around large rock outcroppings and access to the best creek crossings. In addition to improving the surface, the goal of the turnpike company was to straighten the route by removing large rock formations and bridging creeks.

At the same time, not to be outdone by their archrival, Georgetown merchants and investors founded the Falls Bridge Turnpike Company. Like its competition, this company was taking over and improving an older route, the Sugarlands Rolling Road, which gave access to the new Falls Bridge. The company had great hopes of finishing its project first and garnering the trade from Leesburg and beyond.

The Falls Bridge Turnpike Company's route was much shorter than the proposed Alexandria Leesburg Pike. It was only fourteen miles long, stretching from the Potomac to intersect with the Alexandria Leesburg Pike near Sugarland Run. Unfortunately, the job proved to be much more difficult than anticipated. The terrain was very steep in many places, and the route passed over large areas of solid rock. In addition to these problems, there were large creeks in deep valleys that had to be bridged.[10]

As with many new endeavors, the entrepreneurs had seriously miscalculated the time and expense required to build the road. They had trouble finding and keeping a labor force and supervisors. Slaves, freemen, and indentured servants were all used at times. There were long periods when construction stopped due to labor, funds, equipment, or bad weather. Eventually, the road was completed. The Falls Bridge Turnpike—now the Georgetown Pike—opened in 1822 but was not completed until 1827.

To some degree, the turnpikes were a success. They did provide an easier and more direct way for farmers to get their crops to market; however, with the exception of the Little River Turnpike, none of them were profitable. The companies often went out of business. The roads would then fall into disrepair, which made travel very difficult. Eventually, a new company would be founded to reclaim the road. New investors would fund repairs and resurfacing in hopes that the tolls collected would provide a profit, but that was usually not the case.

Nonetheless, these roads had a great economic impact on Northern Virginia. The western grain trade into Alexandria increased dramatically, but so too did trade into Georgetown. It is difficult to determine which town won the competition for the western trade. At times, when a road was in bad shape, farmers traveled on the road that provided the best conditions. Sometimes Alexandria lost business to Georgetown and vice versa, especially during the periods when the bridge at the Little Falls was out. Heavy use and river flooding required that bridge to be replaced several times. But farmers who lived along the roads tended to remain loyal to the town that was easiest to access. Those in northwestern Fairfax County and northeastern Loudoun County continued to trade mainly in Georgetown for the next century.

In addition to providing a way to market, the turnpikes promoted the development of local businesses and, in some locations, new towns and villages. Many new taverns, inns, and drovers' rests were established to accommodate the needs of those taking produce to market. Along with

Dranesville Tavern on the Alexandria–Leesburg Turnpike, c. 1900

food and shelter, businesses developed that catered to the transportation needs of travelers, such as blacksmiths, wheelwrights, and wagon repair shops. Grist and flour mills, hauling companies, and distilleries to provide spirits for the taverns and inns were among the ancillary trades that expanded when turnpikes opened. The ever-moving traffic allowed many people to develop a way to make a living without having to farm.

As the towns competed in taking proactive measures to attract business from the west, all was not well in the surrounding countryside of Northern Virginia.

Chapter 9

FROM ECONOMIC MELTDOWN TO FULL-SCALE DEPRESSION

At the close of the Revolutionary War and during the struggle to create a new nation, some old English customs were abandoned. Spurred by land-poor plantation owners, Virginians used their new freedom to discard the practices of entailment and primogeniture.

During the colonial era, much of the property in large landholdings was entailed, which meant that it could not be sold but must be kept within the family. The practice of primogeniture dictated that the heir—usually the oldest son—inherited everything. These practices did keep large tracts of land intact, but at times they kept the owners land-rich and otherwise short on assets. After 1800, the land was usually divided among all heirs. This situation soon became one of the causes that led to a fall in real estate prices.

At first, the sale of smaller parcels to farmers who could not afford a larger piece of land seemed a positive outcome; however, soon there was too much land for sale, most of which was in poor condition due to bad farming practices, extensive tobacco cultivation, or the presence of clay and rocks. Much of the farmland was unplanted and idle. Travelers through the countryside found the land to be derelict and desolate. Massachusetts congressman Manasseh Cutler traveled through the area in 1802 on his way to inspect the locks at Great Falls and reported that "indolence reigns and the country through which we passed the picture of laziness, negligence and poverty."[1]

Other visitors shared the same opinion. The general dilapidation of the farm country had a negative effect on the region's agrarian economy. To make matters worse, there were a limited number of potential purchasers for farmland. Because most of the land had originally been claimed in large tracts, many farmers had passed through Northern Virginia on their way to western lands. There they could stake their claims to own property instead of leasing it. These independent souls did not want to be tenant farmers. In the post–Revolutionary War years, more western lands in Ohio and Kentucky were opened for settlement. Many residents opted to abandon their worn-out Northern Virginia farms in favor of fresh land.[2]

Migration to the west was not the only cause of the area's diminishing population. Closer to home, the lure of town life and new jobs attracted many from the countryside. Washington, Georgetown, and Alexandria were growing. And all offered job opportunities to those who elected to abandon the hard work of farming.

At the start of the century, the city of Washington was just beginning to be built on previously vacant farmland. The new capital city took many years to develop. For its first twenty years, it was little more than a crude, rough-and-tumble village of shacks mixed with a few nicer homes. At strategic locations, the White House, the Capitol, and several government buildings stood. All were in various stages of completion. The primitive streets were a morass of mud, tree roots, and stumps, making travel dangerous during the daylight hours and positively treacherous after dark. There were very few shops, homes, inns, boardinghouses, or entertainment venues.[3]

Alexandria, on the other hand, at age fifty, appeared to be the sophisticated grande dame of the upper Potomac; therefore, the merchants and shopkeepers in Alexandria were able to profit by supplying goods, services, and entertainment to the early Washingtonians who were willing to cross the Potomac. Due to the poor roads, it was not an easy trip. People could travel by ferry, cross on the Falls Bridge, or, after 1809, use the new Long Bridge—now the Fourteenth Street Bridge. Alexandria had a growing number of silversmiths, tailors, dressmakers, cabinetmakers, bakers, brewers, and distillers. There were also numerous mercantile establishments that offered imported goods and groceries.[4]

Opportunities for entertainment consisted of theatrical plays, concerts, privately hosted parties and balls, and a few other amusements of a less genteel nature. Some congressmen even boarded at Alexandria inns and private homes because there were so few houses in Washington. And the boardinghouses there offered poor accommodations at very high prices.

Away from the environs of Alexandria, the economy of Northern Virginia was declining. From the earliest time of settlement, various entrepreneurs had attempted schemes for different types of industry. Plans for mining, manufacturing, and milling all met with varying degrees of success. It became apparent that the region was not particularly rich in any type of ore, so mining was abandoned. Manufacturing had limited success, depending on the product. Because manufacturers tended to produce items for local consumption, their opportunities for profit were confined to a very small market.[5]

Milling, the best of the industrial operations, was dependent on the crop production rate. As grain became the primary crop, more mills were built. Mills tended to be very local because a load of raw grain took up more room in a wagon than barrels of flour or meal. Sending a finished product to market saved time and freight fees. New, larger merchant mills were established in some areas, where farmers could sell their raw grain to the miller. After processing it, the miller would hope to sell it for a profit.

Colvin Run Mill, Great Falls

Grain milling was dependent on the weather. Drought spelled disaster for millers as well as farmers; not only was there less to mill but often there was not enough water in the streams to turn the mill wheels. With the advent of the steam engine, wool and cotton mills were introduced into the region, but neither was profitable in the long term. Sawmills also converted to steam power. They proved to be more profitable than those producing fabric.

The lack of successful industrial or manufacturing elements for export caused Northern Virginia to retain its agrarian-based economy. Some of the more progressive farmers diversified their crops by adding orchards and vegetables. Others added beef cattle, sheep, hogs, and fowl. The growing towns provided markets for those items. Mainly due to poor farming conditions and recurrent years of drought, however, the economy of the area continued to sink year by year. In the 1830s, the decline culminated in a full-scale national depression.[6]

In addition to the low demand for real estate, the end of the tobacco era and the demise of the large plantation had triggered another consequence. As the large plantations were divided among heirs to an estate, so too were the slaves. Without the labor-intensive tobacco crop, the ownership of these human "commodities" changed from an asset to a liability. Many landowners had too many slaves, a dilemma that was not easily solved. Slaves were personal property, and the owners were required to pay an annual tax for each one. By law, the owners also had to provide them with shelter, food, and clothing.[7]

Shelter and food didn't usually cause large problems, but clothing did. Most farms and plantations had cabins for slaves and food was produced on the land. But clothing and shoes cost money. Clothing was valued, and even slave owners usually only had a few outfits. Unless they were very wealthy, they tended to wear them until they were beyond repair. An indication of the value of clothes is the numerous wills that include named heirs for the deceased's clothing.[8]

Many slaveholders in the area had come to believe that owning another human being was morally wrong and wanted to end the institution. Fairfax plantation owner Henry Gunnell summed up his feelings in his will probated in 1822: ". . . to all my children to use those negroes given to them in a humane manner for I think slavery a cruel thing in the reached *[sic]* world, who can account for it?"[9] However, acts of manumission presented many problems, including how the freed people would find their most basic needs of food, shelter, and clothing.

Robert Carter III, grandson of Robert "King" Carter, was one of the first to take action on the idea that slavery was an abomination and, in 1791, set about freeing more than five hundred people who he owned. About fifty of them lived on his Fairfax County properties. Because of his great wealth, Carter was able to initiate a plan to make sure that those he freed would have a way to live. Very few other owners could afford to make provisions for those they freed.

Some settled their consciences by freeing their slaves in their wills, thus passing on all the problems relating to manumission to their heirs. George Washington followed that plan and freed 123 people in his will.[10]

Large-scale manumission got to be more difficult after 1806, when a state law was passed that often prevented slave owners from granting freedom to more than a few individuals. Under the new law, slaves could not be freed unless they possessed the funds to move out of Virginia to a free state or territory. Freed people who wanted to remain in Virginia had to apply to the county court for permission, a request that was rarely granted. Those who were allowed to stay generally had a skill that was deemed to be of value to the community, such as carpentry, cabinetry, or blacksmithing.[11]

The law does not seem to have been very strictly enforced in Northern Virginia, and several others wrote wills that freed numerous enslaved people. Among them were William Fitzhugh, who freed sixty-one, and William Henry Gunnell, who freed thirty-two. Many other owners freed between one and five people. Some even provided for specific individuals to inherit money, small parcels of land, or an education in another state.[12]

It is difficult to know the true number of freed people who chose to remain in Northern Virginia. The law required them to register with the county circuit courts every three years, but many did not. The US census may provide slightly more accurate numbers. In 1830, the number of free Black people reported for Fairfax County was 311. But that was far surpassed by the number in Alexandria of 1,201. There were probably many more living in the Fairfax farm country than were counted, but census taking was an inexact task. Those who didn't want to be counted could easily avoid the census taker. At times manumission was not a guarantee of freedom for the formerly enslaved. They could still be vulnerable to capture by "slave catchers" from other areas and sold back into slavery in another state. Therefore, many local free people chose to avoid public notice.[13]

Owners could sell their slaves, but some were very reluctant to do so because most of the market for human chattel was on cotton plantations in the Deep South. Often, generations of the owners' families had grown up and lived in close proximity to generations of their enslaved families.

On the large plantations, slave quarters resembled small communities and housed multi-generations of families. In some cases, this caused a mutual affection to develop. Although many owners did sell their slaves, numerous others were not willing to participate in the extreme cruelty of breaking up families as an antidote to their own financial woes.

Unfortunately, the final decision to sell was not always left up to the slave owner. The circuit courts would often order slaves to be sold to satisfy debts or to settle an estate. In spite of the excess population in Northern Virginia, slaves were still valuable. Their sale was a ready source of cash to pay debts, settle the estates of the deceased, or provide an income for owners of derelict plantations. The cotton planters in the Deep South provided a strong demand for laborers who could tolerate working in extreme heat and humidity. And just like the Virginia tobacco planters of the previous century, they believed slavery was an easy fix for their labor needs.[14]

There were numerous slave traders in Northern Virginia, Georgetown, and in the city of Washington to handle these sales. Depending on how many people were to be sold, the owners could hold an auction, consign them to other auctions, or sell them outright to a trader.

The largest firm for human chattel in the entire country was Franklin and Armfield in Alexandria. Advertising in the local newspapers that they would pay the highest prices, the proprietors constantly searched the countryside of Virginia, Maryland, Delaware, and the District of Columbia for slaves who might be for sale. When they had assembled a large enough group in their Alexandria slave pens, they sent them to the slave market in New Orleans either by ship or overland. It is not surprising that many slave owners found this to be an abhorrent practice and struggled to find another solution to their situation.[15]

To alleviate the problem of too many people to support, those owners not willing to sell could hire out their slaves by the year. And some owners allowed their enslaved workers to keep the money they earned to purchase their freedom. This arrangement worked well when the enslaved person

Original Franklin and Armfield slave pen, Alexandria, Virginia

was a trained house servant or possessed a craft or skill. It was not as viable for the untrained. They were hired as unskilled laborers to dig canals and ditches and generally were used to build the new government buildings in Washington. But as time went on, the labor pool shifted more and more toward indentured servants and freemen. By the 1820s, there simply was not enough work for hired enslaved laborers.[16]

Some slave owners salved their consciences and lessened their financial burden by leasing gangs of laborers to planters in the Deep South. No matter which option was chosen, this cruel and unusual practice that had once seemed an easy fix to the labor shortage now presented a socioeconomic conundrum of major proportions.[17]

Added to the other problems of the region was a credit crisis. Real money—which was gold, silver, or copper coins—was always scarce during the colonial era. After the revolution, some states issued their own money; however, there was no universal denomination. This made rates of value difficult to determine from one state to the next. A dollar in

Virginia was worth a different amount than a dollar in Pennsylvania. Even after Congress authorized the Philadelphia Mint in 1792 to produce a universal American currency, coins remained in short supply. As a result, Americans continued to use European currencies. Spanish coins were the most prevalent, including the dollar and various coins of lesser value. English and French coins were also widely used.

Early in the nineteenth century, the Commonwealth of Virginia had issued charters to various banks in Alexandria. During the War of 1812, there was a greater than usual shortage of coins. The banks solved the problem by printing their own banknotes for various denominations. But these notes were not backed by anything more than the bank's assets and reputation. This created an unstable basis for their value.[18]

The purchasing power of money was certainly well demonstrated when banks found it worthwhile to issue notes to represent as little as two cents, rising through increments of one-quarter cent. To circumvent counterfeiting, these notes were printed on elaborately engraved backgrounds. By the time the war ended in 1814, everyone had grown accustomed to this paper money, which was commonly called *shinplasters*. When more coins came into circulation, the banknotes also remained in use.

Northern Virginians also used personal notes to pay their debts. Often scribbled on any convenient scrap of paper, these notes promised to pay the bearer the agreed-upon sum by a certain date.

Many times the noteholder wanted his cash earlier than the note's due date. He would offer the note for sale at a discount. The next noteholder might do the same. Each time the note changed owners, it was further discounted. If the original debtor was clever and had cash in hand, he could purchase back the note for much less than he had originally agreed to pay. In cases of default, the noteholder could go to court and get a judgment against the debtor. Real estate and personal property were then sold to satisfy the judgment.[19]

Unfortunately, the sale of a debtor's property often brought a price too low to satisfy the debt, a circumstance that could cause the debtor to be prosecuted and sent to prison. Social position did not protect anyone from debtors' prison. The famous and wellborn suffered the same fate as the common man. Bankruptcy offered no protection from the penalties of the law. Revolutionary War hero Henry "Light Horse Harry" Lee, a prominent Virginian, went bankrupt and was forced to spend time in prison.

As residents' personal fortunes fell, the economy of the region followed suit. With no Uncle Sam to bail them out, banks suffered debilitating losses from unpaid loans and went broke. The paper notes issued by those institutions were then worthless.

By the mid-1840s, much of Northern Virginia presented a bleak picture of worn-out fields, unemployed laborers, and derelict dwellings. In some cases, whole farms were abandoned. From the earliest settlement, much of the land had been cleared of the native woodland. Many plantation owners had retained virgin forest areas, called *wood lots*, to harvest timber for building, fence construction, and firewood. Now the cleared fields were reverting to woodland and growing field cedar and scrub pine trees interspersed with thick tangles of briars and other weeds. The wood lots remained untouched, since there was not much market for lumber.

The price of real estate fell so low that land was practically being given away. Some properties were offered for as little as $1.56 per acre. But no one really seemed to want them at any price. By 1840, there were 30 percent fewer people in Fairfax County than there had been in 1800.[20]

Added to the list of economic failures was the decline of Alexandria. The town's economy depended on its maritime trade, which was often adversely affected by distant world events. In an era in which world trade was dependent on sailing ships, much could go wrong while crossing the oceans. Bad weather was always a concern. There also was the danger of pirate and privateer attacks. Between 1792 and 1801, French privateers and warships captured twenty Alexandria ships.[21]

More negative trade effects followed due to a war between the English and the French. Even though the United States remained neutral,

French warships began to seize American mercantile vessels, which made sea travel even more dangerous. Then the English began to stop American ships and capture American sailors to impress into the British navy. In retaliation, Congress passed the Embargo Acts of 1807, which prohibited American ships from trading in any foreign ports. These actions stopped much of Alexandria's commerce and deprived grain farmers of their largest markets. Alexandria and the farmers got a brief reprieve from their economic woes when the acts were repealed in 1809. Though that was short-lived, as the United States went to war with Britain in 1812.[22]

Maritime commerce was once again impeded when the Royal Navy blockaded the Chesapeake Bay. Not only did they stop ships; they landed raiding parties as well. This caused great worry to the residents of Alexandria and those along the Potomac riverfront.

The residents' fears were proved correct when the British army invaded and burned much of Washington on August 24, 1814. At the same time, a British naval force was working its way up the Potomac to Alexandria. Fearing they would suffer the same fate as the capital city, the town surrendered. British commodore Gordon agreed to leave the town's homes and shops unharmed in exchange for all merchant ships in the harbor and all merchandise stored in warehouses awaiting export.

The British navy departed Alexandria with twenty-two ships and all the warehouse goods. It was a huge haul. Because the blockade had prevented shipping for two years, there was an enormous stockpile of tobacco, flour, cotton, beef, wine, sugar, and other items. It took three days to load it all on the ships. The town was saved, but it was a major economic loss for the merchants, shipping companies, and farmers.[23]

Aside from international hostilities and war, the fortunes of Alexandria also suffered from various domestic crises. Fire was a constant problem. There were numerous losses of single homes and businesses throughout the years. Those losses were limited compared to the two major conflagrations that occurred less than twenty years apart. A fire on the waterfront in 1810 caused major damage to warehouses and docks. But even worse was the fire of 1827, which destroyed at least fifty-three houses and numerous businesses.[24]

Throughout its history, the residents of the town were often subjected to epidemics of life-threatening diseases, such as yellow fever, cholera, and typhoid. In the first five years of the nineteenth century, four outbreaks of yellow fever occurred in Alexandria. Those epidemics not only claimed many lives; they also caused many people to flee the area. Some residents elected never to return.[25]

The War of 1812 had caused much financial hardship, but Alexandrians were not willing to give up their hope of being a major seaport. The town continued to grow and add new businesses. Within three years following the end of the war, there were six banks, seven bakers, two sugar refineries, two potters, a brass foundry, two nail factories, and two shipyards, among many other businesses. And the merchants were still pursuing their quest to attract western trade.

In addition to developing new roads, the merchants were still looking for an open waterway. When the Potomac Canal was superseded by the Chesapeake and Ohio Canal (C&O), it appeared that Georgetown would derive the main benefit from that route. Those canal boats, which were pulled by horses or mules on a tow path bordering the canal, were not going to use the Potomac to go to Alexandria. Not to be outdone by their rival, Alexandria merchants lobbied to get a connection to the C&O Canal so they could share in the western trade.

Congress chartered the Alexandria Canal Company in 1830. Its aims were to build an aqueduct to carry canal boats across the Potomac from Georgetown to Virginia and to build a canal along the Virginia shore to Alexandria. Unfortunately, Alexandria was far behind Georgetown in its pursuit of canal traffic. The C&O Canal opened from Georgetown to Seneca in 1830 and was operational to Williamsport, Maryland, by 1834. The Alexandria Canal was not completed until 1843. After that, Alexandria did enjoy a share of the C&O traffic.[26]

Owing to the advent of steam engines, coal now surpassed the grain crops as the main commodity shipped from the west. Unfortunately, neither the canal traffic nor turnpikes brought in enough trade to elevate Alexandria to a great shipping center. And while the rivalry for trade continued between Alexandria and Georgetown, Baltimore was far ahead of both towns as a major seaport.[27]

Aqueduct Bridge with Georgetown in the background, c. 1860

A final blow for Alexandria was delivered by the Baltimore and Ohio Railroad (B&O). The railroad company had started the same year as the C&O Canal Company, running from Baltimore to the Ohio country. But because it was the first railroad, many did not believe it would be serious competition to the canal traffic. No one had experience with railroads. After starting with horse-drawn freight cars, the B&O soon switched to steam locomotives. The speed of travel, combined with better prices paid for commodities at the port, soon funneled much of the coal and grain from the west into Baltimore.[28]

The challenging economic landscape in Northern Virginia developed over many years. Recovery would not be quick. There were no government bailouts or tax incentives to stimulate the economy. As bad as the situation was, most people still managed to find places to live and food to eat.

Neighbors helped each other and at times allowed those who had lost their homes to live in vacant cabins or shacks on their property. The Potomac River and creeks were full of fish; there was game in the fields and woods, and even the most worn-out farm could still produce a garden plot. The people of Northern Virginia were used to gardening and hunting. Although they might have missed eating lamb, pork, and beef, they were not starving.

Chapter 10

AT LONG LAST, PROSPERITY

In contrast to the modern era, the economic rescue in the second quarter of the nineteenth century was developed locally and promoted to other regions of the country. Because the economy was agrarian based, rehabilitation of farmland was critical. To that end, several far-thinking farmers began to experiment with soil amendments, crop rotation, and cover crops.

As early as the late 1760s, George Washington and a few other progressive farmers were experimenting with adding lime to their fields to neutralize the acidity. Known as *plaister*, the lime was plowed into the ground before new crops were planted. Those farmers who tried this method had some success in improving the productivity of the land.

John Alexander Binns, a Loudoun County farmer, spent twenty years experimenting with soil amendments. In 1803, having had great success in rehabilitating a worn-out farm, he published an instruction manual of his methods, *A Treatise on Practical Farming*. Binns advocated the use of lime, fertilizers, crop rotation, cover crops, and deep plowing. Those who used his methods did achieve success.[1] But very few Northern Virginians were interested in applying his formula. It took a lot of work and money to purchase the equipment and materials. Seed, lime, fertilizers, and plows were too expensive for some farmers to afford. And it took a team of at least two horses—sometimes four—to pull a deep plow. The purchase price and upkeep of that number of horses was beyond the resources of many.

Commodore Thomas ap Catesby Jones, US Navy, was one of those who embraced the Binns method of farming. He set an example that was very influential in promoting economic recovery—albeit a slow one—through a demand for real estate. While on leave from the US Navy in 1818, Jones began working to recondition his farm, Sharon, which he had recently inherited from his mother. Located near the village of Langley, Sharon had once been part of a prosperous, grand plantation; however, it had suffered the same fate as the rest of the local farmland. It had turned into a derelict wasteland. Jones described the condition of the land and the parameters of the project in an essay published in the *American Farmer* in 1854:

> This isolated patch drawn from a worn-out tobacco plantation of 3,000 acres, was without improvements of any description; there had never been even a Negro Cabin on any part of it; it was not fenced in, nor was there a wheel-barrow load of manure about the premises, nor was there at that day, within my reach, any of the powerful, concentrated manures now so freely used. No agriculturist, young or old, ever embarked on a more forlorn hope than I did when I undertook to renovate worn-out soil in Fairfax. 'Tis true, I had a small income of about $700 per annum, from another source, but what was that compared to my wants? I had houses of every description to build, labor to hire, feed and clothe, farm to stock out and out, and my own personal and somewhat extravagant, wants, real and

> imaginary, to provide for. In short, I had everything to buy and nothing to sell.[2]

This somewhat dark but realistic description offers a picture of the conditions faced by many other Northern Virginians. Of course, not everyone was as fortunate as Jones, as $700 per year was a decent income at the time. As to hiring labor, he did do that, but he also had inherited slaves.

Jones was a man who liked a challenge. Dark picture or not, he was determined to make Sharon productive. He combined deep plowing with different types of soil amendments, planted cover crops, and practiced crop rotation. He tried different methods on each section and kept careful records of the results.

At first, Jones made use of locally available products, such as gypsum, lime, animal manure, and ashes. While on a naval expedition to South America, he discovered an area on the coast of Peru that was thick with partially decomposed bird droppings known as *guano*. Jones loaded tons of guano into the hold of his US Navy ship and brought it back to be incorporated into the soil at Sharon.

His crops began to thrive. He went on to experiment with other types of fertilizers. Jones's land improved year by year. Sharon regained—indeed, surpassed—its former status as a productive farm and grand estate. John Quincy Adams visited Sharon in the summer of 1842 and observed that "Commodore Jones's seat is a paradise in the wild under his cultivation. The house is surrounded by trees which are almost alive with the music of mocking birds and robins."[3]

Jones's published articles touting his successful restoration of Sharon's fields caught the attention of farmers from northern states. A group of New Yorkers came to see for themselves. As often happens in Northern Virginia, real estate prices began to rise when outsiders were attracted to the area. The depressed prices of the Northern Virginia real estate market were appealing to them, as was the climate. Tired of long, cold winters

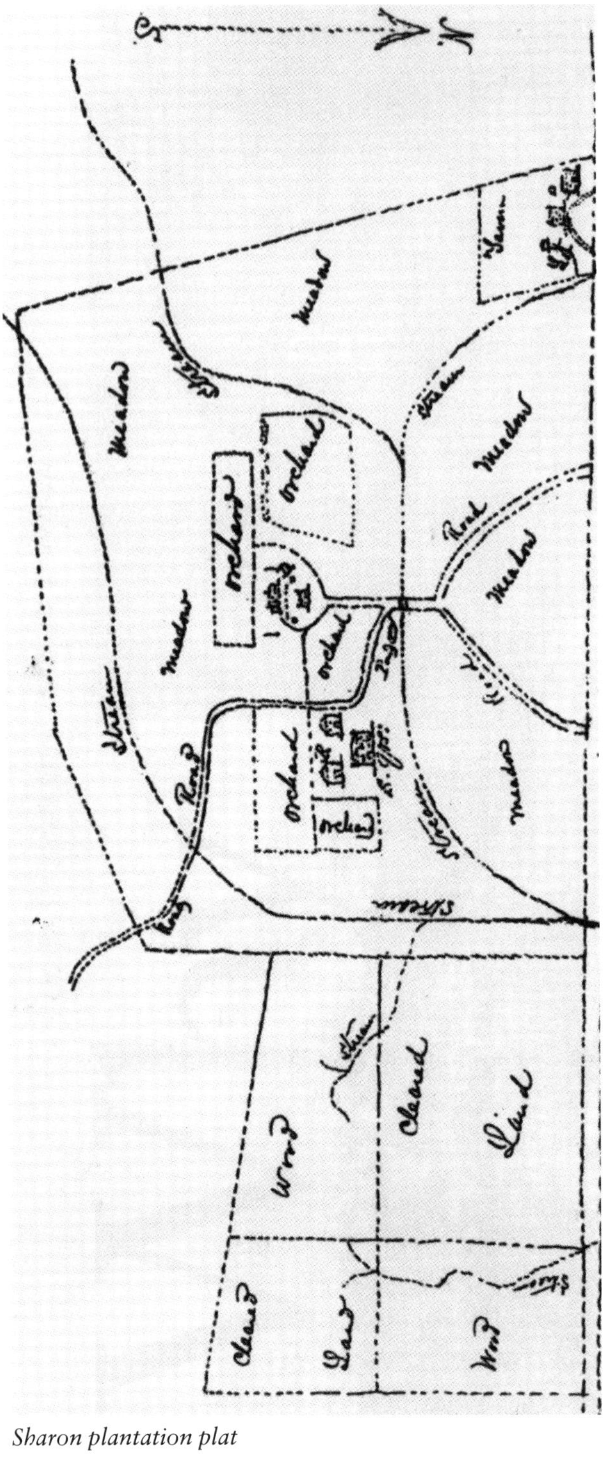

Sharon plantation plat

Bailey's Crossroads, c. 1860

and the high price of land in Upstate New York, they soon began to buy up derelict farms. They were followed by others fleeing various northern states for similar reasons.[4]

Termed by some as the "First Yankee Invasion," this influx proved to be the salvation of the Northern Virginia economy. The first Yankee purchaser appears to have been New York circus entrepreneur Hachaliah Bailey. He bought several hundred derelict acres in Fairfax County in 1837 to use as a winter home for his circus animals. Several years later, his son Lewis purchased part of the farm and settled there permanently. Through hard work and industrious farming, the family was able to turn the land into a profitable farm. While far from being classified as farm country today, the area still bears the family name: Bailey's Crossroads.[5]

The Baileys were followed by other New Yorkers who bought both small farms and larger acreage, according to what they could afford. Wealthy New Yorker Jacob Haight purchased the 750-acre Sully Plantation in western Fairfax County at auction for about $12,000. He soon turned the worn-out land into a prosperous farm. Many other northerners purchased more modest acreages and had similar success.

This spate of Yankee property purchases caused the price of Northern Virginia real estate to rise. In 1840, land was selling for between $5 and $15 per acre depending on location, a factor that remains important in today's real estate world. By 1845, the price for land had almost doubled. Even with this increase in price, it is interesting to note that the purchasers, for the most part, were not speculators but new immigrants to the region who came to establish homes and make a living from their farms. They used many of Jones's farming techniques. And, instead of the more easily used shallow plow pulled by one horse, they practiced deep plowing. A deep plow pulled by one team or two teams of oxen could penetrate the soil up to fifteen inches. The northerners also employed free laborers and did not use slaves.[6]

As the New Yorkers published their success stories in agricultural magazines, other northern farmers were attracted to the area. In the 1840s, four Quakers from Philadelphia purchased Woodlawn Plantation, the former home of Martha Washington's granddaughter Eleanor "Nelly" Custis Lewis. The two-thousand-acre plantation had become so unprofitable that all attempts at cultivation had ceased. Owner Lorenzo Lewis, Nelly's son and heir, had been trying to sell the property for many years. No one wanted the barren land or a mansion in much need of repair—not even at bottom-dollar prices.

But the Quakers were attracted for another reason. Their business was selling lumber to shipbuilders. Woodlawn was home to many acres of untouched white oak forests. The Quakers decided to subdivide the land into tracts of one hundred to two hundred acres, with the stipulation that their lumber firm could harvest the trees. Word of this new settlement spread through the Quaker communities of Pennsylvania and New Jersey. By several years later, forty new families were settled at Woodlawn and on other surrounding land. This area may have been the first commercially planned subdivision in Northern Virginia that was not a town.[7]

The Yankees were successful. By 1847, they had spent $200,000 in Fairfax County alone for farmland that sold for between $5 and $26 an acre. Higher prices were paid for farms that had already been improved. Most land prices ranged between $5 and $10 per acre. For the first time in half a century, the population of Northern Virginia stopped declining

Quaker Mill at Acotink

and began to rise. Growth was stimulated by the more than two hundred northern families who had settled in the area during the previous decade. The population increased by 20 percent from 1840 to 1860. The retrocession of Alexandria County to Virginia in 1847 from the District of Columbia also contributed to the rise.[8]

Farm prosperity led to opportunities for ancillary professionals, including doctors, lawyers, teachers, storekeepers, builders, and millers. New grain mills, sawmills, and manufacturing businesses were built. By 1850, Northern Virginia was a prosperous and attractive region. While not every farm was rehabilitated, many native Virginians had made changes to reclaim the productivity of their land.

Not only had the economy recovered, but it was growing every year. Real estate prices rose too. Farmland near Alexandria increased 400 percent in value over its 1840s prices. Alexandria had also added a substantial number of fishing businesses to its commercial interests. Those businesses tended to be seasonal, but when the shad and herring ran in the spring every year, huge amounts were taken from the Potomac River. The fish were cleaned, salted, and packed in barrels to be shipped to purchasers in Philadelphia and parts of Maryland.[9]

More roads were being built to facilitate the movement of produce to city markets. The population of Washington had grown dramatically since its founding and the city provided a good market for all types of farm produce. Two railroad lines were planned, the Orange and Alexandria and the Manassas Gap, and eventually they were started. Villages of various sizes developed around crossroads, railroad stops, and mills. These communities were no longer just a collection of ramshackle homes like those built earlier. They were new enclaves of solid houses, businesses, stores, post offices, churches, and schools.[10]

By the 1850s, Northern Virginians were enjoying a level of prosperity never before experienced in the region. The area was no longer a wild, sparsely settled, and untamed territory. It was a successful agrarian economy; however, this prosperity came after a long period of hardship. The economy did not "rebound." It had started on its downward path in the last decade of the eighteenth century and hit the bottom at the end of the 1830s. Recovery began in about 1840 and took almost a full decade.

It was a long and hard journey without government bailouts or stimulus packages. The economic recovery was brought about by the experiments of a few farmers and the public's willingness to learn from their examples. Unfortunately, it was not to last for long.

Chapter 11

THE WAR TAKES ITS TOLL

The next economic downturn to strike the region was caused by the American Civil War and Virginia's secession from the Union in 1861. Unlike the rest of the state's pro-Southern population, Northern Virginians' loyalties were divided.

The recent influx of immigrants from northern states sided with the Union. The native element of the population was of two minds: While they embraced the old Virginia customs of hospitality and social order, many lacked enthusiasm for the institution of slavery. There was also the fact that many enjoyed a close relationship, both personal and professional, with residents of the nation's capital. Northern Virginia's populace also included proud career military men and their families, whose consciences were troubled by the idea of going to war with the United States.

In addition to the white population, Northern Virginia was home to small communities of free Blacks who had remained in the area despite Virginia's anti-manumission laws. The 1860 US census lists 672 freemen in Fairfax County and 1,415 in Alexandria. But it is likely there were many more who went unrecorded. Many of George Washington's former slaves had remained in the southern part of Fairfax and had farms on land that had previously been part of Mount Vernon and Woodlawn plantations. In the northern and western parts of the county, there were numerous freemen around Langley, Lewinsville, and Dranesville. Many of these people had been born free due to the manumission of their mothers or grandmothers before they were born. Scattered among those who were free were those still held as slaves whose owners allowed them to rent land or sharecrop and keep their earnings.[1]

Some freemen owned land and businesses and paid taxes but were not allowed to vote. But being barred from the polls did not prevent them from having political opinions. Most of the citizens in this uneasy and unstable political climate wanted to protect their property and homes from whichever side they perceived to be the enemy. Little did they know, they soon would have to attempt to defend themselves and their property from both armies.

Although no major battles occurred within Northern Virginia's borders, its location on the very edge of the US capital and its mixed population of northern immigrants, free Blacks, and native Virginians caused Northern Virginia to become an immediate battleground. A charged situation of opposing loyalties split apart communities and even members of the same families. At the same time, constant military activity, which failed to acknowledge anyone's loyalty, quickly propelled residents from prosperity to penury.

On May 24, 1861, just a day after Virginia's vote for secession, Union troops crossed into Northern Virginia and occupied the city of Alexandria. That act heralded a four-year occupation that brought destruction of property and a climate of fear to the region. Influenced by political loyalty as well as economics, families fled in both directions. Numerous residents, both white and Black, headed for the safer environs of the city of Washington. Some wealthy landowners also had city homes and businesses there, while the less privileged were able to find lodging and

Centreville residents fleeing the war zone, c. 1861

employment. Hoping to distance themselves from the combat zones, other white families "refugeed," taking their slaves with them to live with relatives and friends deeper in Virginia. Many properties were abandoned by their owners. Some were left in the charge of caretakers, both Black and white.[2]

At the start of the war, property owners who remained on their farms hoped the unpleasant situation would soon end. Many men joined the army of their choice. Others stayed and continued to farm. Because land was coveted only by the occupying army, Northern Virginia real estate values plummeted. No one was willing to purchase any property.

At first, money was not a severe problem, but the situation quickly deteriorated and was worsened by the struggle for food and shelter. Both armies needed supplies to support their troops. The Union army, racing to occupy the land along the Virginia shores of the Potomac, secured control of the bridges into Washington and the main thoroughfares that led to the Chain Bridge, the Long Bridge, and the Aqueduct Bridge. Federal troops also quickly seized the railroad lines for military use.[3]

This caused great difficulty for farmers who still delivered produce to city markets. The routes from Virginia into Washington and Alexandria were suddenly very dangerous. People were arrested on many pretexts. Their produce was often confiscated, with no payment, for army

Chain Bridge from the Virginia shore with Union army guard, 1861–1865

use. Access to banks was also curtailed when citizens were denied permission to cross into Alexandria, Georgetown, or Washington.[4]

Because of its easy access to Washington, Alexandria was immediately overrun with Union soldiers. Many homes and business were forced to board officers and staff members. In some cases, it appears this might have been good for business because soldiers could pay for items they wanted. But for the most part, it was just a situation of an occupation force taking what they wanted. And those who had the most lost the most.[5]

Mansion House Hotel, Alexandria, Virginia, c. 1861

James Green, the city's richest man, sustained a great loss when his luxurious one-hundred-room Mansion House Hotel was taken to be a military hospital, and his furniture factory was taken to be a Union prison. Because he had not proclaimed any Southern sympathies, the US government promised him rent. But that was not forthcoming until 1883—long after his death. Not only did his businesses have to close, but the buildings and furnishings were severely damaged as well.[6]

By September 1861, thousands of Union troops were encamped in Northern Virginia. The Union army built a long series of small forts along the banks of the Potomac to protect the approaches to Washington. Property owners were helpless as they were evicted when their homes were destroyed to build forts or taken over for officers' headquarters. Their land was laid waste by camping soldiers. Wells and creeks that had provided sufficient water for farming and family life were used up or polluted from excessive use by the troops.[7]

Salona, the elegant country home of the Smoot family near Langley, became the headquarters of Union general William Smith and his staff after the Smoots relocated to their home in Georgetown. Salona's grounds and those of the two adjacent farms were taken as a campground for more than twelve thousand men, and that was only one division of a growing army. The United States had never fielded an army of the size mustered

Salona plantation, McLean, Virginia, occupied by Union army soldiers, c. 1861

for this war. So it is not surprising that the government was ill prepared to provide supplies for that many men.[8]

Soldiers, left to find their own food from local sources, formed foraging parties to collect garden produce, fowl, hogs, cattle, and horses from surrounding farms. They also took hay and grain to feed their horses. For the most part, they were not careful of crops in the fields. Much was lost to trampling. The Black farmers suffered as much as the white ones as they watched their farms stripped of all crops, food, and animals. Neglecting or refusing to understand that most of these people were already free, the Union soldiers often justified their actions by telling the Black farmers that they were lucky to have them fighting to set them free.[9]

If a landowner was loyal to the Union, the army would occasionally issue a receipt promising later payment for goods that were taken. In the cases of landowners with Southern loyalties, the items were considered to have been captured from the enemy. In either case, ultimately the foraging amounted to theft, which left farm families without enough food. Starvation became a significant problem.

As winter approached, the Union soldiers did not have adequate shelters. They solved that problem by stealing siding from farmhouses and barns. At times they carried off entire buildings, including the stone

Prospect Hill, McLean, Virginia. Union army camp on the Ball's Woodberry plantation, 1861–1865

foundations, to reassemble as huts in their camps. Almost all the trees were cut down to provide wood for heating and cooking fires. When that supply ran low and acquisition seemed too labor intensive, the soldiers took the farmers' fence rails. The seasoned wood made better fires and was easier to harvest than cutting down trees. The army also felled hundreds of acres of old-growth forest deemed to be blocking the view of the artillery units placed to defend the Potomac.[10]

In addition to foraging for items needed for survival, the soldiers indulged themselves in much wanton destruction for their own amusement. Looting was rife, not just by the soldiers but also by neighbors who had stayed. Vacant houses were considered fair game for anyone to steal from. The farms so laboriously reclaimed in the previous twenty years were laid to waste in a fashion much worse than that of the prior neglect. Farms were not the only target either. Whole villages were destroyed: Jermantown and Annandale in Fairfax County and Ball's Crossroads in Alexandria County. In western Fairfax, the town of Dranesville was almost decimated when Union troops under General Edward Ord collided with J. E. B. Stuart's Confederate forces there in December 1861. During the battle, many homes were shot up while the inhabitants took refuge in their cellars.[11]

As if the occupation of Union troops was not bad enough, the Confederate army was on the western edge of Fairfax County. Those soldiers also needed supplies and foraged among the local farms. In the beginning, they paid loyal landowners for their produce. Later, they simply took what they needed, including confiscating homes for officers' quarters. The Confederates also conducted raids into communities closer to the Potomac River to steal horses, pick up young men who could be drafted into their army, and take free Blacks who were conscripted to work for the army or taken further south to be sold into slavery.[12]

The collateral damage to Sharon plantation near Langley on the Georgetown Pike exemplifies the incongruity of the times. The once beautiful home of Commodore Thomas ap Catesby Jones was devastated by the Yankee occupation. Ironically, Jones had served the United States most of his adult life as a career naval officer. He had been a servant to his country and his community, with his work contributing to the financial recovery of the region. Now, with the coming of war, the results of much of his hard work were destroyed.

Sharon's fields, gardens, and orchards were stripped bare. Soldiers ransacked the barns for grain and hay. All the cattle, sheep, hogs, horses, and fowl were taken. Many acres of prime woodland were clear cut for firewood and approximately five miles of fences were stolen for firewood. Entire buildings were carried away, including a stone house, a tavern, ice house, dairy, granary, blacksmith shop and wheelwright shop. Fortunately, Jones, who had died in 1858, did not live to witness the devastation to his life's work; his widow bore the brunt of the military occupation even as their son spent the war serving in the US Navy.[13]

As the War Between the States progressed, thousands of homeless former slaves, known as *contrabands*, fled to the Union lines in the hope of being protected by the Northern army. Unfortunately, they were received with at best indifference and, more often, hostility by their supposed saviors. While many of them eventually made their way into the District of Columbia, thousands camped in shanties constructed with

Sharon plantation building with Civil War damage

lumber stolen from other buildings. These unfortunate souls were also hungry and unemployed. The Union army, which could not supply enough shelter or food for its troops, left these people to find their own. As was the case in the army camps, sanitation was a major problem, and water sources were quickly used up or polluted.[14]

It was a horrible time for Northern Virginians, no matter which side they supported. No farmers were exempt from property destruction and theft. It did not matter which race they were or which side commanded their loyalties. Black or white, Union or Confederate—all suffered the same afflictions. They watched as their land was ruined, and their houses and farm buildings were ripped apart. A writer for the *New York Tribune* reported on conditions in March 1862:

> The fences are gone. Many of the farm-houses ditto . . . Then the crops—all indications of them have disappeared . . . Trees also and brushwood . . . Plenty of recently-hewen [*sic*] stumps suggest . . . the past existence of the former . . . No vegetables, no grass . . . only earth . . . all intersected, cut up and crossed by innumerable tracks of men, horses and vehicles.[15]

Farming was a hopeless chore generally attempted by old men, women, children, freemen, or, in some cases, slaves who had stayed on the land. Most young and middle-aged white men were serving in one of the armies. Because the armies took away most of the available horses and mules, it became almost impossible to work the land. Without horses, there was no way to use the prewar methods of deep plowing or applications of lime and fertilizer to the soil. Those lucky enough to hold on to any farm animals usually had to find a safe place to hide them from foraging troops. Moving and guarding the animals added another difficult chore to the struggle for survival.[16]

People were forced to revert to gardening, hunting, and fishing to provide food for their tables. Food preservation was difficult due to the scarcity of salt and sugar. Anything that farmers were able to preserve had to be hidden to protect it from theft. Money was scarce. Valuables such as silver and jewelry brought very little when offered for sale.

As an added punishment for the Confederates, Congress passed an act in 1862 stipulating that they should be taxed on their property to pay for the extra national expenses caused by the war. The law also required the tax to be paid in person, an impossible situation for Confederate sympathizers. Property owners who were identified as "rebels" were given sixty days to pay the tax or have their property confiscated. The sale of 105 confiscated properties in Alexandria alone was held in 1864.[17]

In 1865, when the war was finally over, the landscape of Northern Virginia was, for the most part, laid to waste. In many places, the once-productive fields sprouted scrub cedar, pine trees, and brambles. Owners had to make hard decisions about whether to repair, rebuild, or seek a new life elsewhere. Farm buildings and houses were badly damaged, if not destroyed. Some landowners had suffered irreparable property loss.[18]

The Ball family returned to their ancestral home of Woodberry near Lewinsville to find everything gone except for a few slave cabins. The prewar property had consisted of three family dwellings, multiple barns, corn cribs, fodder houses, and all the accoutrements of a productive

Union army camp at Prospect Hill, McLean, Virginia 1861–1865

plantation. The occupation of first the soldiers—and later freed slaves—had erased all traces of the Balls' former lives. Eventually, the family decided to rebuild.[19]

Another extreme example was Arlington, the beautiful home of the Lee family in Alexandria County. Claimed early in the war by federal troops, the house still stood and could have been made fit to live in, but its land had been confiscated for nonpayment of taxes and developed into a national cemetery. No one would ever live there again.[20]

While the official hostilities had ceased, it would be a long time before peace and prosperity truly returned to the Northern Virginia countryside.

Chapter 12

RECOVERY

The Civil War caused an extreme decline in the value of Northern Virginia's real estate and the economy in general. Confederate general Robert E. Lee's surrender on April 9, 1865, officially ended the Civil War; however, peace did not come immediately. It would be some time before all military units of the Confederate forces agreed to surrender. The countryside of Northern Virginia, still occupied in places by federal troops assigned to keep the peace, was basically lawless and dangerous. Recovery—both economic and personal—from such a cataclysmic event would not happen overnight.

People who had been away during the war years slowly began to make their way home. In addition to experiencing an overwhelming sense of loss for all things familiar, many grieved for friends and family members who had died during the war. For some, the shock of finding their family farms and homes in ruins left them apathetic and unable to determine how to proceed. Focusing on a goal or purpose that would better their living conditions seemed a hopeless task.[1]

To some, the easy solution to their despair appeared to be forgetfulness or the temporary happiness brought on by the consumption of alcohol. Those entrepreneurs who were not similarly afflicted rushed to open saloons. Within a few months after the war's end, saloons were the most prevalent type of business establishment in Fairfax County and Alexandria.[2]

Those who were able to adjust to their new circumstances began the hard work of rebuilding their farms and lives. Fortunately, the war ended in the spring of the year, so many farmers attempted to grow some type of crop. But planting was particularly hard due to a shortage of laborers and horses. To the farmers' frustration, they found it difficult to find reliable workers, even though there were large groups of hungry, unemployed former slaves living in nearby shanty camps. Further adding to the farmers' troubles was a severe drought that lasted throughout July and August and into the harvest season. At the same time, a hog diphtheria epidemic killed most of the pigs that farmers had managed to keep through the rigors of the war.[3]

Repairs and reconstruction of homes and farm structures presented more challenges for the beleaguered Northern Virginians. Building materials and tools were very expensive. Money was scarce. Citizens who had converted their cash to Confederate currency were left with useless paper, while those who were smart had kept their savings in coins. Some who

Negro contraband camp, 1861–1865

had banked in the District of Columbia or Baltimore still had some funds, but most farmers had earned very little money during the war years. Everyone was seeking lines of credit and loans. The situation was mitigated by merchants who were willing to extend credit to old customers, but shortages caused high prices. The economy began to improve slightly when the US government began auctioning off surplus supplies and horses as it disbanded the wartime army.[4]

In some cases, the farmer's plight during this period of recovery was almost as bad as during the war. Even though armies were no longer descending to steal crops and animals, and farmers again enjoyed access to markets and banks in the District of Columbia, there were still dangers. An atmosphere of general lawlessness made highways and approaches to the Potomac River bridges a haven for armed highwaymen and pickpockets who would lurk in secluded areas and attack an unwary traveler. It was particularly dangerous to travel in the dark. Farmers heading to market before dawn and returning at day's end were at risk, along with their goods, horses, and money. Horse thieves raided fields, barns, and even hitching posts in the towns.[5]

Gradually, though, life began to improve. Land reclamation was not nearly as arduous as it had been during the 1840s. Valuable lessons learned then about fertilizer, lime, and crop rotation still applied. This time, the fields were not worked out and drained of nutrients—they were just neglected. With the exception of clearing brush and scrub trees, farmers could pick up where they had left off.

The labor problem was resolved to some degree through sharecropping, a practice in which tenant farmers gave the landowner a portion of the crops produced instead of money for rent. It was not a new practice and certainly didn't carry the social stigma later assigned to it. It had been used by free Blacks, slaves who were allowed to work away from their master's and to keep their earnings, and some white men.

In the postwar years, when so many young men had been lost or crippled, many families did not have the labor or the money to hire anyone to work their land. This was especially true for widows with young children or those that were elderly. And the produce of the land was their livelihood. Without farmworkers, they had no way to make a living. On the other side, there was a large population of newly freed men, experienced in farming, who didn't have money to pay rent or a home for their families. There were also some who had practiced sharecropping before the war who wished to continue. The tenants usually got a small house or cabin to live in, and both landlord and tenant got an income from the crops when they sold. In some cases, freed slaves who had stayed on their former masters' farms or returned after the war became their tenants.[6]

By 1870, Northern Virginia's economy in general was much improved from the conditions at the close of the war. The railroads were back in private ownership. Bridges had been rebuilt. Some of the old routes had their tracks relaid and repaired. A few new routes were under construction.[7]

Wages for male laborers rose from ten to twelve dollars per month on average. A highly skilled workman could earn as much as fifteen dollars. The women were not as well paid, but their wages increased from five to six dollars per month. As the economy was still largely agrarian, grain and lumber mills gradually replaced saloons as the area's

Orange and Alexandria Railroad repairs at Devereaux Station near present-day Clifton, Virginia

largest commercial enterprises. Mills not only provided jobs for mill workers but also created opportunities for local blacksmiths to repair mill machinery.[8]

Real estate prices were on the rise as both freedmen and new immigrants purchased property. Land prices rose from twenty to forty dollars per acre.[9]

Immediately after the Civil War ended, a large influx of northerners migrated to the area. As in the 1840s and 1850s, most of these new arrivals came from New York. Some had lived in the area during the war while serving in the Union army and, for various reasons, had decided to make it their home. Two outstanding examples were Orrin Hine and Henry Alvord. Hine had served in the Fiftieth New York Volunteer Engineers, a unit that spent the war years building pontoon bridges for the Army of the Potomac. After being mustered out of the army as a major, Hine returned to the area as the local agent for the federal Freedmen's Bureau. He began to buy land in the area that would later become Vienna. Hine exerted enormous influence over the development of the town.[10]

During the war, Alvord, who had served with the Second Massachusetts Cavalry, had stopped at Spring Hill Farm near Lewinsville while on patrol to search for the Confederate partisan Colonel John S. Mosby. There he had met Martha Swink, the owner's daughter. After the war, Alvord's family purchased Spring Hill Farm, and he married Martha. Like Hine, Alvord became an agent for the Freedmen's Bureau in charge of the office for Alexandria County—now Arlington.[11]

Lured by low land prices, many other immigrants found their way to Northern Virginia. The six-hundred-plus Yankee families who had settled in Fairfax County by 1879 were particularly influential in the development of the towns.[12]

As always, the population and commerce followed the transportation corridors. Railroads had been a new innovation in the area just before the outbreak of the war; however, they had not been in place long enough to have much impact. Six years later, though, repaired and running as

Broad Street, Falls Church, Virginia

commercial enterprises, the three railroad lines were becoming increasingly more influential. New towns, villages, and hamlets were developed where country roads crossed the rail lines. Among them were Vienna, Clifton, and Herndon.[13]

Railroad service also allowed the venerable community of Falls Church to become one of the first commuter suburbs in Fairfax County. Attracted by cheap real estate, numerous US government employees made their homes in the village and surrounding area. They commuted to Washington daily. The federal government, expanded during the war, had not reverted to its prewar size. Therefore, there were many newcomers seeking affordable homes.[14]

The rail lines also brought a change to farming. Because of the terrible conditions of Virginia roads and the lengthy travel time to market, railroads provided farmers with an easier way to ship produce. Crop farming did not necessarily guarantee a good return for the labor involved. Profits depended on variables beyond the farmer's control: if the weather was too wet or too dry, the crop would spoil. Different types of pests could also adversely affect the quantity and quality of the crops. Once produce was harvested, the price was determined by the supply and demand of the market, both local and overseas. With the advent of the railroads, farmers were able to diversify their produce to include dairy products.

Dairy farming was an appealing venture to many farmers because milk products were not seasonal. The demand remained steady. Households wanted milk, butter, and cheese on a daily basis. Before the building of the railroads, only those farms within a short traveling distance to the District of Columbia markets could deliver milk to the city before it spoiled. Those with access to the railroads now believed that they, too, could ship milk to market in a timely fashion. *Access* was the key word.

Virginia roads were notorious for their impassable condition. Excessive use by the armies during the war had made them worse than ever. During dry weather, the roads were deeply rutted and full of large rocks, making passage difficult for wagons, horses, and passengers. When the weather was wet, the route was a morass of mud interspersed with the same large rocks. A journey of more than two or three miles could be so time-consuming that daily trips were totally impractical for a hardworking farmer.[15]

Unfortunately, railroad service proved to be extremely unreliable and at times unsafe. Those who depended on rail service were doomed to frequent disappointments. Trains were often late or never arrived at all. All the lines were plagued by accidents, both major and minor. Commuters and farmers alike were forced to seek alternatives. Those who used the train to commute to work in the District of Columbia had to put up

Braddock Road in Fairfax, looking west from the Warrenton Turnpike. The surface of the road is just rocks and dirt.

with the poor service or leave home hours earlier to allow time for a buggy or horse ride into the city—the trip from Falls Church to Washington by horse took two or more hours.

Farmers continued to ship their produce by wagon. To accommodate those who had made the switch to dairy farming, several entrepreneurs established wagon companies to pick up the milk and haul it to creameries in the city. That scheme worked fine for those who were not too far from the city, but it didn't work as well for those who lived in the more remote parts of Fairfax County. Nonetheless, the promotion and development of dairy farming continued and contributed to the economic recovery of the region, as did the formation of new villages and towns.

Chapter 13

POSTWAR LAND GRAB

Northern Virginia's economic recovery was aided by its proximity to the District of Columbia. For more than a century, the markets and ports of Alexandria and Georgetown—and later Washington—were the commercial centers for many Virginia farmers. In the post–Civil War years, the city of Washington began to experience a rapid and steady development, transforming from a town with dirt streets and small wooden buildings into a city of wide, paved avenues lined with stone and brick buildings.

The Civil War and modern technology can be credited with bringing about this building boom. With the advent of countrywide railroad service and the telegraph, Washington finally came into its own as the nation's capital. It was no longer considered a remote outpost inhabited only seasonally by members of Congress. Businessmen from all over the country soon realized that if they wanted legislation to support their goals, it would be wise to spend time at the seat of the government to lobby.

By the 1880s, development had spread far beyond the original city center located between the White House and the Capitol. Wealthy businessmen were building fine homes all along the many avenues and streets. In turn, this development created a new market for Virginia commodities.

While the ports were still important for shipping the farmers' produce, the population of the District of Columbia also required food, lumber, and stone. Virginia sawmills provided lumber for buildings and railroad ties. The new demand for stone for roads and buildings made quarries a lucrative business. There was a large quarry along the Potomac River between the Aqueduct Bridge—near present-day Key Bridge—and the Chain Bridge. Local farmers benefited as well because city residents needed fruits, vegetables, fowl, butter, eggs, and milk. Farmers with as little as five acres of land could make a living from market gardening.[1]

New immigrant farmers flooded the area, bringing much-needed cash with them. Seven former Union soldiers from New York returned to Virginia after the war with their families and purchased land near Merrifield for $25 per acre. Other groups migrated to Herndon, Mount Vernon, and Lewinsville. Sully Plantation in western Fairfax County was sold to Steven Shear of New York and his son Conrad Shear of Michigan for $20,000. In 1870 George Mason's former home, Gunston Hall, with its one thousand acres of farmland, was sold to Edward Daniels of Chicago.[2]

Even the farms that had originally been part of George Washington's Mount Vernon plantation were sold to Yankees. In 1874 the 360-acre property Hayfield was sold to William Clark, who promptly purchased a neighboring tract of land to enlarge the farm to over 800 acres. Clark soon replicated Washington's original sixteen-sided barn at a cost of $30,000.

Through hard work and good financial backing, these Yankees achieved success with their farms. Many of their neighbors, the old Virginia families, did not do nearly as well in the beginning, but their situation improved with time.[3]

Money was the key. Without cash, it was difficult to hire labor or purchase livestock, seed, and fertilizer. Unlike today, land was usually bought for cash. There were very few mortgages on properties. In most cases, if a loan was required, the borrower had at least 50 percent—but more often 80 to 90 percent—of the cash needed for the purchase. Most bank loans were used to start new businesses.

The lending process was also very different from that of the modern era. The borrower would go to the bank, meet face-to-face with the manager, present his case, and submit to questioning about his ability to successfully repay a loan. The bank manager or officer would personally assess the borrower's repayment prospects and the soundness of his plan. The only credit check was based on the borrower's past history with that particular institution and word of mouth in the community. Merchants and storekeepers in the towns and villages could also be persuaded to extend credit using the same system.

On the positive side, getting a loan was not impersonal, and a good spokesman could do well in presenting his case. On the downside, if foreclosure occurred, the borrower was also personally acquainted with the man who would evict him from his property.

While times were hard for farmers in the first years after the end of the war, native Virginians benefited from this Yankee migration. And, given the recent hostilities, it is surprising that there was very little animosity between the two groups. The northern immigrants brought with them new social customs and habits, many of which were deemed to be foreign, unsociable, and rude by old Virginia standards. However, they generally managed to coexist peacefully and learned to practice the better traits of each other's customs. By 1880, the new immigrants were, for the most part, assimilated throughout the region.[4]

Another product of Yankee ingenuity was the development of new towns. Historically, towns and villages had grown around crossroads, mills, or courthouses. In the second half of the nineteenth century, railroads provided the impetus for community development. In western Fairfax County, the new town of Clifton was formed. Prior to the Civil War, the Orange and Alexandria Railroad (O&A) passed through the area with stops at Union Mills and Sangster's Station. During the war, the Union army had built a new siding and called the stop Devereux Station. In 1868 Harrison G. Otis, a Yankee looking for property, arrived at Devereux Station. He liked the area and was able to buy approximately one thousand acres for a little over $9,000.[5]

Otis planned to plant vineyards for winemaking. His idea worked well for quite a number of years; however, his ideas didn't stop with the vineyard. He promoted the area for a village, which would be renamed Clifton Station. Included in the business section were plans to build a hotel. Ten years later, some twenty families lived there. By 1890, Clifton boasted a flourishing lumber mill, a soapstone mill, and blacksmithing businesses. Trains passed through the village almost hourly, supporting the dairy ventures of the surrounding farmers.[6]

The town of Herndon was first established as a stop on the new Alexandria, Loudoun, and Hampshire Railroad in 1858, with a post office at the station. The new town included a locksmith shop, a steam sawmill, and a Methodist church. The Civil War preempted any expansion plans for the town, but after the war, Ancel St.John, a prewar transplant from New Jersey, set about realizing the town's potential. He and a number of friends purchased land on both sides of the railroad tracks,

Orange and Alexandria Railroad at Union Station (now Clifton, Virginia)

Elden Street, Herndon, Virginia

subdivided it into town lots, and offered it for sale. St. John also drew a town map to show how the town would be laid out. By 1878, the assortment of establishments included two steam sawmills, three churches, five stores, and a school. When Herndon was incorporated as a town the following year, the population was 442.[7]

New Yorker Orrin Hine, a former officer in the Union army, had first viewed the tiny village of Vienna when he was serving in the area during the war. Returning to the community as the local agent for the Freedmen's Bureau in 1866, Hine decided to make Vienna his home. He purchased property and immersed himself in the development of the town.

Hine believed the small village of Vienna could develop into a major town. He entered politics and used his previous affiliation with the US government to help build churches and schools. In addition to farmland, he purchased land around the community and promoted its development. By 1885, he owned more than sixty-four hundred acres. Hine became the town's first real estate developer in the 1880s, when he subdivided a portion of his land into town lots and actively marketed them. Apparently, Vienna was developing more slowly than Hine had first envisioned when he moved there twenty years earlier. His honest approach to marketing is evident in an 1884 real estate listing pamphlet:

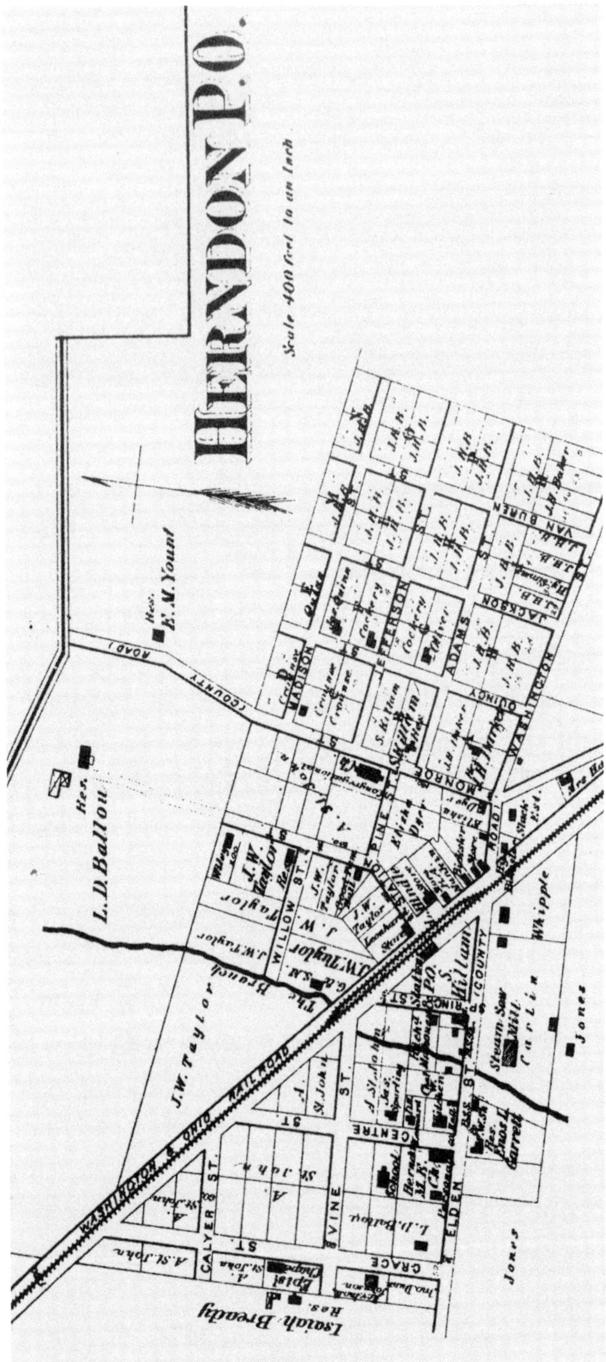

1879 Hopkins Atlas map of Herndon

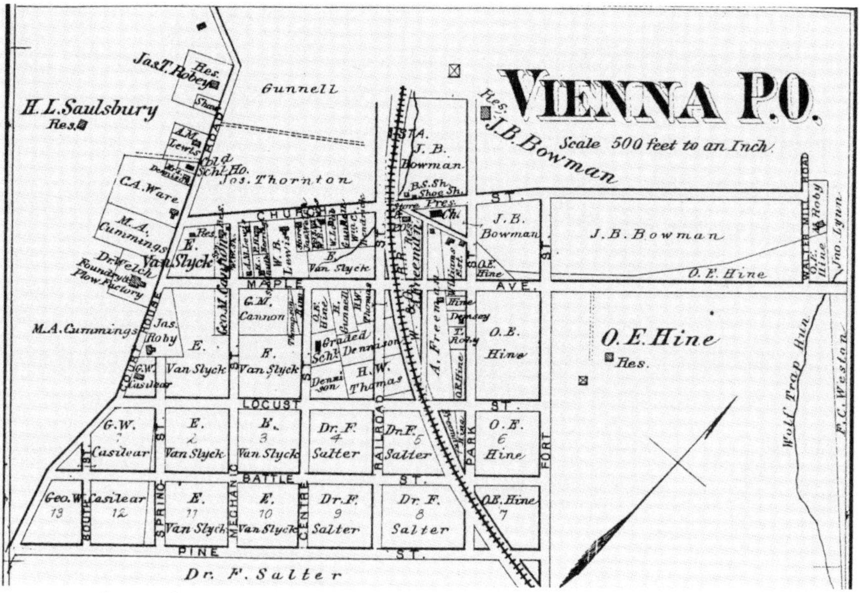

1879 Hopkins Atlas map of Vienna

> **Vienna is regularly laid out, but as yet a straggling village of three hundred inhabitants, situated on the Washington, Ohio, and Western Railroad.**

He went on to tout such attributes as a planing mill, a sawmill, a gristmill, two lime kilns, a shoe shop, and a harness shop, as well as various stores and blacksmith and wagon shops. When Vienna was incorporated in 1890, Hine became the town's first mayor.[8]

It is interesting to note that the general population viewed development as a good idea. Unlike today, there was an abundance of farmland in Northern Virginia, and residents welcomed the establishment of new towns. The fact that development was promoted by outsiders didn't seem to bother anyone. This spirit of acceptance was summed up in a local newspaper article published in 1897 in the *Telephone*, a Loudoun County newspaper:

> To the credit of Major Hine . . . after the late war was over he came back to the very section where, per force of the necessities of cruel war, his men had contributed to the desolation of the country, and has devoted all of the succeeding years in "making glad the waste places" and surely, it can be truthfully said of him that he has restored to this section more than he destroyed.

As the towns were developing, so too were the dairy farms. Every year, more farmers joined the ranks; however, their numbers and rates of production were still limited by the need for proximity to a rail line or main road that made shipping by wagon feasible. In 1881 John Thompson, son of a New Yorker who had a farm at Hollin Hall near Alexandria, rented a building in Washington to process milk from his family's farm. He was followed by John Storm, who had a large dairy farm near Langley. In the early 1890s, Storm rented a processing plant in Georgetown. The example of these farmers inspired others to work for better transportation corridors. At the close of the nineteenth century, entrepreneurs were working to establish more rail lines into Virginia, including electric trolleys.[9]

Thompson's Dairy delivery wagons

Virginia held another attraction for the residents of the District of Columbia. Because of the District's hot, humid climate exacerbated by close dwellings, many residents yearned to escape the city during the summer. Railroads made Virginia towns and countryside accessible for those seeking cooler and healthier locations. Thus, the Northern Virginia tourist trade was born.[10]

Many city dwellers rented rooms or houses, but others decided to buy their own country homes. Not only was farm life healthy, they believed, but the farm promised to earn enough to pay for its upkeep. Of course, due to the horrible conditions of Virginia roads, no city person would want to winter in the country. So these country homes were, for the most part, used as summer places. Nevertheless, they did serve to boost the economic value of Virginia real estate.[11]

Chapter 14

A SUBURBAN LANDSCAPE TAKES SHAPE

Residents and entrepreneurs alike viewed the railroad as the most important key to Northern Virginia's economic growth. For the most part, the roads in the area were still in very poor condition, and trips into the District of Columbia by horse-drawn vehicle were long and hard. In theory, the three rail lines that crossed the area should have provided nearby farmers with a way to ship fragile garden produce and dairy products to market on a daily basis.[1]

In fact, however, the rail service was notoriously unreliable. Trains were late or didn't run at all. The lines were plagued by breakdowns and accidents that could stop operations for hours, if not days. Milk and produce often did not get delivered in a timely manner, and they spoiled. Commuters frequently were late for work or were forced to seek another way of travel; however, none of these facts discouraged either the region's residents or entrepreneurs from believing in the need for more railroads. Those living too far away to use the existing lines clamored for their own railroads. Different groups of investors were constantly hatching new plans to provide for the people's wishes.[2]

As early as 1873, a horsecar railroad was installed in Alexandria; however, it failed to generate enough income to keep it in business for more than a year. Other schemes were launched, but the furthest any of them progressed was the acquisition of the rights-of-way.

The most serious problem that railroad companies faced was finding a profitable market for the line. Small, rural populations did not provide enough traffic to generate a profit. The towns of Vienna, Falls Church, and Herndon, which were already on rail lines, were growing slowly. But many of the new residents were people related to businesses within the town, such as doctors, storekeepers, and mill owners. Even the owners of some of the large surrounding farms had their actual homes in the towns. These people only traveled to the city occasionally to shop and bank. Commuter traffic was sparse. There was no reason to believe that rail lines would greatly increase the number of that group of users.

While Virginia properties and towns were developing, so too was the District of Columbia. Few builders were motivated to build suburban homes in Virginia when they could still buy farmland to develop suburbs in the District of Columbia. Commuters preferred the suburban homes located in the District because they had a shorter commute. In addition, the Potomac River presented a barrier. Any Virginia railroad would have to cross a bridge to get to the city. Development schemes for Northern Virginia were not without risk. This point was proved when the Loring Land Improvement Company tried to market a new Virginia community designed for commuters.

In 1887 William McKee Dunn and his partner, George B. Loring, purchased several thousand acres near the town of Vienna. They planned to develop it as a suburban community for the commuter market. Dunn, the main proponent of the plan, was a retired US Army general who had profited from real estate speculation in the District of Columbia. He

Maplewood, the country home of William McKee Dunn, near Lewinsville, Virginia

owned a home in the District and a large country estate near Lewinsville in Fairfax County.

Dunn enlisted Loring and George H. LaFetra, another Washingtonian, to help finance his development. Located on the Washington, Ohio & Western Railroad line, it was the first Northern Virginia suburban community planned solely for the commuter market. In order to appeal to the greatest number of potential purchasers, lots were offered in sizes varying from as small as 80 by 160 feet up to five acres. Despite advertisements that the land was "situated in one of the healthiest localities . . . 400 feet above tide-water" and "well watered by abundant springs of pure, cool water" and affording "delightful views," the project was unsuccessful.[3]

The advertised forty-five-minute commute into the city, combined with a fare of eighty cents for a round-trip ticket, probably accounted for the lack of interest. Those who had experience with the railroad knew that the commute was liable to take much longer, and the fare was too expensive for most people employed in the city. Dunn died before the first two houses were completed, and the project went on hold for the next fifteen years.

At the same time, another of Dunn's business associates, Dr. Max Wiehle, tried a completely different development scheme. A retired physician from Philadelphia, Wiehle moved with his family to the city of Washington. His idea was to build a planned town where people could live, work, and play without ever needing to leave the community.[4]

In 1886 he and Dunn purchased 6,449 acres on the Washington, Ohio, & Western Railroad near the town of Herndon. They divided the land, with Wiehle taking 3,500 acres for his town. In 1887, even though there was nothing else there yet, he persuaded US postal officials to open a post office in the location of his yet-to-be-built town of Wiehle.

The development moved forward slowly. In 1888 Wiehle built the first house, a summer home for his family so they could escape the heat of the city. Not one to skimp on detail, he hired a professional city planner from Germany to lay out a symmetrical plan for the town. It included avenues named Paris, London, Berlin, Vienna, Washington, New York, and Philadelphia. There were smaller streets named for Wiehle's seven children and for local trees, including Maple, Oak, and Hickory. He had three lakes dug by hand, and a Lakeside Avenue was planned. By 1892, the plans were complete, and the lots were ready for sale.[5]

The town of Wiehle. The building with the steeple was the town hall.

Among the first structures built were a four-room schoolhouse and a brick town hall with a steeple so that it could also be used as a church. Businesses were located near the town to provide prospective residents with employment. There was a brick kiln, an icehouse, a general store, and a hardware store. The Virginia Lumber and Manufacturing Company built a lumber mill and offered all types of framing and furniture for sale. The Maryland and Virginia Serpentine and Talc Company built a mill to process soapstone quarried nearby.[6]

The crown jewel of the community was the thirty-five-room Aesculapian Hotel. Built as a summer resort, it offered concerts; tennis courts; a bowling alley; walking paths; and lakes for swimming, fishing, and boating. The nearby woods had miles of bridle paths for those who wanted to ride horses. The hotel kitchen was run by a well-known chef who had once worked for financier J. P. Morgan. Rooms cost thirty dollars per month. Of all the businesses in the town, it was the most successful and often had a waiting list.[7]

Even though the business sector of Wiehle provided employment for many area residents, residential sales lagged. The primary reason was that many who found employment within the town could not afford to purchase a home there. Most of the town's workforce already lived in the area, had grown up on family farms, and were still farmers at heart. They might have had day jobs, but they also still worked on their farms and gardens. By 1900, only about seven of the residential lots had sold. Dr. Wiehle died in 1901, heavily in debt. His idea of a self-sustaining community went on hold until it was revived as the planned community of Reston in the 1960s.[8]

While Dunn and Wiehle endeavored to profit from the housing market, railroad builders were looking elsewhere. In 1890, a group of men from Philadelphia, headed by Dr. Griffith E. Abbot, identified a new market. They incorporated the Alexandria and Fairfax Passenger Railway Company to provide tourists with transportation to Mount Vernon. The line would be available to farmers and commuters, but until the commuter traffic increased, they believed they could make a profit from tourism.[9]

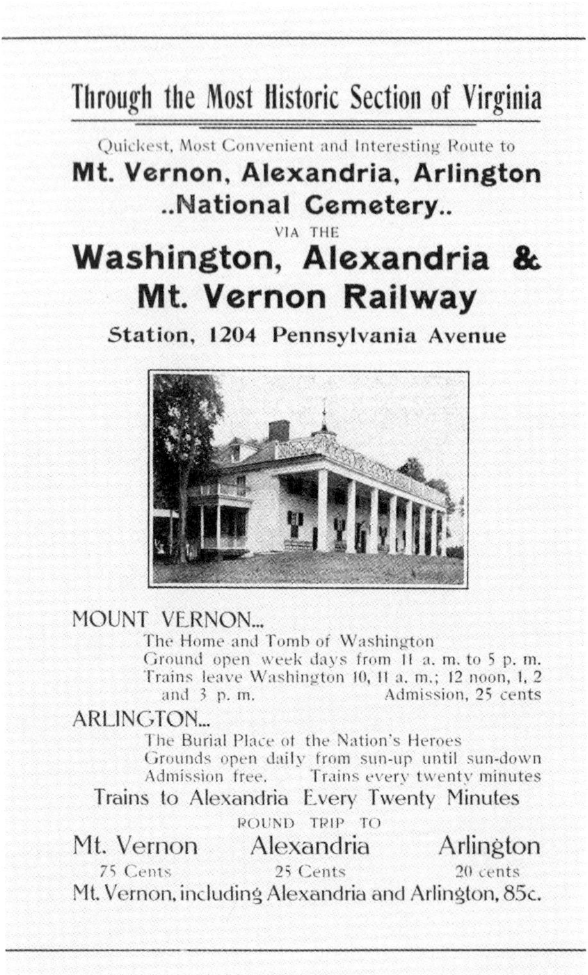

Washington, Alexandria and Mount Vernon Railway advertisement

As these plans were beginning to take shape, the electric trolley, a recent invention, attracted their attention. In 1892 they changed the name of their company to the Washington, Alexandria and Mount Vernon Electric Railway Company. The line opened for business as a trolley between Alexandria and Mount Vernon on September 18, 1892. Over two thousand riders tried it out on the first day. Within two years, the line had expanded upriver to provide access to St. Asaph Racetrack near the site of present-day Reagan National Airport. By 1896, the line went all the way to Rosslyn.[10]

Targeting the tourist market proved to be a good idea for the railroad company. At one end, the line served those who wanted to make the pilgrimage to George Washington's Mount Vernon, which had become a fashionable destination. Before the advent of the railroad, the journey was made by excursion boat and took several hours. The trip by railroad, even with eight stops on the line, generally took about thirty minutes from Alexandria. At the other end, it served a different sort of pleasure-seeker, who bet on the races at St. Asaph or spent their time gambling and drinking in Rosslyn's many saloons. While the tourist trade was a significant part of the railroad's business plan, the company's founders also believed the railroad would promote business and development.

In 1892, the New Alexandria Land and River Improvement Company purchased sixteen hundred acres along the line where it crossed Hunting Creek to develop as an industrial center. Within two years, the industrial center, named New Alexandria, already had several factories and a hotel. To house the factory employees, a number of small cottages had been constructed. Other investors quickly purchased land adjacent to the route

Mount Vernon trolley stop with a restaurant

in anticipation of development opportunities. Those who hoped to capitalize on suburban home development did not do well. Very few homes were built along the line for the next twenty years.[11]

The Mount Vernon trolley line was an immediate success. While the anticipated commuter suburb market was slow to develop, the local population immediately took advantage of the new convenient form of travel. Farmers near the line used it to ship produce and milk. High school students made up another large group of regular trolley riders. As there were no public high schools in Fairfax County before 1906, students who wished to continue their education after seventh grade had to attend private schools or commute to the District of Columbia or Alexandria, where they could attend public schools. The District school system was segregated but allowed Virginia students from both races to attend if they paid a nominal tuition.[12]

In 1893, as different groups of entrepreneurs were working on their development plans for Northern Virginia, a worldwide economic depression affected the United States. The stock market fell, banks failed, and businesses went bankrupt. In many parts of the country, cities, towns, and even states verged on bankruptcy. There were no funds to pay public employees. There were speculations and questions about the soundness of the US Treasury. In some cities, the unemployment rate was as high as 25 percent. No doubt, this depression was one of the factors that delayed development in Northern Virginia.[13]

As a result, there was little or no demand for real estate. Local banks did not have money to lend for speculative projects. Private investors had suffered losses and had little money to invest in new companies. But the Washington metropolitan area suffered less than other regions for a variety of reasons, one of which was that the city was largely funded and supported by the US government.

This depression affected Northern Virginians in different ways. Development schemes stalled or failed. The real estate market ground to a halt. Road and railroad construction stalled. Although most farmers did not own stocks and were not directly affected by the fall of the stock market, they did eventually feel the negative influences through a trickle-down effect. With less money in circulation, consumers spent less. But the lack of competitive produce shipped from other regions in the country generally preserved their market, albeit at lower prices. While people in other parts of the country were starving, Virginians still could feed themselves with the products of their own land.[14]

The most severe effect of the depression was the lack of progress in road and railroad construction. Dairy farmers, who were especially affected by this situation, continued to clamor for improved rail service. As the nineteenth century drew to a close, the economy began to improve. Groups of investors took a fresh look at old ideas for new railroad routes. The advent of the electric trolley was to have a major impact on the delayed development of the Northern Virginia countryside.

Chapter 15

RAILROADS ALTER THE ECONOMIC LANDSCAPE

The final years of the nineteenth century brought positive changes for both the national and local economies. Once again, investors looked toward Northern Virginia as a promising development opportunity. Both Fairfax and Alexandria counties were farmland, interspersed with a few towns and villages. In the eyes of the entrepreneur, the region was a blank slate ready to be developed into subdivisions and factories.

The District of Columbia had strict laws to prevent factories from operating there. Neither Congress nor District residents wanted the capital city sullied by large chimneys continuously belching black coal smoke. But some of the industrial magnates who made their homes in Washington were anxious for a nearby venue for factories. They believed that Virginia, with its deepwater ports and access to raw materials from West Virginia, could become an industrial center to rival Baltimore.[1]

There were other developers who viewed the region as a potential commuter suburb for the District of Columbia. In order to make either plan practical, more railroads needed to be built across Virginia.

Grandiose development schemes notwithstanding, the Virginia farmers wanted better railroad service for their own needs.

The three steam-powered railroads that crossed Northern Virginia did not run efficiently, and there were many miles between them. The distance and the poor conditions of the roads denied many local farmers practical access to the rail lines. While the Mount Vernon Electric Railroad Railway helped the farmers near the line, it ran parallel to the Potomac River. The farmers in the interior of the region were anxious to have new railroads. With that impetus, old plans were revived, and new plans were implemented.

Following the example of the Mount Vernon Electric Railroad, other companies raced to build new railroads. The electric railroad was the single most important catalyst in the conversion of the Northern Virginia countryside from remote farming communities into commuter suburbs; however, the transformation didn't happen overnight, and it wasn't easy. Numerous projects were planned but never built because of a lack of funds.[2]

The first new line to access the region's interior was the Washington, Arlington & Falls Church Railway. It was originally chartered in 1891 with the authority to build a bridge across the Potomac River at the Three Sisters Islands. The bridge project turned out to be too difficult and expensive for the company and was abandoned. After about two miles of track were laid from the end of the Aqueduct Bridge in Rosslyn to the gates of Arlington National Cemetery, the line opened in October 1892. Horses pulled four cars up the steep hill to Arlington House and cemetery, and then the railroad used gravity to bring the cars back down to the starting point. This strategy worked for day-trippers who wanted to visit, but it didn't help farmers or commuters. After experimenting with different electric operations, the company went into foreclosure.[3]

The assets and right-of-way of the company were purchased by the Charles S. Hinchman family, absentee owners from Philadelphia. After relocating to a less steep terrain and being reconfigured as an electric trolley, the line opened in 1896. Its route began at the Aqueduct Bridge in Rosslyn and passed through Clarendon and Ballston before ending in East Falls Church.

On the one hand, this route was good for commuters who lived in the Falls Church area because the electric trolley cars ran more frequently than the steam railroad and were cleaner. On the other hand, the line did not have permission to cross into the District of Columbia, so commuters had to walk across the bridge into Georgetown and then transfer to city streetcars. Nonetheless, it was a good start.

By 1904, the line extended to Vienna, and in 1907, it pushed on to end at Fairfax Courthouse. By that time, bridge access had been successfully negotiated, and the line provided direct access to the city of Washington via the Fourteenth Street Bridge.[4]

The next electric rail line to appear on the scene was the Great Falls & Old Dominion Railroad (GF&OD). Originally planned by a group of Georgetown and Virginia investors, the line had been chartered in 1900 to run from Georgetown to the Great Falls in Virginia. For various reasons, primarily a lack of funds, development of the line lagged. This railroad was more expensive and harder to build than the other lines because of the rough terrain that it would traverse. The crossing of Difficult Run in the proposed route was enough to give the most hopeful investor pause.[5]

Farmers all along the route were anxious for the line to be built. Those who lived in the Arlington Heights neighborhoods above Rosslyn could see all the way to Georgetown, but they could not easily access it. Those who lived farther down the line near the villages of Langley and Lewinsville had an even harder trip to city markets. The farms near Great Falls were so remote that they might as well have been in a different country.

In 1903, a congressional bill was passed that granted the GF&OD the right to build tracks on the Aqueduct Bridge, enabling the railroad to run into Georgetown. This move was a major step in the development of

Great Falls & Old Dominion trolley car on the line to Great Falls

Virginia electric rail systems. The right to cross the bridge had been coveted by many other railroads but had never been approved. After three years of work, the bridge rights and the acquisition of rights-of-way were all the company had accomplished, and it was severely undercapitalized.[6]

But a project savior appeared on the scene just when it looked as if the company would fail. Attracted by the Aqueduct Bridge rights, wealthy real estate developer and newspaper publisher John R. McLean purchased the majority of the company's stock. Once McLean was involved, things moved forward quickly. West Virginia senator Stephen B. Elkins was persuaded to invest in the line. Now properly capitalized, the company started construction.[7]

The motivation of the investors of the GF&OD was somewhat different than that of other local railroads. The Georgetown investors wanted to continue in the old tradition of attracting Virginia business to their city. Those who were from Virginia wanted to use the line to develop the countryside into commuter suburbs.

McLean and Elkins had bigger ideas. Elkins viewed Virginia as a prime spot for manufacturing plants. His vision was to line the Virginia shore with factories and to develop an industrial center that would compete with Baltimore. McLean sought to operate a street railway system that would extend from Great Falls all the way across the city of Washington. Both men hoped to expand the line in the opposite direction and eventually provide access to the coalfields of West Virginia. For the immediate future, however, the practicality of the project dictated targeting a profitable user group.[8]

Past Rosslyn, the rail-line route was across farmland. The villages it passed through might become excellent commuter suburbs eventually, but currently, they were merely farm villages. The farther the line passed into the countryside on the way to Great Falls, the more remote it became. The idea of developing a customer base of commuters in any number from that area did not appear to be a feasible plan for the immediate future. And while the region's farmers were anxious to have the rail line, there was only a limited amount of revenue to be generated from hauling milk and produce. In order to hedge their bets and guarantee a good number of passengers, Elkins and McLean decided to follow the example of the Mount Vernon Electric Railroad and capitalize on the tourist trade. They developed an amusement park at the Great Falls end of the line.[9]

The Great Falls in Virginia had long been a destination for fishermen, hunters, and campers. The area did not attract many day-trippers because the journey was long and rigorous, and only the most intrepid tourists would attempt it. As a result, it was shrouded in mystery and legend. When trolley access to the falls became available on the Maryland side of the Potomac, that site became a popular destination for day-trippers. But the view of the falls was better and much more dramatic from the Virginia shore. And there was the added attraction of a stroll through the remains of the village of Matildaville and viewing the Potomac Canal locks.

In spite of all the well-laid plans, it took three years to extend the track to Great Falls. On March 6, 1906, the long-awaited trolley opened for business between Difficult Run and Georgetown. The cars were crowded from the first day, especially with people from the neighborhoods near Rosslyn. The entire route to Great Falls opened on July 4, 1906, and the trolley was almost overwhelmed with day-trippers to the falls. The *Washington Post* estimated that six thousand people used the rail service that day, although that number might have been exaggerated given the

Great Falls Park, Virginia, observation tower and dance hall. The observation tower had electric lights to illuminate the falls at night.

capacity of the cars. Still, the tourist trade for the line was well established from its first day, and the commuter traffic was soon to follow. In the meantime, though, the farmers had their railroad.[10]

The advent of the GF&OD stimulated a change in farming produce along the rail line. Farmers who had not been able to ship milk to the District of Columbia now had that opportunity. Many farmers changed from grain crops to dairy farming. As railroads were established all across the United States, western grain was shipped east to compete in the local market. Economically, dairy farming began to appeal to Virginia farmers as a more stable source of income.

In 1903 the Department of Agriculture issued a report stating that the residents of Washington consumed less milk per capita than any of the other fifteen largest cities in the country. This made the dairy business in the District of Columbia very competitive. Only twelve thousand gallons of milk a day were processed through the city. The main reason was that there was only a small amount used in manufacturing. Other cities had large manufacturing plants, and Washington did not. In fact, much of the District of Columbia was still farmland, and the city had 136 operating dairy farms, which produced about two thousand gallons of milk per day. Both Maryland and Virginia farmers were competing for a share of this market. To be successful, however, they needed a faster way to ship their milk to the city. The change in Fairfax County due to the rail lines was so dramatic that it became one of the top milk-producing counties in the state for the next fifty years.[11]

The establishment of electric rail lines changed the character of the Virginia countryside forever. The most immediate effects were along the routes of the Washington, Arlington & Falls Church and the Great Falls and Old Dominion railroads, both of which now provided easy commuter access to the District of Columbia from Virginia. The result was an increase in real estate values; however, it was not an instant change. Real estate investors had to wait a few years for the idea of the commuter suburb to gain in popularity.

In 1900, Washington realtor James. E. Clements offered Virginia properties for sale in the following advertisement: "Cheap fruit, poultry, and garden farms—on electric roads, within short ride of city-28 acres, house, and barn for $300 down; balance in monthly payments." Clements also advertised lots in the town of Ballston for $100 each, with the terms of $5 cash down payment and $1 per week for the balance. Two years later, he was still offering the same deal.[12]

Matthew Middleton unloading milk cans at the Herndon Railroad Station

Then the prices began to rise. In 1905 Dominion Heights subdivision lots were offered for $125 to $200. At the same time, builder Will W. Douglas offered 25-by-125-foot lots in West Ballston for $150 to $175 for $10 cash down, with the balance to be paid off at $5 per month.[13]

One of the most successful developers was Frank Lyon. A lawyer and newspaper editor from Alexandria, Lyon branched out into suburban development. In 1904 he purchased a tract of land near Clarendon, which he divided into 130 lots. In one year, he sold 120 lots, and twenty-three new homes were built. A year later he purchased an existing subdivision of fifty acres divided into 312 lots on Fort Myer Heights. That subdivision had been on the market for almost ten years; only twenty-five houses had been built. At 250 feet above the Potomac, the high ground was very desirable. It afforded great views of the city and cool breezes in the summertime. In the first year under Lyon's ownership, another twenty-five houses were constructed, with twenty more projected for the next year. Planned to be affordable for government employees, these were small houses on small lots priced at about $2,500 and financed with payments of only $25 per month.[14]

When the GF&OD opened in 1906, the development spurred by the electric railroads was progressing at a rapid rate. The area of Alexandria County located on the hills above Arlington Cemetery and Rosslyn came to be known as Arlington. Between 1900 and 1906, the population was estimated to have increased by more than 50 percent. Rosslyn, known during the previous century as nothing more than a collection of saloons, gambling halls, and brothels, had undergone a change in character. About a dozen factories had been established there between 1895 and 1906.[15]

Frank Lyon

While the GF&OD line was under construction, many of its investors, including members of its board of directors, acquired land along the route for subdivisions. They created a one-hundred-acre subdivision in Arlington called Livingston Heights—named for Colin Livingston, an investor in the project and a director of the railroad. This site was marketed as a step up, both literally and figuratively, from the Fort Myer Heights subdivision.

Promoted as the highest point in the county, Livingston Heights was situated approximately 450 feet above the Potomac. Ever mindful of the swamp-like climate in the low parts of the city, Washingtonians considered high ground to be healthier. In addition to its purported healthy atmosphere, this land was very desirable for the views. The lots were considered to be some of the choicest in suburban Virginia. A writer for the *Washington Post* real estate section enthusiastically described Livingston Heights as having:

> Lots with sewer, water, electric lights, fire plugs, macadam roads, granolithic walks, and every convenience known to a high-class subdivision. This property has every advantage that nature could bestow, and with unlimited means to add all the comforts invented by man, the result will be that at this point on the Great Falls road will rise the most attractive suburban town adjacent to the National Capital.

All other advantages aside, the idea of a home with electric lights was an appealing asset provided by the electric railroads, which sold their excess electricity to neighboring communities. Electricity was not available from other sources in the countryside.[16]

Alexandria County was not the only place where new railroad-stimulated subdivisions were springing up. Others were being developed along the GF&OD in Fairfax County. There the railroad had selected a route midway between the old established villages of Langley and Lewinsville, but there was not an immediate benefit for either place.

When planned in 1905, the stop named McLean appeared to be in the middle of nowhere, yet there were those who thought it prime for a subdivision. Therefore, the Mackall-Laughlin Company designed the community of Ingleside. They advertised it as the "Handsomest Subdivision on the Great Falls and Old Dominion Railroad" and offered lots of 100 by 150 feet for $150 to $350 apiece. They also offered adjoining properties priced at $200 to $400 per acre.[17]

Franklin Park, located in a hilly area straddling the Alexandria-Fairfax county line, was next. According to its promoters, in 1909, it had something for everyone and was advertised as the "Queen Suburb On the Hills." Developers were busy clearing dense woodland to create a parklike setting. A broad range of street-front "villa sites" was offered to fit the size of everyone's budget. Lots measuring 25 by 150 feet were sold starting at $100, with a $10 down payment. One-acre lots were offered for $600 to $1,900, and five- to ten-acre lots ranged from $2,500 to $7,500.

Moore and Hill of Washington marketed Franklin Park. They advertised financing with no interest and no taxes. Furthermore, the firm was willing to pay the carfare for anyone wanting to look at the property. In a particularly outrageous statement, Moore and Hill claimed that purchasers would "live fifty percent longer and fifty percent better" in Franklin Park. And just in case anyone's estimate of their personal longevity was in error, and they died within two years of the purchase, the company

Franklin Park railroad stop

guaranteed a refund with 6 percent interest. If they died two or more years after their purchase, the company would give them a free deed. All this within an "easy" commute to the city that cost only eleven cents in carfare.[18]

The Northern Virginia commuter subdivisions had arrived, ushering in a boom in real estate values. And while the subdivisions were all different, they shared a proximity to the electric rail lines. Because Virginia's roads were not commuter friendly, Northern Virginians brave enough to purchase homes in the countryside soon realized how very dependent they were on the railroads.[19]

Chapter 16

TROLLEYS AND TRAINS BRING TOURISM AND DEVELOPMENT

As housing developments were being added to the Northern Virginia countryside, at the same time those developers had to compete with many new housing communities being built in the District of Columbia. But land was cheaper in Virginia, so homes there could be offered at lower prices than those in the District.

Virginia also attracted commuters who could afford higher prices and who wanted to live in or near the country. Country living was considered to be much healthier than city living. Falls Church and Vienna, which had been home to commuters from the steam railroad days, saw population boosts when the electric trolley arrived. Farther down the line, the communities of Franklin Park and Ingleside, which offered lots in all sizes up to five acres, were much slower to sell. Franklin Park, on the Great Falls and Old Dominion Railroad line, was too far removed from any commercial centers. Some of those who did purchase property used it for summer homes and lived elsewhere during the rest of the year.[1]

Falls Church railroad station, c. 1898

Ingleside, also on the GF&OD line, had two stops, Ingleside and McLean, but the area was rather isolated. Even though those stops were only about a mile from either Langley or Lewinsville, road conditions in wet weather meant that travel was slow and difficult. Because of the railroad and the bad roads, however, a commercial center developed there. A store was built at the McLean stop, and a post office was installed in 1910. Lewinsville and Langley faded into obscurity, known only by the local residents.[2]

The electric trolley systems were largely responsible for the significant economic development of Northern Virginia. It was definitely a case of "build it, and they will come."

Due to the extreme heat and humidity, Washington was considered unhealthy during the summer months. Life-threatening diseases, such as cholera and typhoid, often plagued residents of the nation's capital. Even when conditions were not unhealthy, they were just plain miserable. For those Washingtonians who could afford to leave the city, it had long been the custom to flee to more salubrious locations, including the nearby Virginia countryside. Some District residents rented houses on farms or in villages; others rented rooms in family homes. Virginians were glad to have the extra income. The electric trolleys gave a healthy boost to the summer boarding business.[3]

On the Mount Vernon line, just south of Alexandria, Wellington Villa was established as a summer resort. Its owners purchased several small buildings from a former amusement park and moved them there on a railroad flatcar. The structures were distributed on half-acre lots near the Potomac River and rented as summer cottages. Vacationers could enjoy the quiet, rustic atmosphere, where they could fish, swim, and boat. And it was only a short trip to Alexandria to shop.[4]

Franklin Williams ran a successful summer resort on his 434-acre Woodford Farm near Vienna. Originally, because it was close to a stop on the steam railroad line, Williams rented rooms to summer boarders. Woodford was ideally located to attract summer guests. Built on a hill that always enjoyed breezes, the house had large porches and a swimming pool as well as woodland walking trails, a pond for boating and fishing, and meals featuring food grown on the farm.

Woodford grew in popularity every year. Even though the Williamses expanded the house and added porches, there were still more guests than the main house could accommodate. Williams's sons built their own homes on the farm and took in the overflow of paying guests. In 1904, the Washington, Arlington & Falls Church Railway extended its trolley service to Vienna, passing through Woodford on what is now Electric Avenue and making the resort more popular than ever. The trolleys ran on a frequent schedule. Summer visitors could easily go into Vienna or Fairfax to shop or visit.

Aiming to capitalize on the resort business, Williams's son Herbert built a new complex on the property that included his personal home and three rental structures. In the center of the complex was a large combination dining hall and ballroom. Herbert employed both a cook and a chef to prepare the meals. The farm provided most of the food from its orchards, gardens, chickens, and dairy cows. Ice cut from the pond in the winter was stored in deep pits and used all summer long to chill drinks and freeze ice cream. On Saturday nights, there was music for dancing in the ballroom.[5]

Camping at Great Falls. These men were there to fish during the day but are dressed in suits and ties and even brought along a Victrola.

For a more dramatic—and less civilized—setting, the summer visitor could rent a campsite and pitch a tent in Great Falls. A bit farther upriver at Trammell's Camp, small cottages by the river were available for rent. The Trammell's had a boathouse with rowboats for rent, a dining hall, a swimming beach, and a rustic restaurant. Great Falls Park offered a choice of two restaurants, the Great Falls Inn and Dickey's Tavern, as well as a sandwich shop. There was a dance hall with live bands on weekends. An electric light show illuminated the falls at night.[6]

There were many other homes throughout the Northern Virginia countryside where a family could rent a room or two for the summer. Since the idea was to escape the city heat, visitors often stayed all summer. Before the advent of the trolley, mothers and children would move to the country, but fathers who had to work could only visit on weekends. With the advent of the trolley, fathers could also stay all summer and commute daily to city jobs.[7]

While the trolleys promoted economic development for Northern Virginia in many ways, they were also the source of much angst and trauma. The principle behind the trolley was fast, reliable, and cheap transportation. Unfortunately, all the lines failed miserably in the first two categories. And to make matters worse, all the commuter development was completely dependent on them. Most of the commuters had no other way to get to the city. Advertisements for the small-lot developments emphasized every convenience based on the trolley. There was nowhere to put up a stable for a horse or a shed for a carriage. There were no taxis. The developments farther out in the countryside did include lots with room for horse stables, so those people had other ways to commute if necessary.[8]

The cars were crowded from the opening day of each line. Not only was it standing room only in the interior of the cars; it was standing room only on the back platforms and steps—and if there was more than one car, riders sometimes stood on the car couplings on their way into the city. Because it was a new technology, the motormen and others charged with running the trolleys were often poorly trained. The cars could achieve an amazing speed of forty miles per hour—compared with horse-drawn vehicles, which averaged four miles per hour.[9]

The motormen were often fascinated with speed. Even though the trolley stops were planned at intervals of about one-tenth of a mile, a motorman whose cars were full or who had built up a high speed might whiz through a stop without picking up any more passengers.

Accidents were common. In places where the rails were shared with steam railroads or where junctions with sidings allowed other rail cars to pass, trolley operators sometimes ignored the signals and raced to be first on the track, often with bad results. Each line experienced severe crashes caused by reckless driving, a lack of attention to signals, and fog. There were also collisions of varying degrees of severity with horses, wagons, pedestrians, and embarking and disembarking passengers.[10]

No sooner did the trolleys begin operating than the passengers started to complain about poor service, life-threatening encounters, late service, no service, and dirty waiting facilities. Most of the stops only had a three-sided shed to shelter waiting passengers. To make matters worse, the trolley companies operated on a narrow profit margin and in some

Rosslyn Trolley Depot, c. 1908

years did not make any money. As the result, there were never enough cars to handle the volume of traffic at peak hours.

Local farmers who had happily anticipated the trolley as a fast way to ship milk to city processing plants added their complaints to the commuters' list of grievances. Trolley employees frequently would not pick up the full milk cans from the platforms or, worse, would forget to unload them at their destination. In the latter case, the smell of sour milk would remind them and their passengers of their error for days to come. Even when the milk was properly delivered, the farmers still found cause for complaint when the trolley operators forgot to return the empty milk cans or dropped and dented the cans and lids. Nevertheless, those who dairy farmed along the trolley lines had two choices: ship their milk by trolley or change to another type of farming.[11]

While the trolley companies were the catalyst that opened Northern Virginia to suburban development, their ultimate nemesis, the automobile, appeared almost simultaneously. The first automobile in the District of Columbia arrived in 1897. Originally a rich man's toy because of its high purchase price, the automobile caught the attention of everyone in the city. Within five years, it became the preferred form of personal transportation. As prices came down, more people could afford to own an automobile.

Due to the wide and smooth city streets, electric autos were the favorite choice of most purchasers. Others favored those powered by steam or gasoline engines. Because of their still-substantial cost and the terrible road conditions, however, automobiles were slow to appear in Northern Virginia. The economical electrics, which resembled glorified golf carts, were not suitable for Virginia gravel roads. And there was no electricity available to charge their batteries.[12]

In 1903, the *Loudoun Times* reported that one brave driver and his companion drove through Falls Church and all the way to Leesburg. In 1907, the Washington Automobile Club staged an outing to Great Falls Park and commented that if a driver could get his auto to the falls, it was proof that it was indeed a good machine.

In spite of all the challenges, by 1910, developers opening new communities in Alexandria County began installing paved roads and advertising that their sites were just a short drive from the city. This change was spurred by the Model T, introduced in 1908 by Henry Ford. The Model T, simple in construction and very adaptable, had a four-cylinder gasoline engine and could be purchased in three styles: the Runabout, the Touring Car, and the Town Car. It was later offered as a pickup truck. All these styles were tough enough to tackle Virginia roads. This versatile machine was unique in that the new models got cheaper every year as Ford perfected his manufacturing techniques. In 1908, the Touring Car sold for $825, a bargain at the time. By 1916, the price had fallen to $260.[13]

While the Model T was very popular, it wasn't the only automobile to penetrate Virginia farm country. In 1911, Daniel Cornwell became the first automobile owner in the vicinity of Great Falls when he bought a Stanley Steamer. This was an appropriate choice given that he owned a steam-driven sawmill and had installed steam heat in his Forestville farmhouse.[14]

The mechanization of the Virginia countryside did not immediately impact the business of the railroad companies. The roads were still in

Automobiles were often stuck in the mud on Virginia roads.

terrible condition, and automobiles were only practical during dry conditions. In the wet months, the roads became deep morasses. Early automobile drivers soon learned that their magic machines could not plow through foot-deep mud nor could they run in snow. Most automobile owners put their machines away for the winter. The time of the automobile as a practical commuter transport was still years away, and commuters were dependent on the trolleys.

Encouraged by the early success of the Great Falls & Old Dominion Railroad, principal owners John R. McLean and Stephen Elkins decided to branch out to a larger project. In 1910 they began negotiations with Southern Railway to lease its fifty-four-mile-long Bluemont Branch, a steam railroad that ran from Alexandria to Bluemont as both a freight and passenger service. Farmers used the line to send produce and milk to market. McLean and Elkins proposed converting the line to an electric railroad.

The line would still serve the farmers and carry freight and long-distance passengers. An added bonus would be the ability to run more cars on the line to pick up commuters from as far away as Herndon and at all the stops along the line to Rosslyn. The Bluemont would provide commuter transportation to an area that to date had only been able to use the slow and expensive steam trains.[15]

Elkins died before the lease was signed, but the original planned commuter community of Dunn Loring finally began to sell when the Bluemont Branch changed to electric trains. The towns of Herndon, Vienna, and Falls Church all acquired commuter residents and no longer existed just to support the farming communities. McLean, the trolley stop in the middle of nowhere, expanded into a bustling village with a mix of farmers and commuters.[16]

The economy of the region grew with the population. Real estate prices rose slowly but steadily. Even with the increase in tourism and the commuter population, however, the base for Northern Virginia's economy remained agrarian.

Chapter 17

A LANDSCAPE TRANSFORMED BY MACHINERY

By 1915, the region was enjoying unprecedented prosperity. Farmers had embraced many new systems, but at times they found new innovations to be overwhelming. On the eve of World War I, the area was experiencing a slow and somewhat reluctant shift to mechanization and modern living.[1]

It was a strange time, as technological advances arrived faster than most residents could assimilate them. Horses provided the main power for farm work and local transportation, while automobiles began to penetrate the region. With the success of the Wright brothers' flight, man had taken to the air. A farmer plowing his field behind his horses could look up and see an airplane flying overhead. The city of Washington had electric lights, paved streets, a street railroad system, automobiles, and houses with indoor bathrooms and central heat.

Across the Potomac in Virginia, the dichotomy between the lifestyles of members of the same community and same socioeconomic class was at times startling. The trolley companies brought electricity to the countryside and sold it to homes near their power stations. New commuter developments offered houses with indoor plumbing and electric lights, while farmers continued to light their homes with kerosene lamps and bathed in washtubs placed in front of the kitchen stove.[2]

New houses were constructed with small kitchens equipped with electric or gas stoves and iceboxes for cold food storage. Ice was delivered, and many homes were built with a door in the exterior wall so the iceman could slide the ice block into the icebox compartment without entering the kitchen. In contrast, farm families cooked on wood-fired ranges in large country kitchens that were the central gathering place in their homes. Their cold food was stored in their springhouses on shelves or submerged in water. If they had ice, it was because they cut it themselves from their ponds in the winter and stored it in their own icehouses.[3]

Commuters' homes had small kitchen cupboards to store a limited number of canned goods. Farm kitchens often had a separate pantry to store the canning jars with that year's garden produce, large sacks of flour, sugar, and buckets of lard. Root vegetables were kept in a dirt-floored cellar.

Newspaper ad for the new electric washing machine, complete with wringer.

The new commuter homes were built over basements outfitted with furnaces that provided steam heat to radiators in every room. Farmhouses were generally heated by wood or kerosene stoves and the kitchen range. Commuter homeowners could purchase electric wringer washing machines to do laundry, while farm wives had to set their wash boilers on kitchen stoves or on open fires in the yard and scrub clothes by hand.

In spite of their different lifestyles, the commuters and farmers got along fairly well. They lived in an atmosphere that could best be described as mutual tolerance. Assimilation into the community was a slow process for newcomers. The farmers were still divided between the cultures of the old Virginian and the Yankee newcomer. At times, the old Virginians still viewed their Yankee neighbors with rancor and suspicion for deeds done a generation or more before during the Civil War. This situation did not abate until the last of that generation passed away.

The farm community, despite its varied backgrounds, did unite, while the commuters formed the opposition on many issues. Nonetheless, for the most part, they lived without active animosity and participated together in various community organizations. They belonged to the same churches and clubs. Their children went to school together. Citizens from both groups ran for public office, but political activities created some acrimony at the level of town and county governments. The commuters wanted more modern improvements and, as always is the case in Northern Virginia, it was the newcomers who stimulated change.

The native population still tended to prefer the old ways. They also felt that the newcomers could not really understand their way of life. On two subjects, however, there was universal agreement: the poor service offered by the trolleys and the horrible condition of the roads.

Bad roads notwithstanding, Northern Virginia was becoming mechanized. Cars and trucks shared the roads with horse-drawn vehicles. While the horse still provided most of the power for farm machinery, the tractor was slowly making an appearance. The early steam-powered tractors were large, noisy, and unwieldy machines. Their great value was that their

George Johnson on a steam tractor in Great Falls. The barrel on the back of the tractor held the water for the steam engine.

steam engines could also provide power for other farm machinery such as threshing machines.

It was commonplace for farmers who invested in tractors and auxiliary machinery to work for neighbors; however, it was necessary to notify the entire neighborhood when the machinery was going to be moved on the roads to prevent frightening horses. Sudden encounters with these infernal behemoth engines would often cause horses to bolt at top speed, to the peril of those who were riding or driving them. Farmers had to introduce horses carefully to tractors and other machines because the horses were still needed for many jobs, such as hauling grain to and from the threshing machines.[4]

With the improvement of the internal combustion engine, smaller tractors that ran on kerosene and gasoline were introduced. They came with a great many attachments and could perform all manner of cultivation work, from plowing to seeding to harvesting the crop. The manufacturers claimed that a tractor could do the work of several teams of horses and numerous men in a fraction of the time. They also pointed out how economical the tractor was because the owner would not have to feed it. While horses did have to be fed every day, no one offered any price comparisons between the cost of horse feed and tractor fuel.[5]

Based on the time-saving attributes of tractors, the manufacturers proposed that farmers would be able to cultivate more acres than ever before. Virginia farmers, however, had a few problems with this theory, including the high cost of the basic machine. Priced at about $600 without all the necessary attachments, tractors were too expensive for the average farmer. The claim that much more acreage could be cultivated did not apply because most of the farmers had no access to property besides what they were already farming. As a result, most Northern Virginians relied on horses and helped each other during the harvest when more hands were needed.

Generally, farmers were doing well and felt no inclination to switch to tractors. But that was about to change. To start with, there was a sudden increase in the cost of living that reached even into the pockets of farmers. A long, cold, wet spring in 1916 was followed by a hot and dry summer. Crop production was negatively affected. Farming had changed from a diversified production aimed at providing the farm family with their needs to specialty crops raised for sale. In short, farmers no longer worked just to feed themselves and their families. They worked for money. With the increase in property values, real estate taxes had gone up, and so had the price of many other items.

World War I had broken out in Europe in 1914 and soon spread to Africa and the Middle East. Americans viewed the conflict from afar with some detachment until the effects began to be felt on the local level. Soon the war caused an increase in the prices of all manufactured products used on the farms. Fertilizers were in particularly short supply because of the presence of warships and German U-boats in the Atlantic Ocean. In addition, there was increased demand for all types of manufactured goods, horses, and food in Europe. That scenario, coupled with a poor growing season, caused prices to rise in the United States. In fact, the cost of living rose almost daily.[6]

Because much of America's prosperity was based on agricultural products, the federal government decided to help the farmer. A rural credit system of federal farm loan banks was created to loan money to farmers at low interest rates. The theory behind the loans was that if farmers could afford tractors and machinery, then farm productivity would rise. It seemed like a good idea at the time.[7]

Local farmers continued to resist switching to tractors. They still saw little need to try anything new while they were still adjusting to the changes in their lives brought on by the boom in commuter housing. Many were very wary of incurring debt, especially with the ever-rising cost of living. Reluctant or not, the farmers were about to be spurred into mechanization by an outside force.

Chapter 18

SOCIETAL SHIFTS BROUGHT ON BY WAR

On April 6, 1917, the United States declared war on Germany and its allies, a decision that had an immediate and lasting effect on Northern Virginia. With the drastic increase in the size of the armed forces, the government found that keeping the military operating in good order required the efforts of more people than ever before. As a result, workers from all over the country rushed to Washington to participate in the war effort. Their roles ranged from top-level company executives to engineers, clerks, typists, mechanics, nurses, doctors, veterinarians, architects, and others.

Within one month of the declaration of war, thirty-nine hundred people had been hired by the Civil Service Commission in Washington alone, with salaries ranging from $600 to $4,800 per year. The following month saw the addition of another six thousand clerks, stenographers, and typists earning yearly salaries of about $1,200. Nearly fifteen hundred of these hires were women, now in positions traditionally held by men. This great influx of people ushered in a wave of prosperity greater than any previously experienced in the nation's capital. That prosperity quickly spilled into the surrounding suburbs, and Northern Virginia got its share.[1]

The city of Washington was not prepared to house this new population. Hotels, boardinghouses, the Young Men's Christian Association, and the Young Women's Christian Association quickly filled up. Many who could not find a home in the city moved across the river to Virginia. At the outbreak of the war, farsighted speculators quickly leased apartments and houses, which they sublet to war workers for two to three times more than the original rent prices. Many owners with both city and country homes moved to the country and vacated their Washington homes to offer them for rent. Those who could afford to do so bought houses as fast as they came on the market.[2]

Real estate prices rose daily. Week after week, real estate companies posted record-breaking sales figures. The housing shortage immediately led to a building boom—a bonus for the Virginia suburbs, where the highest demand was for smaller homes of six to eight rooms. But building supplies became scarcer as contractors depleted stockpiles and the army built new barracks for soldiers.[3]

When the United States entered the war, there was a serious lack of military training facilities. As the number of troops increased, the government scrambled to expand old facilities and acquire new ones, particularly in the Washington area. Northern Virginia was home to two army posts: Fort Myer, next to Arlington National Cemetery, and a small garrison at Fort Hunt in Fairfax County. Fort Myer, established during the Civil War as part of the defense system for the capital, was the home base of a premier cavalry unit.

Shortly after the United States entered the war, Fort Myer added an officer's training school and facilities for engineers, artillery, and infantrymen. As a result, it gained an additional twenty-five hundred men almost immediately. The "doughboys," as they were called, became a common sight in the Virginia countryside.

Troops on parade at Fort Myer, 1917

Initially, these soldiers had to live in tents due to the lack of barracks space. The army awarded building contracts to several private contractors, who quickly built new barracks alongside the old polo field. In between training sessions, soldiers helped with the construction. When new recruits overflowed those facilities, the army leased the old St. Asaph Racetrack nearby and built more stables and barracks.[4]

The army was not the only branch of the armed services suffering growing pains. The US Navy and Merchant Marine had a serious shortage of ships. To fill the gap, many private shipyards sprang up all over the East Coast. It was a perfect opportunity for Alexandria to return to shipbuilding.

At the end of 1917, the Virginia Shipbuilding Corporation signed a contract with the federal government to build a shipyard at Jones Point in Alexandria. Construction started almost immediately on the new facility. The company had federal contracts to build twelve ships and raced to complete the shipyard, which would have four large shipways, administration buildings, barracks for workers, a cafeteria, and even its own hospital. By April 1, one thousand men were employed there, and that number soon increased to fifteen hundred.

Many Alexandrians were thrilled at the thought of a having a busy port again. The *Alexandria Gazette* offered the following opinion:

> All have waited long and patiently for capitalists to appreciate the advantages offered by Alexandria. While Norfolk, Newport News and other Virginia cities have been forging ahead we have bided our time. All rejoice that the commercial importance of Alexandria is now assured and within the next few months' operations on our river front will enthuse us as nothing has heretofore in our history.[5]

That may have been somewhat of an optimistic overstatement. While the shipyard and the employment it offered were certainly good for Alexandria's businesses, they were not problem-free. Because of the war, there was an all-around shortage of manpower. And in spite of having a barracks for the workers, there was insufficient housing. The government advertised in the local newspapers, begging citizens to do their patriotic duty and rent rooms in their homes to shipyard workers.

The shipyard and its workers also generated a lot of traffic on the narrow streets of the town, and residents suddenly found it very difficult to drive or find anywhere to park their cars. They complained vigorously while enjoying the extra income brought in by those who caused the traffic problems.[6]

Virginia Shipbuilding Corporation in Alexandria, 1917

Nonetheless, the shipyard forged ahead and laid the first keel on May 30, 1918. President Woodrow Wilson arrived to drive the first rivet for a ship named the *Gunston Hall*, after George Mason's home. Three other ships were immediately started. In spite of a tremendous effort, the shipyard did not launch the first ship until February 27, 1919.[7]

All over Northern Virginia, citizens held rallies and pledged their support for the war. Many men rushed to enlist in the army. By early June 1917, more than fifteen hundred men in Fairfax County between the ages of twenty-one and thirty-one had registered for the Selective Service draft. This exodus of drafted and enlisted men caused a serious labor shortage on farms and in mills, stores, and businesses. There was even some discussion in Congress about instituting a draft for farm labor, but nothing came of the idea. Consequently, the labor shortage had one beneficial side effect.[8]

Women had been working for years to change their status in society. Many wanted careers and occupations besides housekeeping and motherhood. Prior to the war, working women primarily served as teachers, maids, cleaners, store clerks, laundresses, governesses, and telephone operators. Their wages were much lower than those of their male counterparts. Live-in maids earned about $1.25 per week, along with room and board. Store clerks worked for about $3.00 per week. Now women hurried to fill the higher-paying jobs that the men had vacated. Those who did not take government work signed on as bank clerks, delivery vehicle drivers, and farmworkers.

This employment shift caused a labor shortage in the field of domestic help; however, no one dared to complain too loudly about the difficulties of hiring a maid, because the women were deemed to be doing their part for the war effort. Even the daughters of the wealthy did their part to help win the war by doing farm work. In 1918, the Women's Land Army of America was formed to encourage women to work on farms.[9]

The influx of war workers resulted in an increased demand for food in the city markets. The cost of food continued to rise. Unfortunately, the farmers did not reap much of the profit from the increase in prices. Minor

Poster displayed to attract women to sign up for the land army, c. 1917

food shortages were caused more by speculation and transportation problems than by production issues. With the advent of railroads across the entire country, consumers had become accustomed to food offered in their markets that was imported from distant locations. The railroads were now used to move troops and war supplies instead of produce for city markets. Local farmers could produce plenty of food, but it was of limited varieties and restricted by the growing season.[10]

Rumors of food shortages caused consumers to worry and vendors to raise the prices. One month after the United States entered the war, food prices rose substantially in the Washington markets. This was especially true for dairy products and all types of meat. Cheese doubled in price. Fish was still a bargain, though, and trout was available for fifteen cents a pound. The scarcity of potatoes, which went to feed the army, led local housewives to experiment with the novelty of macaroni, rice, or dried beans in place of the potatoes that had been served at almost every meal.[11]

Shortages of food and manufactured goods, both real and engineered, promoted the general public opinion that it was patriotic to live frugally. Women formed clubs in which they pledged not to buy unnecessary luxuries. Their definition of *luxuries* included all types of household items and new clothes. Because stores were well stocked with most of those items at the beginning of the war, this trend initially had a very negative effect on the local economy. But that was soon corrected.[12]

One item in short supply was the automobile. Soon after war was declared, Washington-area automobile dealers sold all their inventory and had trouble filling orders for new vehicles. People had to wait months to get a new car.

While city consumers worried about food prices, local farmers planted gardens. Able to grow plenty of fruits and vegetables to sell in the city markets and to their commuter neighbors, they now felt that they were working for the war effort. Borrowing from their example, the Washington Boy Scouts got permission from the District of Columbia City Council to plant a garden at Potomac Park.

Seeing an opportunity to promote his company's tractor, Henry Ford donated one with all necessary attachments to the park project. He also sent two of his employees to teach the scouts how to use the machine and to supervise the planting of the garden. In several days, fifty boys cleared more than one hundred acres of parkland and prepared it for planting. More than two hundred boys worked on planting the land and tending the garden. The end-of-season harvest yielded more than $5,000 worth of corn.[13]

In general, the summer of 1917 was a good gardening season. Farmers transported a large amount of produce to the city markets. By August, the previously scarce potato was again available. Prices for all produce, fowl, and dairy products dropped back to normal levels. Prices for meat, which was shipped in from western states, remained high due to curtailed rail shipments for domestic consumer goods.[14]

Massive government purchases to feed the army created shortages in eastern markets; however, everyone adjusted fairly well to the economic changes brought on by the overseas conflict. Most locals accepted shortages as their own personal contribution to winning the war.

Chapter 19

EXPLOSIVE GROWTH COMES TO REMOTE BELVOIR TRACT

As the civilian population was learning to cope with all the wartime shortages, so too was the military. It quickly became apparent that even with its expansions, the space at Fort Myer could not accommodate the cavalry, infantry, and artillery, plus the engineers. The chief of engineers, Major General William M. Black, wanted his branch to have its own training camp, with space to teach the skills necessary for war.

To solve this crisis, in April 1917, the federal government leased ground on Belvoir Plantation, the former home of the Fairfax family, on the Potomac River. P. F. Gormley Company, a civilian contractor, was hired to quickly build a camp for eight hundred men there.[1]

The camp established at Belvoir, the most remote in the Washington area, was surrounded by farmland and acres of woods. The closest commercial center was the village of Accotink. While much of Northern Virginia was experiencing growth and development stimulated by the electric railroads, the Belvoir area of Fairfax County remained, for the most part, untouched by progress. The closest electric trolley stop was at

Accotink village street scene

Mount Vernon, more than four miles away. The Southern Railway line passed the camp on the opposite side, four and a half miles away. The roads leading to the camp were some of the worst in the county, making access difficult.

As soon as the camp was established, the army was convinced that Belvoir, with all its undeveloped acreage, was an ideal place to build a major training post for the Army Corps of Engineers. It was decided to name the camp in honor of Major General Andrew Humphreys, an engineer who had served with distinction on General Ulysses S. Grant's staff during the Civil War.[2]

Crossed by creeks and ravines, Camp Humphreys's rough and rugged land provided a natural training ground to teach men how to build bridges, roads, and railroads. Camp expansion began in January 1918 during the worst winter on record. Day after day, the high temperatures remained in the single digits; the lows dropped to zero degrees or below. Added to the cold were frequent snows, ice storms, and high winds that caused blizzard conditions.[3]

Contractors attempting to construct buildings discovered that the ground was frozen to a depth of eighteen inches. Motor access to the camp, not easy in good weather, became almost impossible under the harsh winter conditions. To deliver supplies to camp, army engineers had to resurrect road-building techniques from the previous century. They constructed a fifteen-foot-wide plank road to connect with the main highway from Alexandria; however, all other roads in the area, including the Alexandria Highway (now Route 1), were also in poor condition. When temperatures rose above freezing, the roads thawed out and turned into a deep and impassable muddy mess.[4]

To aid in moving supplies, the government began building a spur line to the camp from Accotink Station on the Southern Railway. An additional one thousand men from the Army Corps of Engineers were assigned to the camp to build the rail line. With that move, the army could accomplish two goals at once: the supply transportation problem would be solved, and their engineers would be trained to build railroads. The War Department also helped to finance an extension of the Mount Vernon rail line to the camp. Neither railroad progressed very quickly. Saddled with a dishonest contractor, the Mount Vernon line was never finished.[5]

Ultimately, the army was forced to ship building supplies on boats down the Potomac and to build a two-mile internal railroad to move the supplies from the riverbank up to the plateau where the camp was being

Narrow gauge railroad built by the army engineers at Camp Humphreys to move building supplies delivered by ships on the Potomac into the main camp area.

constructed. In spite of all the problems presented by weather and transportation, the contractors kept their crews building at the camp.[6]

The positive economic effect on this previously remote area was substantial. Suddenly there were jobs that paid good wages available close to home. Local men hired on with the contractors as carpenters, woodcutters, cooks, and general laborers. Women were hired as stenographers, typists, and bookkeepers. By March, another three hundred laborers were hired by the War Department from distant locations and transported to Camp Humphreys to supplement the local workforce. All these workers were paid top wages. They also were provided with food, living quarters, and medical care. The latter was acutely needed because many working on the project suffered from frostbitten hands and feet and had to be hospitalized before they could return to the job.[7]

Housing and feeding all these workers also provided local businesses with an economic boost. The P. F. Gormley Company rented at least fourteen houses for them, and one local store sold them $10,000 worth of blankets. Other local businesses sold them clothes, food, and household items.[8]

On the negative side, the civilian population was adversely affected by the overuse of local roads caused by the influx of military vehicles

Soldiers at Camp Humphreys digging a foundation for another building

Soldiers' tents at Camp Humphreys

traveling from Alexandria to Camp Humphreys. Terrible road conditions, combined with gasoline rationing, made travel very difficult for residents. Two years earlier, Fairfax County had issued a road bond for $90,000 to pave the main roads south of Alexandria. Unfortunately, the water-bound macadam pavement that was installed was no match for the heavy military supply trucks. The money spent on the project literally went down the drain. As a result, the Fairfax County Board of Supervisors felt justified in requesting that the federal government repair the roads.[9]

Recognizing the need for access to the camp, the government quickly agreed to repair the old Alexandria Highway in a magnificent fashion, allocating $200,000 for army engineers to build a concrete road on top of the old roadbed. The new eighteen-foot-wide surface would benefit area residents while simultaneously attracting tourists to visit Mount Vernon, Woodlawn Plantation, and other historic sites in the Virginia countryside.[10]

Another positive side effect from the location of the camp was the construction of electric power lines. When the government's original plan to build a power station at the camp proved to be unfeasible, an eleven-mile-long line, strung with thirty-three miles of wire, was constructed to carry electrical currents from Alexandria. While providing power to Camp Humphreys, ultimately the line also provided electricity to the residents of the neighboring countryside.[11]

Bad weather notwithstanding, the camp was built in record time. By April, two hundred buildings had been completed. When the camp formally opened on May 4, 1918, over eight thousand soldiers were already stationed there. The camp population quickly outgrew the facilities when the number rose to seventeen thousand by the end of the month. Approximately five thousand men were living in tents while waiting for permanent quarters and barracks. To speed up the necessary construction, the army hired another two thousand civilian carpenters and laborers.[12]

The sudden huge increase in population to this previously isolated area brought many benefits to the local economy even as it created problems. Transportation was a major issue. On weekends, there was no easy way for soldiers with weekend passes to travel to Alexandria or Washington. Their options were to take a boat from the Belvoir dock, hitch a ride on an army truck, or walk the four miles to the Mount Vernon trolley stop. To make matters worse, the new concrete highway to Alexandria was only half finished, so traffic was diverted to other, less direct routes. The military added its voice to those of the local citizens demanding better roads and rail service to the area. In early June, the situation improved when the first three miles of the spur railroad opened, connecting with the Southern Railway at Accotink.[13]

Throughout the summer and fall of 1918, Camp Humphreys continued to grow. The federal government concluded that, having invested so much money in the site, it was the ideal place for a permanent military post and training facility for the Army Corps of Engineers. On October 2, 1918, the *Washington Post* reported that 963 acres of the Belvoir tract had been purchased by condemnation proceedings from its owner, John S. West, for $53,695.40. In one short year, the property had advanced from a remote and isolated tract to a valuable location.[14]

The fortunes of war were good for Mr. West's finances. Those same fortunes also had a lasting effect on the entire countryside south of Alexandria. In 1935, at the request of President Franklin D. Roosevelt, the name of Camp Humphreys was changed to Fort Belvoir to commemorate the Fairfax family.[15]

Unfortunately, in spite of all the benefits to the area brought by the establishment of Camp Humphreys, the winter of 1917–1918 was a particularly difficult time for all the civilians in Northern Virginia. The economic gains spurred by military expansion did not necessarily offset the deprivations and hardships caused by the war.

Chapter 20

THE ADVENT OF RATIONING

Many Northern Virginians spent a winter of misery brought on by the effects of the war and the extremely cold weather. There were shortages of wheat, meat, sugar, and fuel. With the exception of those items, there was plenty of food available. Food supply deficits were more inconvenient than life threatening. But the government felt it necessary to regulate the consumption of those items that were in short supply—probably because the shortages resulted from government purchases to feed the army and a curtailment in railroad shipping for nongovernment supplies.[1]

To balance out the supplies available to the civilian population, in December 1917, sugar was rationed to three pounds per person per month. The government also halted all brewing of beer and other alcoholic beverages. In the hope of avoiding additional rationing, the food administration issued guidelines for meal planning, suggesting at least one meatless meal a day and totally meatless Tuesdays. Individuals were

Northern Virginians bought their fruit and vegetables from vendors in the District of Columbia markets.

advised to forgo wheat on Wednesdays and pork on Saturdays. Eating fowl was permitted on any day.[2]

To most citizens, these instructions were just another added annoyance, as meat was already scarce in the markets. Except for sugar rationing, the farming communities of Northern Virginia were not too troubled by these shortages, because they grew or raised much of their own food.

A month before food rationing was instituted, Americans began experiencing a severe fuel shortage. The "coal famine," as it was called, first affected the Virginia farming communities in the upper Potomac corridor. Next, government officials began to worry about coal supplies for the city of Washington. Anthracite, or hard coal, was used to heat most homes with modern furnaces as well as public buildings and government offices. Coal also provided the power to generate electricity and run the steam engines of ships and trains. Because of the capital area's sharp population increase over the previous year, coal consumption had increased by 60 percent. Washington ran on coal, burning twenty-five hundred tons of it per day. Without coal, all business would come to a screeching halt.[3]

One factor contributing to the coal shortage was the military's reliance on the fuel to run the railroads, ships, and factories that produced its equipment. With so many young men in the army, mines were experiencing labor problems. Miners who remained on the job were either men deemed too old or unfit or boys too young for military service. Many of the miners, unhappy with the low wages they earned for their hard and dangerous work, went on strike.

Then there was the problem of shipping. The railroads were overwhelmed with the movement of war supplies and stymied by a severe labor shortage. Miners returned to work after negotiating a pay raise, but it was impossible to quickly make up for the coal production lost during the strikes. By November, coal shipments into Washington had dwindled to between fifty to one hundred tons a day. The government advised everyone to practice fuel economy.[4]

As the extremely cold weather continued, the coal shortage assumed catastrophic proportions. In Washington, Georgetown, and Alexandria, the poor, sick, and elderly were in danger of freezing to death. Trolley system administrators agreed to conserve coal by cutting their scheduled runs and making fewer stops. They also stopped heating the cars and waiting stations, adding to the hardships felt by commuters who had to walk farther and wait in frigid stations.[5]

Northern Virginians were affected by the coal shortage in similar ways. Those who lived in towns, villages, and new suburban homes had the same dependence on coal as the city dwellers. They found it hard to heat their homes, and many suffered from frozen water pipes.

Early in November, the government decided that hard coal would not be delivered south of the Potomac River. If Virginia got any coal, it was bituminous (soft) coal, which burned faster and provided less heat. Any deliveries to the coal dealers were very limited and were in turn sold in small quantities. Many smaller dealers were forced out of business. The local fuel board attempted to prevent hoarding by requiring everyone who purchased coal to swear an affidavit that they did not already own more than two tons.[6]

By the first of December, the price of coal had risen to ten dollars a ton, a fifty-cent increase from the month before. The price increase was moot, however, because no one could find a whole ton to purchase. When Smoot Lumber Yard in Alexandria received a delivery, the firm deployed all its horses and wagons to deliver coal to customers. In an effort to be fair to all, the largest quantity that anyone could purchase was fifty cents' worth.[7]

The region's farmers did not suffer nearly as much as the residents of the cities and towns. The primary heat source for most of their homes was still the wood burning range in the kitchen, and there was no shortage of wood. As the coal crisis continued, however, kerosene, a coal by-product, also became scarce. Many farm homes depended on kerosene lamps for light and had auxiliary stoves that burned kerosene.[8]

By January 1918, the government had added more regulations in the hope of conserving the small amounts of coal coming into the region. Heatless Mondays were decreed. All businesses not directly involved in the war effort were required to close on Mondays or operate without heat. Most businesses elected to close. Grocery stores only stayed open until midday. Without heat, the employees and owners could not function. Alexandria billiard and pool parlors remained open, but patrons played in their overcoats.[9]

In a move similar to the response to the gasoline crises of the 1970s, the US Geological Survey announced there was no need to panic; there were huge deposits of coal underground, enough to keep the country running for centuries to come. According to the report, the whole problem was transportation—it took as long as a month for coal to travel from the mine to the consumer. That statement was of scant comfort to freezing people who were unable to heat their homes, or to commuters who suffered from frigid waits for delayed trolleys. A week after the agency's report ran in the *Washington Post*, another snowstorm hit the area, bringing all coal trains to a halt.[10]

Warmer weather eventually resolved the heating crisis; however, the negative impact on local businesses, including the trolley lines, lingered. Some businesses took years to recoup their financial losses caused by the lack of fuel. During the summer months, the government strongly suggested that people order their winter coal early. Northern Virginians were urged to substitute wood for coal whenever possible. To ensure that supplies would last, restrictions were imposed on electric lighting for all commercial establishments.

In the fall, the government announced that 1918 was the greatest coal production year on record. War work for the railroads was blamed for the lack of deliveries. But that was a small comfort to those who couldn't heat their homes and business owners who suffered from lost revenue.[11]

Extreme cold and a lack of fuel did not stop the growth of the government during the war. New jobs were constantly created, and the population in the Washington metropolitan area continued to grow. That was good news for property owners because the real estate market remained very strong.

There was still a serious housing shortage. Builders were having a difficult time getting supplies to build single-family dwellings due to restrictions on railroad shipping. Materials that aided the war effort had priority on the rail lines, and the production of single-family homes was not considered a factor in winning the war. The same philosophy did not apply to apartment buildings. The government, understanding the dire need to build housing for war workers, encouraged apartment house builders to get on with the job.[12]

US government poster from 1918 encouraging residents to order their coal early.

Messenger boys employed in the District of Columbia, c. 1918

The City of Alexandria and its neighbors experienced a large housing problem when the government decided to build a torpedo factory on the waterfront there—the site of the present-day Torpedo Factory Art Center. Suddenly it was necessary to find or build new accommodations for another 450 to 500 workers and their families.[13]

New government jobs were not restricted to adults. With the surge in paperwork and interoffice deliveries, the Civil Service added many new jobs for messenger boys and girls between the ages of fourteen and sixteen. The annual salary offered was $360—about fifteen cents an hour. Those messengers who performed well could advance to a subclerical job paying $480 per year. As odd as the concept of the government employing children seems today, many children at the time found it necessary to go to work before the age of fourteen. Children as young as ten found employment in the private sector. The fact that the government required a minimum age of fourteen was a concession to the anti-child labor movements in the country.[14]

Child labor in Northern Virginia's farming communities was considered normal. Public schools still consisted of one- to two-room schoolhouses. And while some offered high school classes, there was no requirement that children attend. Many children left school after the fifth, sixth, or seventh grade. The basics of reading, writing, arithmetic, spelling, and some geography were viewed by many as sufficient formal education. Children who lived on farms were expected to help with chores by the time they were five or six years old. By age ten or twelve, they were often considered old enough and strong enough to learn the serious business of farming, or, for girls, housekeeping.[15]

Increased government employment did not necessarily translate to prosperity for the average citizen. In 1918, the cost of living in the nation's capital and the surrounding suburbs was among the highest in the country. The price of housing and fuel was certainly a primary cause, but the high cost of food topped the list.

Food price increases across the country in the previous five years averaged 66 percent. The Washington area, as usual, was ahead of the average and added another 7 percent for the fiscal year ending June 15, 1918. The statistics startled economists, who were at a loss to explain why a small city surrounded by high-producing farmland should generate such high prices. The profits certainly did not end up in the pockets of the farmers or the grocers. To prevent war profiteering, the government fixed prices and profit levels on most comestibles. High food prices stimulated people to plant their own gardens.[16]

Bicycle messenger boys, c. 1918

Certain items were scarce. For the most part, though, residents of the region had plenty to eat. Voluntary rationing was still encouraged, but with the exception of sugar, which remained in short supply, it was not generally enforced. As the June fruit-canning season approached, householders were allowed to exceed the ration if they signed a statement that it was to be used exclusively for that purpose. But the shortage worsened when German submarines sank two ships, sending sugar cargos of twenty-four million pounds to the bottom of the Atlantic Ocean. The sugar ration was then set at two pounds per person per month.[17]

In addition to the high cost of living, other factors negatively affected the Northern Virginia economy. During an exceptionally hot summer, temperatures advanced to over one hundred degrees for many days in a row, ruining crops in the fields. Apples and other fruits literally cooked on the trees before they could be harvested.[18]

In July 1918, an outbreak of typhoid struck Alexandria. This highly contagious disease caused much personal hardship and grief among the victims and their families, and it negatively impacted the local economy. Fearful of an epidemic, the commander at Camp Humphreys banned all soldiers from eating or drinking anything in Alexandria. The lost revenue for restaurants and bars was substantial.

By September 1918, the general population was fatigued by the frantic pace of war work and the oppressively hot weather. As the days cooled down, there was good news from the war front that the Allies might have a victory before the end of the year. A general attitude of hope pervaded all aspects of daily life. As gardeners harvested their produce, they even changed the name of their "war gardens" to "victory gardens." After a challenging year, everyone was looking forward to an easing of hardships. Unfortunately, the worst was yet to come.[19]

Chapter 21

OBSTACLES TO PEACE AND PLENTY

Earlier in 1918, an especially virulent strain of influenza had flared up in Europe and other parts of the world. This airborne virus, known as the Spanish flu, quickly spread from soldier to soldier in the trenches in France and was carried back to the United States by soldiers returning home from the front. A situation that had begun as localized epidemics was soon a pandemic. The virus arrived in the Washington area in September and cut a devastating swath through the entire population.[1]

Outbreaks of flu viruses were not uncommon, especially during the winter months. It was a part of life; however, the victims rarely died unless they were elderly or very young, or had other health problems. This particular flu was often fatal, and those at the highest risk of catching it were in their midteens to early thirties. Symptoms included high fevers, general aches, extreme chills, coughing, and hemorrhagic pneumonia. The speed of the progression of the illness was especially frightening. A person could feel well in the morning, fall ill by midday, and be dead before daybreak of the next day.[2]

The Spanish flu arrived in Washington and Alexandria simultaneously in September and quickly reached epidemic proportions. Its spread through sparsely populated Northern Virginia farm country was much slower. In an effort to control the spread of the contagion, public health officials closed all schools and public meeting places. People were afraid to leave home, but certain necessities of life required some public contact. Riding trolleys, shopping for food, and going to work were all potentially dangerous activities.

So many people became ill that hospitals were filled, and churches had to be used to house the overflow of flu-ridden patients. The death toll mounted so fast that all available coffins were used up. Gravediggers could not keep up with the demand for their services. Bodies and coffins piled up in front of hospitals and mortuaries. In some cases, entire families died.[3]

Most commerce in the region came to a halt, it was hard for farmers to get their harvest in from the fields, and even more difficult to ship it to market. They were already experiencing a labor shortage due to the war, and now, with some laborers ill with the flu, the lack of available help became an acute problem. Many grieving families were hit not only in their hearts but also in their wallets.[4]

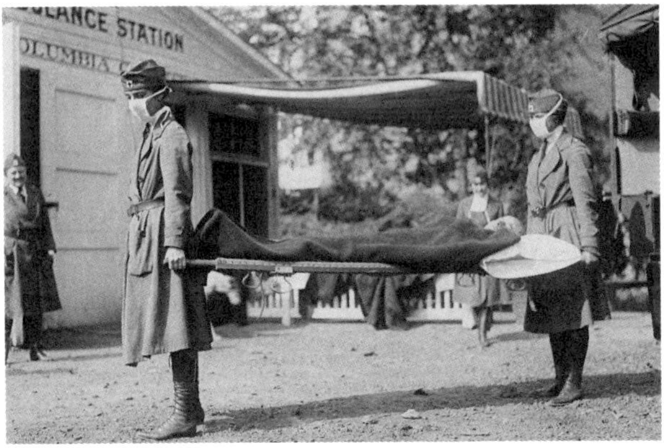

Red Cross demonstration, 1918

October was the worst month, with the highest number of flu cases. By November, the number was winding down. The joy brought by the end of the war on November 11, when the armistice was signed, was greatly tempered by the struggle to survive. The number of cases escalated again in December. It was not until late spring of 1919 that the deadly virus disappeared.[5]

The influenza epidemic had far-reaching consequences that lasted for years. The population of Northern Virginia suffered enormous losses. Fairfax County alone had the second-highest death rate in the state of Virginia. Out of a population of about 21,000, the county lost 530 of its citizens to the virus.[6]

Those who survived found it very difficult to resume a normal life. The negative impact went beyond grief for lost loved ones. In some cases, families were left without an income when the father died. Other families experienced the loss of the mother, leaving young children with no one to care for them. As relatives took in orphaned or motherless children, many family budgets were stretched to the limit or beyond. Some families were reduced to a life of poverty that they had not previously experienced.[7]

In general, most people had hoped the end of the war would bring back a quieter, more normal lifestyle and that the high cost of living in Washington and its suburbs would be reduced. But the many deprivations brought on by the war could not be quickly corrected. In the years immediately following the war, the entire country suffered an economic recession.

One cause of the economic downturn was a general change in jobs and labor. A large part of the population had traveled away from their hometowns and had been introduced to different lifestyles. During the war, many jobs normally done by men had been taken over by women. At the end of the war, men released from their military duties reclaimed their jobs. In other cases, men who returned to their former jobs were no longer satisfied with the old terms of employment. They wanted higher wages, better working conditions, and fewer hours. When their demands were not met, they went on strike. This attitude pervaded almost all types of labor and caused another increase in the already high cost of living.[8]

A year after the signing of the armistice, strikes at coal mines caused another serious energy shortage. By December 1919, the strikes were settled, but it would take months to replenish the coal supplies. In an attempt to manage the situation, Congress resumed the wartime fuel rules. This severe rationing required all manufacturing plants to cut back to a three-day workweek. No ornamental electric lights for businesses were allowed, including shop windows. Stores, except for those that sold food, could only use electric lights six hours a day. And probably worst of all, electric railroads had to operate on restricted schedules.[9]

This cutback in commerce had a very negative effect on the economy. If businesses could not operate, they did not pay their employees nor did they make any money. While Northern Virginians suffered another bleak and cold winter along with the rest of the country, the local economy was propped up to some degree by the population of government employees with guaranteed wages.

On the positive side, builders and real estate agents were predicting a rise in sales. The population explosion in the region caused by the huge expansion of the wartime government appeared to be permanent. While the government was downsizing some departments, others were growing.

People who had endured cramped living quarters during the war now wanted better homes. High rents in Washington stimulated many to look to the suburbs and consider buying a home. Young married couples were tired of living in one-room apartments, with the kitchen facilities consisting of a single burner located in a shallow closet and one shared bathroom per floor. They wondered why they should continue to pay rent if, for a few dollars more every month, they could own a home. The banks and mortgage companies were working hard to help them make their dream come true by lobbying Congress to enact legislation for higher mortgage credit and a plan for amortization of mortgage loans.[10]

Builders and developers hurried to complete new subdivisions and houses in Arlington County—formerly Alexandria County—and Fairfax County. But their profit margins were limited, and the anticipated rush to purchase did not materialize. Building supplies, almost impossible to get during the war, were readily available but at a higher price. Craftsmen and laborers who worked on the construction also demanded higher wages. The end result was higher-priced homes that were slow to sell. By 1922, desperate builders were advertising homes at "prewar prices." At the same time, older homes sold in less time.[11]

Farmers in the region were also suffering from this recession. In spite of the spreading developments of commuter communities, the local economy was still based on agriculture. While the effects of the recession caused some hardships for the commuter population, farmers suffered the most. Food prices remained very high for consumers, but farmers made less on the products of their labor. Just as the recession was a nationwide problem, so too was the farmer's plight. By 1922, the secretary of agriculture pronounced that the American agricultural economy was in a state of very serious depression.[12]

During the war years, farmers had been encouraged to mechanize their farms for greater production. Many mortgaged their property to raise the money to update their farms with electricity and purchase new equipment. On some farms, tractors replaced horsepower, but the majority of Northern Virginia farmers still relied on horses for farm work. For transportation, most had upgraded to automobiles and trucks. The expenses involved with mortgage-financed upgrades, coupled with a depressed market, caused financial problems for many farmers. A survey conducted in 1924 found that more than 20 percent of the farmland in Fairfax County was mortgaged. Given the condition of the produce markets, this rate of mortgage debt would soon have a negative effect on the local economy through foreclosures.[13]

Market prices were lower than the cost of production. Ironically, increased mechanization had caused the market for farm products to fall.

Fairfax County dairy farmer Jesse Smith, c. 1920

American farmers in general were producing more crops than the world markets needed, and exports had declined. In addition, the cost of running their new machinery absorbed much, if not all, of their profits. No matter how necessary the farm-grown products were, farmers' wages were lower than those of any other working group. It is not surprising that the farmers' children often tended to seek jobs in nearby cities.[14]

In 1923 one writer for the *Washington Post* summed up the economic situation in an astute manner when commenting on the rush to upgrade to indoor plumbing, electricity, motorized vehicles, and other luxury items:

New motor-driven farm machinery on display in Herndon

> In this the farmers were not different from city dwellers. All classes of the American community have learned how to spend money as fast or faster than they make it. The farmer has kept up with the procession in turning luxuries into necessities.[15]

To help the farmers recover financially, various programs were introduced. Harry B. Derr, who had been appointed the agricultural agent for Fairfax County in 1917, spent the next twenty-one years advising and educating farmers on all phases of agronomy and animal husbandry. His job was not easy. He recommended fertilizers and high-quality seed. Farmers who could not afford to purchase those went without fertilizer and used inferior seed. The result was a diminished yield or a failed crop.

Derr also advised on the breeding of dairy cattle. Those who followed his advice generally had better success than those who did not. Dairy farming was the strongest farming industry in Northern Virginia. Local cows constantly won awards as top milk producers and usually exceeded the national milk production average per cow by 25 percent. Nonetheless, a drop in consumer milk prices from seventeen cents to fifteen cents per quart made headlines in 1919. Derr also encouraged farmers to form cooperatives and associations to learn about the latest farming techniques and to give them a voice within the government and

Great Falls Grange

in the marketplace. For instance, in 1920, the Maryland and Virginia Milk Producers' Association worked to restore the price of milk to seventeen cents per quart.[16]

Another strong farmers' organization was the Patrons of Husbandry, a national fraternity of farmers with local chapters known as Granges. Northern Virginia Granges included Pioneer, Great Falls, Floris, and Providence. The Granges, which included both men and women from local farming communities, were designed to improve the lives of farmers through education and legislation. They also served as a community outreach program in rural areas, where members united to help each other in times of trouble.[17]

Chapter 22

MOONSHINERS, GENTLEMEN FARMERS, AND REAL ESTATE DEVELOPERS

In Northern Virginia, farmers were not the only ones suffering from the effects of the postwar recession. The county governments of both Arlington and Fairfax were also trying to cope with a lack of funds.

The explosive commuter growth cultivated in the decade before the war had seemed beneficial at the time. The prevailing theory was that a larger population translated into more tax money to fill the county treasuries; however, boards of supervisors from both counties had failed to recognize that additional taxpayers would require additional services.

Neither Arlington nor Fairfax was prepared to immediately provide the infrastructure necessary for the expanded population. While farmers were having trouble adjusting to the lifestyle and habits of the commuter population, both groups agreed on several major concerns.

Better roads and transportation headed the list. Now that so many people were dependent on the automobile, everyone wanted paved roads. Many citizens were unhappy with the railroad services provided by private rail companies. Railroad users complained that the schedules were insufficient, the service was unreliable, and the cars were dirty and cold in the winter.[1]

Residents also demanded improvements to existing school buildings and the establishment of high schools, as well as sewer and water service for the towns and sprawling new subdivisions. The cost for all these improvements was astronomical and quite beyond the budgets of the counties. The task of building better roads alone was beyond their scope, since the counties were still responsible for road construction and maintenance within their jurisdictions.[2]

As far as the county supervisors could see, raising taxes and selling bonds were the only ways to fund the needed improvements. But the taxpayers were not agreeable. They did not mind the bonds, but they did mind a rise in taxes—especially the beleaguered farmers. They were already struggling with a high cost of living and low income in a time of economic recession. What is more, they did not believe they were getting fair value for the tax dollars they already paid. Nonetheless, the counties passed a few bond issues, and some improvements were slowly implemented.[3]

The hard times of the recession, coupled with new state and national legislation, provided an impetus for the development of a new type of local business. In 1919 Congress ratified the Eighteenth Amendment to the US Constitution, which established the prohibition on the manufacture, sale, or transportation of intoxicating liquors. The law went into effect in January 1920 and immediately spawned businesses across the country that manufactured and sold illegal liquor known as *moonshine*. The product was marketed and sold by *bootleggers*.[4]

Virginia moonshiners and bootleggers were already well established because the commonwealth had passed Prohibition for the state in 1916. Poor country roads made remote wooded areas ideal places to establish homemade distillery operations known as stills. Some entrepreneurs were bold enough to build their stills within the town limits, but most favored sites along the Potomac River. If the law caught up with a business owner or his employees, the river offered a good escape route. It also provided for easy boat transport for bottles and jars of the finished product.[5]

In spite of diligent work by the federal law enforcers known as *revenuers*, the cottage industry of moonshining provided a living wage to some of the farmers and a few others. Unless the still operator was blatant, the county sheriff's department often turned a blind eye to the business. Indeed, it was a dangerous business because some law enforcers were trigger-happy. There was the additional risk of being arrested, tried, and convicted. If that happened, the still owner would serve a term in jail. Yet moonshining could be lucrative. In fact, some bootleggers made a fortune.[6]

The Eighteenth Amendment killed the legal sale of liquor, but it didn't cure the thirst. Since advertising could only be done by word of mouth, and potential customers had to be carefully vetted, it took some time to start a new moonshining enterprise. Once his business was started, a moonshiner could establish regular delivery routes in Georgetown and Washington. Customer lists often included congressmen and senators who might have voted for the law but certainly did not intend to abide by it. It was not unusual for farm trucks loaded with market produce to carry the other product hidden beneath.[7]

During the 1920s, another social element, the gentleman farmer, was added to the local farmer-commuter population mix. It had long been the

Law officers with a still captured in Fairfax County, 1929

custom for the wealthy to maintain both city and country homes; however, the farms that served as country homes were working farms. Depressed prices for farms and country properties offered at foreclosure auctions or private sales began to attract members of the upper middle class.

It became fashionable for city dwellers to purchase these properties, especially those with historic homes. New owners restored and rehabilitated old structures, often installing a grandeur that went beyond the original style of the home. Since they were not farmers, these new owners would usually employ a local farmer to work their land.[8]

While these efforts did offer some employment to the community, often gentlemen's farms were not farmed to the maximum or with the idea of making a profit. To make matters worse, a 1924 survey conducted by the University of Virginia found that these properties were usually taxed at only one-quarter of their true value. It appears the tax assessors were reluctant to offend this particular group of owners. This reticence may have been based on the theory that some money is better than none. Because of the depressed real estate market for farms, the assessors may have believed that the land would lie idle and produce little or no tax revenue if it were not for the gentleman who owned it. Working farmers, however, did not subscribe to this theory.

Cameron Run fox hunt, Fairfax County, c. 1920

To add insult to injury, many gentleman farmers enjoyed fox hunting. To ensure good sport, they imported foxes and fed them before releasing them into the countryside. In addition, they resisted all local legislation to curb the fox population. Poultry farmers often incurred large losses when foxes killed their flocks, and they were bitter about laws that protected the "idle rich."[9]

At the beginning of the 1920s, parts of the country started to recover from this recession. Northern Virginia real estate development played a major part in the local recovery.

The large number of employment opportunities offered by the expanded US government during the war years did not decline with the end of the war; therefore, the population of the Washington area continued to grow. The housing shortage that first became an issue in 1917 had not abated. Real estate developers with an eye on the large number of potential buyers began to launch new projects.

One of the most successful was Lyon Park in North Arlington, planned and developed by Lyon and Fitch. Established in 1919, Lyon Park became the model for many developments that followed. Frank Lyon, one of the partners and the developer of Lyon Park, had first ventured into subdivision development in 1904 near Clarendon. Given his success rate and the magnitude of the projects that he started, it is somewhat surprising that a writer for the *Washington Post* described suburban development as Lyon's hobby.[10]

A lawyer and a newspaper editor, Lyon believed the infrastructure for the community should be in place before the lots were offered for sale. The forested land that became Lyon Park was cleared of small trees and undergrowth. Large trees were retained; streets and sidewalks were laid; and electric, water, sewer, and gas lines were installed throughout the entire development before the first lot was offered for sale.

After several winters of coal shortages, the idea of gas heat must have been very attractive to potential purchasers. Lyon also planned and built a group of brick buildings as a commercial center. A chain-store grocery,

Lyon Park, Arlington County, 1921

a pharmacy, and a meat market were slated to be opened near the trolley stop that served the community.[11]

When Lyon began to market the property in 1920, sales were initially slow, no doubt due to the recession. The following year, he added another innovation to his marketing methods. Instead of the traditional male real estate sales agent, he employed Ruby Lee Minar as his sales manager. With Lyon's development skill and Minar's marketing strategy, the project took off.[12]

Lot buyers had the option of purchasing homes from Lyon or another builder. Lyon's company would help arrange the financing. The initial advertisements offered the following enticement: "LIVE IN LYON PARK Washington's new suburb. Don't pay rent all your life. $20.00 a month will start you."[13]

By the end of July 1921, the company was reporting sales of more than $100,000. During the first year, almost all the sales were to homebuyers. As the economy got stronger, however, investors began to buy lots. A record-breaking transaction occurred in October 1921, when one investor purchased eighty lots at once. This was the single largest sale of finished building lots anywhere in the Washington area since before the war. The purchaser intended to invest $300,000 in building five- and six-room houses.[14]

As the recession started to fade, the momentum for development increased. In July 1922, Ruby Lee Minar reported that her office registered $75,000 worth of transactions in only one week. She also predicted unprecedented development in Arlington in the next ten years. To capitalize on her prediction, Minar opened an office in Cherrydale with a staff of six agents specializing in real estate sales in Maywood, Thrifton, Dominion Heights, Park Lane, and Livingston Heights. Not wishing to miss out on any possible business, Minar also included a special department to handle farm sales.

New subdivisions arrived on the scene in Arlington as fast as they could be drawn on paper and recorded by the county. In five short years, a farming community with small villages and dirt roads was transformed into a modern twentieth-century commuter suburb. Financing was easy, interest rates were low, and banks helped to spur sales by making second trust mortgages readily available. The price of real estate steadily increased every year.

New home in Cherrydale, 1920

Chapter 23

BUILD IT, AND THEY WILL COME

Several major transportation projects helped to stimulate the great demand for real estate in Arlington. Originally, the trolley systems provided commuter transportation and made homes in Virginia a practical choice for those employed in the District of Columbia. Although many commuters were still using the trolley system, by the 1920s automobiles were becoming increasingly popular.

Virginia's dirt and gravel lanes compared poorly with Washington's wide, paved streets and boulevards—a fact that caused some potential homeowners to question the wisdom of moving to Virginia. With increased development, however, came road improvements in areas near the new subdivisions. Aware that good roads would attract buyers, developers took on much of the roadwork themselves. But they were only inclined to spend their money on road improvements that were in close proximity to their projects.

Road quality had been a constant issue with Virginians since the time of the first settlements. Now the residents of the new subdivisions added their demands to those of longtime residents. The Lyon Park and Clarendon citizens' associations mounted a successful campaign to lobby the Arlington County government for a road bond. The result was a measure to widen and pave the mile and a half of Lee Highway (Route 29) between Halls Hill and Falls Church.[1]

The new pavement dramatically affected the price of real estate. Land adjacent to and near Lee Highway that sold in 1922 for $250 to $500 per acre increased to between $2,500 and $5,000 per acre in 1925.[2]

During the flurry of road improvements, Congress authorized two major bridge projects from the District of Columbia to Arlington. The Francis Scott Key Bridge was constructed to replace the ancient and decayed Washington Aqueduct Bridge that ran from Georgetown to Rosslyn. The old wood-surfaced bridge, originally built to take canal boats across the river, had been in poor repair almost since the day it opened. Potomac River floods and winter ice dams constantly eroded the bridge piers and resulted in frequent closures for repairs. When the Key

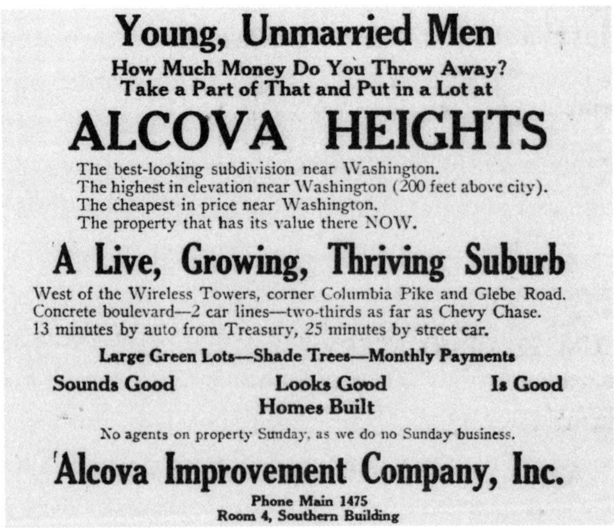

Advertisement for Alcova Heights in the Evening Star *newspaper*

Memorial Bridge under construction

Bridge opened in 1923, the new span provided a smooth and easy ride into Georgetown.[3]

Thanks to the bridge and the newly paved Lee Highway, economically priced homes in Arlington were now a viable choice for commuters. A prime example was the development of Alcova Heights, where four hundred lots were offered for sale in 1923. Almost three hundred lots sold within the first few months. Real estate ads began to reflect these road improvements. While agents still touted proximity to a trolley line, they promoted good roads and short automobile commutes even more. Alcova Heights was advertised as being only a fifteen-minute drive from the Treasury Department.[4]

A second bridge project of a larger magnitude provided an even greater stimulus to Arlington real estate sales. In 1925, Congress authorized the construction of the Arlington Memorial Bridge to run from Constitution Avenue past the Lincoln Memorial and across the Potomac River to Arlington National Cemetery. Even though construction took six years (it did not open until 1932), the bridge had a positive effect on real estate values as soon as it was authorized. No longer would Arlington commuters bound for Washington have to pass through Georgetown.[5]

Washington real estate maven Ruby Lee Minar applied the lessons she had learned from her work experience with Frank Lyon. She took

Advertisement for Lee Heights in the Evening Star *newspaper. The realtor made it very easy for prospective purchasers to view the new subdivision.*

advantage of road and bridge improvements to start her own development. Never one to take a small approach, Minar collected a two-mile-long assemblage of properties that stretched between Lee Highway and the Potomac River. She started by purchasing a forty-acre tract known as Livingston Heights and went on to buy Lee Heights from Ashton C. Jones.[6]

Minar continued to buy various other adjacent parcels, including one hundred acres of prime land adjacent to the Washington Golf and Country Club. Originally accessible only by a dirt road, this parcel was part of a large farm purchased by Admiral Presley M. Rixey, MD, in the 1890s as a country home. He particularly liked the land because of its four-hundred-foot-plus elevation above Washington and its fine views.

Following the 1906 opening of the Great Falls & Old Dominion (GF&OD) trolley line, which ran right by the property, Rixey began to see development opportunities for his land. In 1908, he sold a large parcel to the country club for a golf course. His intention was to continue development of the property, but he never seemed to find the time away from his career in the US Navy—and later as US surgeon general. Now in his early seventies, he was happy to sell to Minar and let her plan the development.[7]

According to a *Washington Post* article, Minar planned Lee Heights as a "Model Home Colony," stating that "restrictions will be imposed which will assure homes of a high class in keeping with the natural beauty of the property." Villa sites with even stronger restrictions were laid out along the golf course. Accessed by new concrete roads and only a ten-minute drive from the new Key Bridge, the sites sold rapidly when the development opened in spring 1923. Two years later, new sections were added, and they sold at a blinding speed. Prices ranged from $15,000 for an attractive bungalow to $20,000 for a luxury home.[8]

Section seven of Lee Heights opened in August 1926. It was almost sold out in three weeks. Minar raced to open the next section and achieved record-breaking sales in November. To handle all the new business, she expanded her sales force to include one hundred agents.[9]

There certainly was a large demand for houses, but Minar's success also grew out of her innovative marketing style. She ran large display ads in the Washington newspapers, emphasizing location and amenities. Home styles were merely implied in these ads, as if they were afterthoughts. To facilitate site visits, Minar hired buses to take potential purchasers from her New York Avenue office in Washington out to the subdivision every Sunday.

Minar did not restrict her sales activities to her own projects. She was willing to list and sell any piece of real estate offered to her. Some buyers preferred older homes to the new construction. Tapping that market, she took time out from her busy subdivision activities and sold the historic Glebe House to Virginia state senator Frank L. Ball.

This wonderful old Arlington County landmark had originally been on a large property of one hundred acres. Subdivided after the opening of the GF&OD, the property eventually was reduced to a two-acre parcel. Just before Ball's purchase, Glebe House had been updated to include electricity; plumbing; a heating system; three modern, tiled bathrooms; and a state-of-the-art white enamel kitchen. Wide porches accented with

Advertisement for Greenway Downs in the Evening Star *newspaper*

lovely millwork marked the home's facade. Set in mature gardens, this jewel of a home stood out as an extraordinary property.[10]

The unbridled success of her Lee Heights project caused Minar to cast her eye farther afield and venture into Fairfax County. In 1926, she bought five hundred acres in the county with plans to develop the land later. That venture was followed by the purchase of the one-hundred-acre Tripp Farm just west of Falls Church, where she established the Greenway Downs subdivision. Despite wet weather, Minar sold thirty-eight lots in two days on the first weekend of sales in June 1927.[11]

Continuing on her westward course, Minar set her sights on the four-thousand-acre Sunset Hills Farm (now Reston), which she listed on behalf of the heirs of the late Dr. Hugh B. Hutchison in August 1927. The property was the largest single tract of land within an hour's drive of Washington. Hutchison had purchased it in 1908 with the idea of subdividing it into small poultry and truck farms. But World War I delayed his plans, and he operated a large dairy farm on the property instead.

Minar received inquiries from people all over the country who wanted to purchase Sunset Hills Farm for various uses, including subdivisions, a religious boys' school, and a recreation center for railroad men. The property sold in two months to A. Smith Bowman for $200,000. Bowman intended to continue the dairy farm and add a breeding program for thoroughbred horses while he worked out plans for subdividing the land. He also brought a pack of foxhounds with him and started the Fairfax Hunt.[12]

While Minar enjoyed healthy sales in the subdivision market, she was not the only player in the field. Developers of other new subdivisions, such as Aurora Hills, Virginia Highlands, and Lyon Village, saw similar success. Lyon and Fitch, developers of Lyon Village, built ninety-seven homes in two years. By 1926, the company predicted a $3 million building operation at Lyon Village, with luxury homes selling for as much as $50,000.[13]

Rampant development in Arlington County created wealth for some but caused headaches for others. Between 1920 and 1925, the population increased 100 percent to thirty-five thousand. The Board of Supervisors was hard-pressed to meet the demands for new schools, waterlines, sewage lines, and electricity. Even the telephone company failed to keep up with new orders for service. A survey revealed that the average real estate tax paid in Arlington and Fairfax was about 70 percent lower than that of most other Virginia counties because the assessor's office could not keep up with the rising property values.[14]

By 1927, the rapid rise in real estate prices was giving pause to some cautious souls, including real estate agents. The AlexandriaFairfax Real Estate Board joined the various chambers of commerce to publicly lobby the county governments for better planning and stricter zoning. These groups believed the counties needed to plan ahead to be able to provide the needed infrastructure to support a growing population.[15]

Chapter 24

GROWING PAINS AFFECT COMMUTERS AND FARMERS

Northern Virginia's business economy was growing steadily and had shaken off the effects of the postwar recession; however, much of the farming community continued to experience the negative effects of the recession.

Fairfax County still had an agrarian economy, while Arlington County was shifting away from farming at an almost daily rate. The influx of commuters into both counties accentuated the economic division between commuters and farmers. The commuters worked for steady paychecks, paid their taxes, and demanded public improvements to enhance their communities. Meanwhile, farmers struggled to make a living in a climate of fluctuating prices.

In the years immediately following World War I, while the United States' economy in general suffered from a recession, the farm economy experienced a full-scale depression. By the mid-1920s, the farmer's plight was improving; however, the agricultural economy did not fully recover until nearly the end of the decade. The federal government had instituted numerous programs to aid farm recovery, but some made matters worse. Land banks made loans easily available to farmers so they could afford to modernize their operations, thereby increasing production and income. Unfortunately, the land bank loans created long-term negative impacts. Farmers' incomes were dependent on uncontrollable variables: weather, animal health, crop health, and a demand for the farms' products. Loans that appeared within a borrower's means for one growing season could become insurmountable burdens after one or two bad seasons.[1]

Many farmers in Northern Virginia turned to truck gardening and dairy and poultry farming to circumvent fluctuations in weather and crop prices. The field crops that they produced, such as hay, oats, barley, and corn, usually served as food for their animals. Grain production was down, and only a few farmers still grew grain for sale.

Farmers did not work for a guaranteed income. Seeking more control over their markets, they formed associations. The largest and most influential organization among dairy farmers was the Maryland and Virginia Milk Producers' Association. By 1924, 97 percent of the milk delivered daily to the District of Columbia was handled by only nine different processing and distribution companies. To get a fair price for their product, farmers relied on the strength of the Milk Producers' Association. Even so, they were only paid thirty cents a gallon for their milk. And this price was often depressed by cheaper foreign imports of milk products, such as butter and cheese. Hot debates in Congress led to tariffs on imports to protect the market prices of American farm products.[2]

Additional legislation resulted in still more costs and complications in the American milk industry. In 1925 Congress passed a bill requiring all dairy herds to be tested annually for tuberculosis. Animals carrying the disease had to be destroyed. Fortunately for Northern Virginia farmers, not many of their cattle were infected. That same year, however, low prices, large debts, and increased feed and labor costs, combined with an intense summer drought, drove some to abandon dairy farming. This led to a shortage of milk in Washington. To encourage more milk production, processors agreed to raise the price of milk by one cent per quart. As a result, a quart of milk cost thirteen cents at the store and fifteen cents for home delivery.

Three years later, Dr. William Fowler, the chief health officer for the District of Columbia, decreed that dairy farmers selling milk in the city could no longer have straw ricks or compost piles in their barnyards. This measure outraged local dairy farmers, who threatened to boycott the city markets. Farmers maintained that they had always operated this way and that hauling straw and manure away from their barnyards would be a hardship. Fowler backed down and amended his rule, allowing straw ricks and compost piles in the barnyard if they were at least fifty feet from the milking barn.[3]

While some farmers were leaving the dairy business, others were entering it. In 1925, developer Frank Lyon moved his family from North Arlington to a 150-acre farm (modern-day Ballantrae) near Langley. Not one to do things in a small way, he built a luxurious house for his family and a state-of-the-art dairy barn for his pedigreed herd of Guernsey cows. A new $35,000 dairy processing plant was built that same year in Lyon's North Arlington development, Lyon Village.[4]

Chestnut Farms Dairy was a large milk processing company in the District of Columbia. Many Virginia dairy farmers delivered their milk there. Pictured here is their fleet of home delivery trucks with some of their drivers.

Despite the advantages of electricity and plumbing, farming—especially dairy farming—was hard work. Thanks to improved feeds and breeding programs, farmers were able to increase production, but labor costs also increased. Nonetheless, milk remained the major farm product for Northern Virginia on both large and small properties. By 1927, many saw their first year of real profit since the end of World War I. Fairfax County led the state in dairy production with a gross revenue of $516,000. It was sixth in the state for poultry products, with a gross revenue of $592,000.[5]

Northern Virginia housing developments simultaneously benefited local farmers and created hardships for them. Those who owned land near areas of development and wished to give up farming could sell for good prices as land values steadily increased. Property owners beyond the development zone could not yet sell for higher prices, even though the assessed land values and property taxes had increased.

Higher taxes caused an additional hardship for farmers already struggling to make a living. They often felt that they were getting little value from increased real estate taxes. Although they wanted better schools for their children, they did not feel responsible for the added student population caused by the influx of commuters nor did they benefit from new sewer or waterlines extending to the housing developments.

Farmers and commuters agreed on one topic: the need for better roads. In 1906 Virginia established the State Highway Commission to construct and maintain a primary system of highways. But little happened until 1918, when the Virginia General Assembly created a state highway system. The remaining roads were still the responsibility of the counties. Suburban development led to a public outcry for improvements of existing roads and construction of new roads. With county treasuries already overextended, limited funds were available for road projects.[6]

Arlington, in particular, suffered from a lack of funds because of other required improvements. By 1925, its school system was running at a deficit and required severe budget cuts to remain in operation. The Arlington Board of Supervisors was learning the hard way that increased

Typical Fairfax County road in the 1920s. Notice two license plates on the truck.

tax revenue provided by new development did not cover the cost of the necessary infrastructure. Fairfax County residents watched the turmoil in Arlington with great interest.

Meanwhile, farmers in both counties wanted better farm-to-market roads, and commuters wanted better neighborhood streets. In spite of this united appeal for better roads, Virginia voters defeated a 1923 bond issue to fund roads, approving instead a gasoline tax of three cents per gallon.[7]

Additional road maintenance funds were raised through automobile license tag fees. To collect more revenue, the commonwealth required regular users of its roads to pay for and display Virginia tags. Owners of country property in Northern Virginia who were legal residents of the District of Columbia resented having to pay for extra car licenses. Business owners saw the tag fee as unfair since they often had to license their trucks and delivery vans in two jurisdictions. Everyone wanted better roads, but no one wanted to pay for them.[8]

Some answers to the road and tax conundrum appeared on the scene in 1925, when Harry Flood Byrd was elected governor of Virginia. Byrd's ancestors included two prominent plantation owners: William Byrd of Westover Plantation and Robert "King" Carter, who was the land agent for the Fairfax family's Northern Neck Proprietary in the early eighteenth century.[9]

Only thirty-eight years old when elected governor, Byrd brought a wealth of experience to his post that many twice his age could not claim. He grew up near Winchester, Virginia, where his father owned an apple farm and published the *Winchester Evening Star* newspaper. By the time Byrd was born in 1887, the family's wealth was depleted. While the Byrds were not poverty-stricken, there certainly was no money for luxuries. Like many other Virginians, they were still suffering from the long-lasting ill effects of the Civil War.[10]

As a young man, Byrd developed a lifelong aversion to debt. In 1903, at age fifteen, he left school to manage his father's nearly bankrupt newspaper. He quickly discovered that a $2,500 debt owed to a paper supply company threatened to stop the publication because the supplier refused to extend any more credit. Byrd dealt with the issue on a daily basis, scraping together the amount of cash for each day's paper order. Therein he established the financial philosophy that he brought to public office: "the pay-as-you-go system."[11]

Byrd gained valuable experience with roads when he became the president of the Valley Turnpike Company in 1908 at the age of twenty-one. He supervised the daily operations of a ninety-three-mile-long toll road that ran over rough terrain from Winchester to Staunton. Twice a month he drove the entire length of the road, checking on needed repairs and operations—a time-consuming task at an average speed of twenty to twenty-five mph. For the next seven years, he ensured the road was maintained by using only toll-generated revenue.[12] Thus, Byrd was able to apply his no-debt policy to another business while gaining valuable experience with transportation issues.[13]

In 1915 Byrd began his political career with his election to the Virginia state senate. He became a lifelong leader of the Democratic Party. Parlaying his experience, he ran on a platform of good roads and efficient government. Once elected, he served on several Senate committees, including Roads and Finance. Byrd was a chief proponent of a gasoline tax as a fair method to finance road construction. Always eschewing debt, he also led a fight against road bonds to pay for new roads.[14]

A man of strong opinions and enormous energy, Byrd became the Democrats' candidate for governor in 1925. By then, his outspoken opinions on road issues and government debt had gained him publicity throughout Virginia.

In addition to his political and miscellaneous business roles, Byrd was a farmer who owned apple orchards. Adhering to his platform of good roads and a fiscally responsible government, he set out to win the farmers' votes. Even in that era of poor roads and slow transportation, he managed to visit many farming communities while campaigning all around the state, including numerous stops in Northern Virginia. He was not just the farmers' friend—he was one of them and understood their problems. Byrd also promoted his idea that increased government efficiency would lower costs and allow for tax reductions.

After his statewide travels, no one was more familiar with the poor road conditions than Byrd. Preaching his pay-as-you-go plan, he strongly supported road construction and repair and advocated a one-cent gas tax hike. At the same time, he recommended removing the state tax on land and personal property, believing that collection of those revenues should be left to the counties.[15]

Byrd also thought that automobile licensing fees should be graduated according to the weight of the machine instead of the horsepower of the engine. His message was popular. He won the governor's seat by seventy thousand votes. He confirmed his support for the farmers in his inaugural address, stating, "The prosperity of Virginia depends primarily upon agriculture. Virginia should always be mindful of her duty to the farmers, and the advancement of agriculture should never be neglected."[16]

True to his campaign promises, Byrd immediately set about making state government more efficient by eliminating many offices and departments. As a proponent of better roads, he created the Department of

Harry Flood Byrd

Highways as a new state agency and got on with road construction. During his term as governor, two thousand miles of roads were built using gas tax revenue.[17]

Byrd's automobile license tag policy based on vehicle weight did not sit well with some residents. In 1927 the price of the tags jumped from five dollars to seven dollars, depending on the model of the vehicle, leading several Arlington residents to comment that their tags should be gold plated. Some Virginia residents who commuted to work in the city tried to bypass the expense by licensing their cars in the District, which had cheaper fees. Police roadblocks were set up to monitor morning traffic. Automobiles with district tags leaving Virginia in the morning were stopped. If it was discovered that the vehicles were owned by Virginia residents, the drivers were fined.[18]

His greatest contribution to the condition of the roads came after Byrd completed his term as governor. In 1932 the General Assembly passed a measure that he had worked on for years. Called the Byrd Road Act, the statute called for the state to take over the care of all secondary roads that had previously been the responsibility of the individual counties. Therein began the modern road system still in effect today.[19]

Due to an improved general economy and both state and federal legislation, Northern Virginia farmers enjoyed a dramatic improvement in the agrarian economy. Evidently, their proximity to the nation's capital gave them a boost not enjoyed by the farmers elsewhere in the state. In 1929, while farm incomes in the rest of the state showed a decrease, Northern Virginia's were the highest since before World War I. Fairfax County led the state in dairy products. The volume of butter produced was double that of 1922; the amount of cheese had multiplied 400 percent. Farmers were finally able to make a reasonable living.[20]

Chapter 25

HARD TIMES

In the fall of 1929, just as farmers were being congratulated on a profitable year, US financial markets began showing signs of instability. Starting in September, the New York Stock Exchange experienced volatile periods. Prices rose and fell with increasing frequency until everything bottomed out on October 29, later called Black Tuesday.

In an attempt to prevent a full-scale depression, various companies and individuals reinvested their money in the hope of promoting consumer confidence. Newspapers emphasized these efforts, but to no avail. Too many people had lost all their investments, and those who had salvaged some of their money were not inclined to throw it back into a risky gamble. By the end of the first week of November, even the most optimistic investor had to confront the final diagnosis: the stock market had crashed. The resulting failure of many businesses created significant unemployment and severely curtailed the quantity of money in circulation.

While cities and towns across the country and throughout the world were feeling the first negative effects of what was later named the Great Depression, residents of Northern Virginia were, for the most part, not in a panic. They were concerned but hopeful that the poor economic situation would soon be resolved.

To some extent, the Washington suburbs were protected from the immediate disastrous effects of the stock market crash because so many people were government employees; however, it didn't take long for those with secure jobs to become fearful of the events that were occurring elsewhere and to restrict their spending habits. The trickle-down effect of less spending was negatively reflected on the balance sheets of local businesses. Those who wanted to stay in business had to cut their expenses, which included laying off employees.[1]

The region's farmers kept an eye on produce prices, but they were far removed from any dealings with the stock market. They had just come through a long agricultural depression and hoped that the improved circumstances of the past two years would continue. After all, people had to eat, and while they might eschew luxury items, they could not skip feeding themselves.

The national economic picture was grim, but people went on with their daily activities. In January 1930, the Fairfax County Chamber of Commerce lobbied the state government for funds to widen Chain Bridge Road. Fairfax County teachers petitioned the County Board of Supervisors for a pay raise.[2]

In March, the board proposed the establishment of a new county position, superintendent of public welfare, with an annual salary of $1,800. It is unclear whether this idea was stimulated by worries about a continued economic decline or the fact that there were already many poor farming families in the county. There was a great deal of public opposition to this new office because farmers felt that most of the burden of taxes rested on them and believed it was time to reduce taxes instead of creating new ways to spend money. They must have made their voices heard. Two days later, the Board of Supervisors cut the county budget dramatically.[3]

Farmers had not been lured into a false sense of security by the farming successes of the late 1920s. A good year merely meant breaking even and putting food on the family table. The following year gave them a better return and allowed them to expand their production. Farm labor was still relatively cheap at twenty-five to thirty dollars a month with room and board.

Many Fairfax County farmers had followed the advice of agricultural extension agent H. B. Derr, diversifying their crops so their income would not be dependent on the successful harvest of one product. It was not unusual for dairy and poultry farmers to also have truck gardens and orchards. The summer of 1929 had brought a sharp reminder that a good crop was dependent on good weather. The growing season that year had ended in a two-month drought.[4]

Fortunately, the drought came after the crops were established, and most farms produced a good harvest. The winter months of 1930 were exceptionally cold, with many days of single-digit temperatures. Warmer days between cold snaps brought rain and one large snowfall, partially replenishing the water supply.[5]

Fairfax County Agricultural Extension agent H. B. Derr counseling a young farmer.

The end of the drought was the last good news of the year for farmers. Things started to go wrong when the cold snaps extended far into the spring. Apple, peach, and pear orchards were all damaged by sudden frosts and a hard freeze. The end of April ushered in another drought, denying farmers a successful fruit harvest. As spring turned to summer, drought conditions became extreme. Hay and corn crops were stunted and dried up in the fields. In some cases, it was possible to water vegetable gardens from creeks or wells, but that supply was soon reserved for farmers' livestock.[6]

To make matters worse, the region suffered a record summer heat wave. On July 22, after four days of 100 degrees or higher, localized thunderstorms with high winds and a small amount of rain plagued the area. Some farms got both; others got wind only. By August 8, the temperature had passed the 100-degree mark on ten of the previous twenty-one days. The highest temperature recorded was 106 degrees.[7]

As creeks, wells, and springs dried up, desperate farmers herded their stock to any water supply they could access, sometimes at a distance of two to three miles. The Potomac River fell to an all-time low, with large expanses of exposed mud that dried and cracked in the blazing sun. The countryside literally burned up.

Crops of corn, peas, beans, hay, apples, peaches, and pears were severely damaged or destroyed. Total production of those crops for the entire state was down by more than 50 percent. The hay harvest was only one-fifth of the normal volume, and it was of poor quality. With the pasture grass all burned up and no good hay to feed the cows, farmers saw their dairy production fall by 50 percent. Finally, the temperature fell to eighty-nine degrees, but the damage could not be repaired.[8]

The situation was bleak for Virginia's farmers, few of whom would be able to sell enough of what was left of their crops to pay for seed and fertilizer for the next year's planting. Many farmers already had mortgaged their crops in the spring to purchase that year's seed and fertilizer. When those crops were diminished, they were unable to make their mortgage payments and faced foreclosure.

Additionally, they were forced to purchase feed for their remaining livestock or turn them out into the hay and cornfields to gain what nourishment they could from eating the stunted growth.[9]

Those opting to give up the thankless job of farming had trouble finding anyone who would buy their stock. Young cows that had sold for eighty to one hundred dollars a head the year before now went for twenty dollars each. Sheep purchased for fifteen dollars now sold for three dollars. Even the farmers' gardens failed. Previously, in bad times, farmers could feed their families from their own plots. Now they were unable to can enough produce to see them through the winter months.[10]

The plight of Virginia farmers was shared by farmers in other states. The severe drought and heat affected much of the country. President Herbert Hoover called a meeting of the governors of the twelve states most affected by the crisis, including Virginia, to discuss ways to help. He also asked the Red Cross to stand by to help, if needed.[11]

Local farmers' granges and the Fairfax County government gave Virginia governor John Garland Pollard a list of resolutions to present at the meeting with the president. It proposed a year's suspension of penalties on all late tax payments. They went on to recommend that Hoover declare a state of emergency and prevent the federal land banks from foreclosing on farmers who were delinquent with mortgage payments. They also called for a plan to give emergency credit to worthy and needy farmers to buy seed and fertilizer and to reduce railroad rates for transportation of farm commodities.[12]

One day after Hoover's summit, rail rates for farmers' shipments of produce and farm supplies dropped to $2.40 a ton. The rest of the pleas went unanswered for months as Congress debated how best to help.[13]

Governor Pollard turned to former governor Byrd and asked him to chair the state's drought relief committee. Byrd was the perfect man for the job. He was a farmer with an astute business sense and great executive ability, but this was the most difficult task he had taken on in his long career.[14]

As the dry summer dragged on, the situation worsened. When the days cooled off in the fall, there was still no rain. By October, the drought had become the most prolonged and widespread in the history of national weather records. Congress continued to debate how to relieve the farmers' situation but did not reach a conclusion or provide any help.[15]

The state began offering drought relief loans toward the purchase of animal feed, but many farmers were reluctant to incur the debt because they were afraid they would not be able to repay the loans. At the end of October, Edmund Allen, chairman of the Fairfax County Drought Relief Committee, and H. B. Derr, the Fairfax County agricultural agent, filed a grim report with Byrd's committee.

In addition to huge crop losses, there was no cattle pasturage for the winter months. Even timber and wood pulp could not be harvested, due in part to forest fires. Allen and Derr estimated the loss of income for the county's farmers at about $1 million. They requested $150,000 of drought relief loans for those who had "no banking credit but were excellent moral risks." Unemployment was a serious concern because there were no jobs for farm laborers and forestry workers. Allen and Derr estimated that the Red Cross would need to provide approximately $25,000 worth of food.[16]

Meanwhile, Byrd was working hard to wring more aid out of the federal government, which had allocated only a small amount of relief funds so far. Vociferous in his criticism, Byrd pronounced the "drought aid far inadequate," going on to say that the aid that was available was so bound up in restrictions that it would never in any way be available to those most in need. Out of the $200,000 allotted to Virginia, only $43,000 had been used because of the strict qualifications for the loans.[17]

In his forward-thinking and creative way, Byrd suggested that Congress authorize a road appropriation to be matched by the states, allowing funds to be spent on many small, local construction projects that would provide employment opportunities close to home.[18]

Byrd also called for another year's extension of farm tax credits against the next year's crops without penalty. Further, he said, the federal government should purchase large quantities of seed, fertilizer, and feed for sale to farmers at much-reduced prices.[19]

In November, Northern Virginia farmers were given a small reprieve when a third of an inch of rain fell on the area. While the rainfall did nothing to replenish depleted water supplies, it did help the pasture vegetation.[20]

The Depression had caused prices of various commodities to fall drastically. In spite of produce shortages, farm prices fell to 1912 levels. Poultry farmers could not make enough money from selling eggs to pay for chicken feed. The price for chickens was so low that farmers felt they would be better off keeping them for their own families' dinner tables. Sheep prices dropped to two cents a pound. Dairy farmers got less than seven cents a gallon for milk and could not even give away their cows. It was generally agreed that Virginia farmers had not suffered this degree of destruction and destitution since the Civil War.[21]

Meanwhile, Congress continued in a deadlock over a bill to aid farmers. Finally, in January 1931, President Hoover signed the Drought Loan Appropriation bill, allocating $45,000,000 in loans to farmers toward the purchase of feed, fertilizer, seed, working stock, and tractor fuel.[22]

There is no doubt that farmers suffered the most from the havoc and deprivation caused by the drought; however, the lack of water also had far-reaching implications for other residents of Northern Virginia. While the new neighborhoods in Arlington County were supplied with city water, those in Fairfax County and western Falls Church depended on wells, many of which were only thirty to thirty-five feet deep. The lack of surface water caused the wells to dry up, leaving 40 percent of the homes in Falls Church without water. No one was prepared for this water shortage.[23]

The city requested a federal government loan of three water tanks, along with trucks and drivers, to deliver water to households in Falls Church. Officials were able to obtain three three-hundred-gallon tanks, but the city had to supply the trucks and drivers. For a small charge, water was delivered to homes where wells had gone dry, but the homeowners had to supply the buckets. When the days got colder in the fall, the heat was out in many of those same homes because they were outfitted with boilers designed to circulate hot water. Fairfax County also faced the possibility of closing schools that had no water.

Area volunteer fire departments often were unable to find water for pump trucks. Firefighters usually pumped water from nearby creeks or ponds when responding to fires. Now those water sources were dried up. When a Vienna store caught fire, the nearest creek with water was half a mile away—too far for the pump to create the necessary pressure—and the building burned to the ground.[24]

By fall, area residents looked forward to cooler temperatures, but they were not prepared to deal with a sudden blast of Arctic air. On November 28, the mercury fell to fifteen degrees. People began to believe that their weather-related miseries would never end. Throughout the winter months, there were intermittent periods of light rain or snow, precipitation that at best kept the drought from worsening.[25]

When the spring planting season arrived, the farmers were in despair. Finally, on May 8, 1931, a heavy downpour provided the region with six-tenths of an inch of rain. The *Washington Post* called it the "$1,000,000 Rain." Everyone hoped that the drought was broken and that better times were coming. But it would take a lot of rain to replenish the depleted water supply and many years to end the Great Depression.[26]

Chapter 26

A RAPID DOWNWARD SPIRAL

The hard times suffered by Northern Virginia farmers in 1930 were not isolated to one specific area of the region. The effects of the Great Depression were broadcast over all aspects of the local economy.

The government, especially at the county level, also suffered from a lack of revenue. The enormous amount of development during the preceding decade in Arlington and parts of Fairfax had often left the supervisors of those counties scrambling to find funds to provide the necessary infrastructure for their growing populations. Roads and schools in particular were high on the list of necessary improvements.

The Fairfax County Board of Supervisors was working on a project to consolidate many of the county schools. They began closing old one- and two-room schoolhouses and moving students into modern facilities. This plan certainly made sense because it was more efficient to operate fewer sites. Improved transportation routes enabled students to travel slightly longer distances to school. In addition, with the recent growth in population, accommodations for many more schoolchildren were needed.

River Bend School on Runner Road near Forestville (now Great Falls) was typical of the one-room schoolhouses across Northern Virginia.

The eventual sales of old schoolhouses helped defray the cost of building new schools.[1]

Population growth in Arlington also meant that more school buildings had to be built. Structures that had been built only a few years before now required expansion. Washington and Lee High School had opened in 1925 with twenty-five classrooms. Five years later, thirty-two more classrooms were being added, making Washington and Lee the largest high school in Virginia.[2]

At the beginning of the Great Depression, many hoped that voluntary budget cuts would keep government operations running close to normal. In March 1930, the Fairfax County Board of Supervisors cut its budget. But by June, it was apparent that even more stringent cuts would be required. Due to the extreme reduction in farm revenue and the collateral negative effects on local businesses, many citizens could not pay their real estate taxes.

Fairfax County was besieged by property owners appealing their real estate assessments. The Board of Equalization met in June and agreed that assessments would be reduced to 50 percent of the sale value of the property.[3]

The City of Alexandria had one thousand tax-delinquent properties. The normal policy was to send the property to a foreclosure auction. The city would buy the property and then negotiate a tax payment with the previous owners so they could buy it back. Because of the large number of foreclosures, the city decided to forgo auctioning the properties and to instead negotiate with owners to recoup at least some of the back taxes.[4]

Arlington County, because of the high percentage of property owners who were government employees, only had 260 cases of tax delinquency. All were prosecuted in the normal way, and the supervisors did not adjust the tax rate.[5]

Even though Arlington County had less trouble than other jurisdictions in collecting real estate taxes, the supervisors did recognize that many of the county's residents had suffered a reduction in their incomes. Therefore, the supervisors asked the electric power company to reduce its rates. Many of the new homes built in the county in the previous ten years were all electric, except for furnaces, and the rate reduction resulted in substantial savings to those households. Houses with electric refrigerators received a 50 percent reduction in rates, while all other homes were charged a flat rate of fifty cents a month.[6]

By the close of 1930, Fairfax and Arlington counties and the City of Alexandria had to make more changes. Fairfax citizens continued to appeal their assessments on the basis of the falling price of real estate. Alexandria reduced its real estate assessments by 50 percent and drastically cut the city budget. Meanwhile, Arlington County saw a rise in assessments based on real estate sales.[7]

The Depression's effect on the Northern Virginia real estate market varied drastically from one area to the next. After a slight price reduction, Arlington real estate was still selling, though not at the rampant rate experienced in previous years. Sales were steady and new homes were being built. Several factors could be credited for the stimulation of the residential real estate market while many parts of the local economy were declining.

First, Arlington was a favorite close-in location for government employees. Second, the developments were supplied with public water. Most housing developments in Fairfax County were dependent on well water. With the drought of 1930, when many wells went dry, homes with public water supplies became much more desirable. Third, mortgage money was still available at rates of 5 percent to 6 percent. Last, new construction was on the market at attractive prices. Building materials and labor had dropped in cost, allowing builders to offer new homes at reduced prices. But new home competition caused prices to fall in the resale market. Nonetheless, developers continued to start new projects, with some building around golf courses.[8]

In November 1930, homes in the 1,311-acre planned community of Strathmeade were offered for sale. Located in Fairfax County on Lee Highway (Route 29) near Falls Church, Strathmeade was the former site of Camp Alger, a military training post during the Spanish-American War.

This development offered a twenty-seven-hole golf course, a community clubhouse with tennis courts and a swimming pool, walking and bridle trails, and covenant restrictions to protect the views until 1970. The Brumbach Realty Company offered homes to be built in a price range from $10,000 to $50,000 and advertised the homes as "easily within reach of the man of modest income."

The developers spent a fortune building the golf course and advertising the venture. As they were completing the golf course, they also signed a contract for road paving. That was as far as the project went. The anticipated rush of purchasers did not materialize. Only a few lots were put under contract. The Strathmeade Corporation went into default, and the property went to foreclosure auction in 1932. It sold for $100,000 to the previous owner, who held the mortgage.[9]

Strathmeade's failure had many negative side effects. Those unfortunate people who had paid a deposit on their new dream home lost their money at a time when most could ill afford to do so. The building of the

REAL ESTATE. THE EVENING STAR, WASHINGTON, D. C., SATURDAY, AUGUST 22, 1931. REAL ESTATE. B-5

Advertisement for Strathmeade in the Evening Star *newspaper, 1931*

golf course and the roads had provided employment for many local men, but suddenly they were without jobs.

Country Club Hills, a high-end golf course community in Arlington, did manage to survive the lean times. The 130-acre Grunwell estate had been sold to the Brumbach Realty Company in 1928. Brumbach planned a development where the prime lots overlooked the golf course of the Washington Golf and Country Club. When the new development opened in 1930, "English-type" homes were offered in a price range from $16,500 to $42,500.

Purchasers were given a choice of designs, and the homes were built to order. By June of the following year, fifteen homes had been sold at an average price of $20,000. Although the project was deemed a success in those difficult times, by August the Brumbach Realty Company had lowered its prices. It was now possible to purchase a "studio-type" home for $12,500. Later in the fall, as the Depression worsened, prices were lowered again. One model, originally marketed as a "true colonial masterpiece" and priced at $42,500, was later offered for under $30,000. Lesser masterpieces were offered for as low as $10,700; however, this was still high-priced residential real estate. Purchasers who were willing to travel 30 minutes from Washington could buy a new home in Fairfax County near Falls Church for $6,750.00 in Devonshire Gardens.[10]

Through careful pricing and cost-cutting measures, some of the new housing developments managed to continue selling houses. By May 1931, the cost of building materials had fallen to 1917 prices. Even so, many builders were reluctant to start new homes, and buyers were hesitant to pay deposits for built-to-order new homes. Potential buyers feared losing their deposit if the home was not completed or, worse yet, was not even started. This impasse was resolved only when a few builders braved the market and offered finished new homes for sale.[11]

While the builders' actions stimulated the real estate market somewhat, there was still another snag in the process. Real estate professionals called it the "old house problem." Many potential purchasers of new

Advertisement for Country Club Hills in the Evening Star *newspaper, 1929*

construction already owned a home that they needed to sell before they could buy another. Because new-home construction prices were down and many buyers wanted new instead of used homes, it was difficult to sell existing homes.

New homes offered the latest in modern conveniences, which were not found in many older homes. Real estate agents had to work very hard to persuade their clients to price their homes for the market conditions. Agents pointed out that if the client was getting a new home at a bargain price, then that person would have to sell the old home for a bargain price. All prices had fallen, not just new construction. Nonetheless, many sellers refused to adjust the price of their property to the market conditions. Instead, they spent many months hoping in vain for a sale. Frustrated agents pointed out that the rental market was good so if the property did not sell, it could be rented, but cautious sellers often gave up and stayed in their old homes.[12]

While suburban real estate was suffering from pricing conundrums, the market for farm property was much worse. The severe drought of 1930 had caused so many problems that few people wanted to buy farmland. The farm economy had declined dramatically. Spurred by the loss in farm products, taxable income reported in 1930 by Fairfax County residents had fallen by 50 percent from the year before. The 1931 growing season was helped by rain, but the extensive drought damage could not be reversed in one year.[13]

Added to the other problems of farming was a large decline in prices for farm products, prices that continued to slide lower every month. On the positive side, the return to more normal weather patterns allowed most farmers to grow enough food to feed their families. In fact, many who had given up country life the year before to seek work in the city had returned to the farms. On the negative side, many farmers were in debt and behind on mortgage payments and real estate taxes. Due to a limited market for country properties, farms often went into foreclosure.

THE FARM

BEST HOME OF THE FAMILY

MAIN SOURCE OF NATIONAL WEALTH

Foundation of Civilized Society

129 ACRE Fairfax County, Virginia Farm, only 25 MILES from Washington, to be sold at

AUCTION

Wed. Dec. 23, 1936, on the premises at 1:30 P.M.

LOCATED ON THE LEE-JACKSON STATE ROAD HIGHWAY from Fairfax to Middleburg, 9 miles from Fairfax, 15 miles to Middleburg.

Known as the J. I. LOCKHART FARM; 120 acres tillable, balance timber.

NEVER-FAILING STREAM OF WATER running through the entire farm.

1500 FEET OF STATE ROAD FRONTAGE, making this desirable property. Valuable, farm is level, no waste ground.

SOIL FACILITIES SUPERIOR to the average farm.

ALFALFA IS KING IN DAIRY PRODUCTION. What an opportunity in the purchase of this splendid farm, where tons of this wonderful cattle pasture and hay can be grown. Corn, wheat, barley, oats, potatoes, beans and cabbage will thrive upon this well-balanced soil.

THERE ARE ABOUT THREE ACRES OF FRUIT—apples, peaches, pears, cherries, plums.

UNSURPASSED FOR THE POULTRY BUSINESS, in connection with the Dairy, an income can be realized every day in the year.

THERE HASN'T BEEN A FARM SOLD IN VIRGINIA for a long time that should attract the attention this farm offers in its superior location and the price it will sell for; surrounded by some of the best farms in the good, old State of Virginia, near MIDDLEBURG and UPPERVILLE, two of the outstanding communities in this part of the country, affords a pleasure as well as a privilege in the purchase of this ever-increasing valuable farm.

BUILDINGS CONSIST OF 7 ROOMS AND BATH, frame house, recently painted, located just far enough from the State Road to be desirable.

NEW DAIRY AND STOCK BARN, other out-buildings.

EXTRA GOOD WELL OF WATER—a driven well which never fails.

Buy on the road where value increases, R. F. D., school bus, telephone, electric by the door.

CONDITIONS: 10% of the purchase price is to be paid when the farm is bid off to the highest bidder, balance and final settlement to be made on or before 60 days from date of sale. Terms can be arranged.

INFORMATION: Call, write or phone District 5232, COL. J. CLINTON BOWDEN AUCTION CO., Inc., Office, 204 Chandler Bldg., 1427 Eye St., N. W., Washington, D. C.

J. I. LOCKHART, OWNER
P. O., HERNDON, VA.

How to reach the farm from D. C.: Over Key Bridge, then Lee Highway or Route 211. Turn right on Lee-Jackson Highway when you reach the Fairfax Junction. Drive eight miles to Auction sign.

Advertisement for farm auction, 1936

But depressed prices for farmland did bring about an economic boost for the region, one that grew out of an unexpected source. City dwellers were provided with an affordable opportunity to try out the life of a gentleman farmer. Army officers, mid- to high-level government employees, and socialites began to purchase farms where they could spend weekends or vacations. Some even moved to farms permanently.[14]

In some cases, this shift was motivated by those who enjoyed fox hunting with the Fairfax Hunt, founded in 1927 by A. Smith Bowman. The kennels for the foxhounds and the hunt's clubhouse were located on Bowman's four-thousand-acre Sunset Hills Farm (now Reston). Even though it was a very young hunt club, it provided good sport and grew in popularity every year. The hounds went out at least twice every week, covering territory that went from Tysons Corner to Great Falls and Herndon on one side and went all the way to Oakton on the other. Soon foxhunters were purchasing homes in the hunting territory or nearby.[15]

The pilgrimage of the city dweller to the country, foxhunter or not, provided multiple benefits for many different areas of Fairfax County and provided income at numerous levels. The biggest benefit was an influx of outside money injected into the various communities.

Gentleman farmers did not do their own farming. They paid local men to manage the farm, plant crops, feed livestock, and care for their

Fairfax Hunt

riding horses. They also had to keep farm buildings and fences in good repair. In turn, farm managers employed local laborers, some full-time and some as seasonal help. Depending on the wealth of the gentleman farmer, local women were hired as household help to cook, clean, and do laundry. Most of the animal feed, groceries, and other supplies needed on these farms were bought locally, which was some help to small-business owners. For some of the properties purchased, there was another, longer-lasting community benefit: the preservation of large tracts of land and historic homes.[16]

In 1930, Catherine Filene Shouse, a resident of the District of Columbia, purchased Wolf Trap Farm as a country home for her family. She paid $5,300 for the fifty-three acres and its antique house and outbuildings. Though not a farmer, Shouse loved the countryside and firmly believed that her children would benefit greatly from experiencing life on a farm.

Thus began a love affair with a farm that lasted for the rest of her life. Without experience in farming, she had a lot to learn, and 1930 was not a particularly good year to start. But she worked hard to learn what she needed to know and hired knowledgeable people to help her.

Before long, the farm produced corn, wheat, alfalfa, and oats, all of which were used to feed Shouse's fowl, hogs, angus cattle, and milk cows. A vegetable garden supplied the family table with fresh produce. It was a true working farm. Always generous, Shouse provided neighbors who did not have their own dairy cows with milk for below-market prices. Later, she built a kennel and employed local workers to raise several different breeds of dogs, many of which were sold to foxhunters as pets.[17]

Shouse took great pleasure in horseback riding. The proximity of the farm to the Fairfax Hunt territory may have influenced her decision to purchase that particular piece of land. She built stables, raised riding horses, and spent many years foxhunting with the Fairfax Hunt.

While there is no doubt that Wolf Trap Farm provided a wonderful country life for Shouse and her family, there were also great benefits to the community. She employed local people and put much-needed money back into the local economy during the dark and lean years of the Depression.

Catherine Shouse seated on a hay wagon on her Wolf Trap farm.

Chapter 27

BANK RUNS AND MONEY HOARDING

By January 1932, Northern Virginians had suffered through two years of the negative impacts of the economic downturn. The economy continued on its self-perpetuating downward spiral. Consumer confidence was at a low point. Most of those who still had any money were reluctant to invest because they feared losing it. At the same time, they did not want to spend money for fear that they would not be able to earn more. Everyone practiced some degree of frugality that became more stringent as time went on.

Matters worsened when the banks began to fail. At the slightest rumor of a bank's financial trouble, depositors rushed to withdraw their cash before it was too late.

Hazel Sanders Thompson, a lifelong resident of Great Falls and the daughter of a local dairy farmer, vividly recalled one such bank run. Her father and grandfather were at work in the fields one day after milking their cows and sending the milk to Washington. Oswald Carper, who had trucked the milk to the city, rushed back along his milk route, alerting his customers that the Potomac Bank was failing. Hazel's father ran in from the fields, changed his clothes, and raced into the city to join the long line of depositors waiting to withdraw their money. This scene occurred at many other banks throughout the country.[1]

Withdrawals of all deposits led to bank failures. Unfortunately, the banks were not insured, and most could not pay all their depositors. Even salaried government employees were not immune to this loss. As a result, many people stopped keeping their money in banks, choosing instead to literally put it under their mattresses or in other secret hiding places on their property. Some who had more money to lose rented bank safe deposit boxes, keeping their cash safely locked up rather than depositing it.

The economy could not recover if money did not circulate. President Herbert Hoover attempted to discourage money hoarding, giving an impassioned radio speech on March 6, 1932, in which he pleaded for the $1 billion in hidden currency to be returned to circulation. As reported in the *Washington Post*, Hoover appealed to every man's sense of patriotism:

> The safest risk in the world is a share in the future of the American people. The American people have at this moment one of the greatest opportunities in their history to show an assured confidence and an active faith in their own destiny, which is the destiny of the United States—and by that faith we shall win this battle.

He closed by saying that every dollar out of circulation deprived a potential wage earner of his pay. While his points were certainly correct, the sad fact was that many Americans had lost confidence in the government's ability to return the economy to pre-Depression prosperity.[2]

The president's appeal to put money back into circulation was also supported by Charles G. Dawes, president of the Reconstruction Finance Corporation. According to the *Washington Post*, Dawes echoed Hoover's warning:

> As long as this currency is out of circulation we must remain as a people for an indefinite time under the terrible hardship of an unprecedented business, industrial, and commercial stagnation with all its consequent human misery.[3]

In the battle against money hoarding, the US Treasury issued so-called baby bonds in denominations as low as fifty dollars that paid 2 percent interest and could be cashed on sixty days' notice. The night before the bonds were launched, Frank Knox, chairman of the Citizens Reconstruction Organization, issued a wonderfully metaphorical statement, as reported in the *Washington Post*, explaining the purpose of the bonds:

> Most emphatically the drive to be launched tomorrow is not a drive to sell Government bonds. It is however, broadly speaking, a Nationwide campaign to put money back to work. We have organized a national employment agency to find jobs for idle dollars. We do not care what the job is so long as the dollar goes back to work.[4]

These strong appeals to end money hoarding were not immediately successful. Consumer confidence was at such a low point that much of the missing currency remained in storage in unusual places.

While Hoover and his agency chairmen were working to solve the problems of the entire country, Virginia's state and local governments were also attempting to make ends meet. The Depression caused so many new issues for local governments that the Fairfax County Board of Supervisors had to increase its meetings from once a month to twice a month. In addition to their normal duties of running the county, the beleaguered supervisors were hard-pressed to cope with the increasing population of homeless and hungry people. Their work was further complicated by a significant reduction in county revenue. In March 1932, Arlington County officials begged property owners to pay their taxes on time because the county needed to borrow $140,000 to meet expenses.[5]

At the state level, the General Assembly had passed a bill designed to shift some of the burden of infrastructure from the counties to the state. Called the Byrd Road Act after its chief proponent, former governor Byrd, this law provided the means for the state to take over all responsibility for the counties' secondary road system. Here was real relief for the financial problems of the counties because so much of the tax revenue collected had to be allocated to road building and maintenance. Every county had the option to transfer its road burden to the state if the citizens voted to do so.[6]

Therein began the fights. Northern Virginians had long felt somewhat removed from the rest of the commonwealth. Many viewed the road transfer option with deep suspicion. Byrd estimated that if all counties turned over their roads, real estate taxes could be reduced and could save taxpayers $3 million statewide. In fact, Fairfax County's supervisors were so certain of public support for the measure that in March they lowered property taxes by eighty cents per each $100 of assessed value, even though the Byrd Road Act was not scheduled for a vote until August.[7]

Even the promise of a large tax cut did not win over everyone. Throughout Arlington and Fairfax counties, citizens vociferously opposed the plan. They believed it would give the state too much control, that the counties might lose their share of the gasoline tax, which partially supported the roads, and that those in charge in Richmond could not possibly know what was needed in Northern Virginia.[8]

To make matters worse, the state highway department proposed to have about eight hundred convicts supply the labor for their new secondary road system. Citizens in Arlington and Fairfax counties were horrified. This would never do. Aside from the inherent danger of having prisoners in their neighborhoods, convict labor would take jobs away from local people. And even if the highway department did employ local men, it would only pay fifteen cents an hour for general labor and a mere seventy-five to eighty-five dollars per month for job supervisors. Arlington County paid forty cents an hour for general laborers.

These statistics proved to opponents of the plan that Richmond had no clue about the high cost of living in Northern Virginia. Charles Pickett of Fairfax summed it up when he stated that the new system would violate the principles of local government and transfer control to Richmond, and that the people would have no direct voice.[9]

While citizens debated the pros and cons of the Byrd Road Act, the Arlington Board of Supervisors hastily put all of its pending road projects out for bids. That was done as an insurance policy. If the roadwork had already started, and if by chance the citizens voted to join the state road system, the Department of Highways would have to accept the contractors and pay for the completion of the projects. The state would not be allowed to neglect Arlington roads.[10]

When Arlington and Fairfax voters went to the polls on August 9, 1932, Fairfax voted to join the state system, but Arlington rejected it. That decision was not a surprise given the demographics of the two counties. Arlington had a wealthier tax base because of its large amount of suburban developments. Fairfax was mainly agrarian, and the farm economy was suffering badly.[11]

In spite of fears to the contrary, the state highway department did not forget Fairfax. After the vote, it immediately allocated $150,535 for the county's secondary road system and scheduled the work to commence early in September. The county got an extra boost to its flagging treasury when all of its road equipment was turned over to the state highway department for an additional allotment.[12]

It was just as well that Fairfax accepted the Byrd Road Act because the trolley systems throughout Northern Virginia were falling victim to the Depression. The trolleys had never been particularly profitable. Maintaining the lines cost more than the fares that could be charged. While trolleys were still a popular mode of transportation, especially among those who could not afford to own a car, the Depression economy had an impact on the trolley companies.

Riders anxious to save every penny possible would opt to walk several blocks rather than pay extra fares. Others walked longer distances and did not ride at all. Freight hauling declined. As portions of different lines were closed, buses took over the routes. The Mount Vernon line closed south of the City of Alexandria, parts of the Arlington and Fairfax line were abandoned, and the Washington & Old Dominion curtailed its schedule on its line to Great Falls.[13]

No matter what measures the local, state, and national governments were taking, the economy was still falling. The real estate market was struggling along in Arlington and Alexandria, but at much reduced prices. In most of Fairfax County, the real estate market was very slow. There were an alarming number of properties under foreclosure or about to go to foreclosure. Many of the pending foreclosures were because the loans were coming due rather than a failure to make payments.

Due to reduced incomes, many people who had managed to scrape together their monthly payments did not qualify to refinance their properties and lacked the cash to pay off the loan. The downward shift in market values also prevented them from selling the property, which left foreclosure as the only option. To allay the problem, President Hoover had proposed to Congress that a Federal Home Loan Bank system be instituted. Under this plan, the government would finance loans through local banks to accommodate borrowers who could not qualify under the normal bank regulations. As usual, however, the bill got hung up in congressional debate, with no relief forthcoming.[14]

In April 1932, the Virginia Real Estate Association met and passed a resolution to support the bill and to ask Governor Pollard to appeal to the president to ask mortgage holders to refrain from foreclosures on homes. Their resolution included the statement that foreclosures were "subversive of financial and moral soundness and good citizenship." They believed that more foreclosures would only exacerbate the falling economy.[15]

Advertisement in the Evening Star *newspaper, 1932*

Congress finally passed the bill in July 1932; however, it was not until September that the funds became available to those under threat of foreclosure. The new loans had reduced interest rates to as low as 5 percent.

While the local governments were working hard to cut their budgets and to stretch their revenue, the federal government was also taking stock of how to find funding for the relief programs that had been introduced. Like the local and state governments, the US government had also suffered a severe drop in tax revenue. In November 1931, the Internal Revenue Service announced that the 1930 individual income tax returns reflected an income drop of $7 billion and that returns for 1931 were expected to look even worse.[16]

Meanwhile, the whole country was expecting miracles of financial relief to be delivered by the federal government. As part of the search for funding for relief agencies, the government examined the viability of other departments. In the course of that investigation, and at the behest of many lawmakers and citizens, Prohibition came under scrutiny. Those who did not favor the law had been arguing against it since 1919, when the Eighteenth Amendment to the US Constitution had made it illegal to manufacture, sell, or transport alcoholic beverages.

It was argued that the law was one of the greatest mistakes the federal government had ever committed. The prohibition of alcohol stimulated an enormous amount of crime and required huge expenditures by local, state, and national governments to enforce the law. Now the shortage of tax revenue caused various members of the government to take a long, hard look at Prohibition.

Sara Lee Fain, the first woman to be elected to the General Assembly, summed up conditions in Virginia when she addressed a meeting of Democrats in Arlington. "More money has been spent by the Federal Government in mis-enforcement of the Prohibition law than the present deficit in the National Treasury," she said, as reported by the *Washington Post*. Fain went on to point out that although she personally was not in favor of whiskey, it was impossible to prohibit the use of it. Furthermore, Prohibition had given birth to the greatest gang of criminals ever known in this country. As a result, she, like many others, believed the only sensible thing to do was to allow alcohol to be sold legally by stores managed by the government.[17]

The enforcement of Prohibition was a nationwide problem, and Virginia certainly had its share of trouble. In 1930, 3,844 Virginians were arrested for owning or operating stills or transporting liquor. Law enforcement personnel confiscated 1,966 stills and 38,794 gallons of liquor. As the Depression worsened, so too did the liquor violations.[18]

The City of Alexandria cited 1,545 arrests related to alcohol use, manufacture, or sales in 1930. The Arlington Court docket was choked with violators. In Fairfax County, the number grew every month. During the September 1931 term, eighty-eight out of one hundred cases were liquor violations.[19]

Enforcement of the law became a great burden to local jurisdictions. The police and sheriffs' departments and the courts were forced to expend an enormous amount of time and money chasing, capturing, and trying lawbreakers. It was a frustrating situation in which monetary fines and jail terms did nothing to deter the miscreants from repeating the same offense. And it was costing the local governments money from their already reduced treasuries.

For example, Arlington's liquor violation fines for June 1932 totaled \$455, and the costs were \$462.15. The statistics for Fairfax and the numbers of stills broken up were shocking. At least once every month or two, there would be a police raid that would capture twelve hundred to fifteen hundred gallons of whiskey from one manufacturer. These were interspersed with the capture of other smaller operations.[20]

To exacerbate the situation, both counties needed new jail buildings and were having trouble finding space to lodge those who were convicted. No matter how one looked at the situation, enforcing Prohibition was

Large still operation captured in Fairfax County.

expensive; however, if alcoholic beverages were legalized, they could be taxed and could provide the governments with an income. As was the case when the Eighteenth Amendment was introduced in 1917, the matter was hotly debated by the "wets" and "drys." Now when its repeal was proposed, those same groups continued their vehement arguments. Prohibition finally ended when Congress passed the Twenty-First Amendment in December 1933.[21]

As 1932 drew to a close, many residents of Northern Virginia despaired over their economic circumstances. The help provided by the state and federal governments was a start, but it did not relieve the poverty many endured. This may have been because their poverty was new, brought on by the current economic situation. People who had always been able to earn a living were reduced to being poor; their pride did not allow them to take what they considered to be charity. In Fairfax, sixty-six businesses had closed in that year alone—a grim statistic for an agrarian county. Those closings did not take into account how many farmers had gone out of business; however, farmers who had managed to keep their land were able to grow enough food for their families.[22]

President Hoover's programs to end money hoarding and put cash back into the economy were showing little success. With so little cash in circulation, resourceful farmers reverted to the barter system used by their ancestors. Country doctors accepted chickens, butter, eggs, firewood, and other locally produced items in payment for their services. Country stores also took produce on trade to add to their stock. Farmers traded with each other for different types of produce, animals, and labor. As long as farm families could raise vegetables and a few chickens, they would not starve. One of the Fairfax County weekly newspapers even joined the barter system. It agreed to accept as payment for printing, advertising, or a subscription any of the following items: grain, vegetables, eggs, meat, milk, canned goods, insurance, hardware, gas, oil, tires, wood, coal, paint, or services.[23]

The close-knit farming communities also looked after their own when someone lost his or her property to foreclosure. At such times, old buildings on other farmers' property were suddenly converted into dwellings in exchange for farm labor when neighboring families became homeless.

When one family in Great Falls lost their farm to foreclosure after the father was severely injured, they moved to a neighbor's property, where a basement had previously been dug and lined with cinder blocks to build a new home. The building had stopped, and the structure was uncovered. By spreading tarps over the top, the space was enclosed for the family to live in for the next year. The kitchen stove, salvaged from the farm that they had lost, provided for cooking and heating through the long winter months. These primitive spaces were not at all comfortable, but they provided shelter in the family's community and allowed them to keep their work ethic, pride, and dignity.[24]

Times were hard, but most people were not willing to give up. They just struggled on and helped each other when they could.

Chapter 28

HOPE INSPIRED BY THE NEW DEAL

While the average citizens of the region were working on creative ideas to earn a living, the governments were also working on ways to draw money into the area. Former governor Byrd was an enthusiastic proponent of tourism. He believed the many historic sites in the state should be advertised nationally to attract as many tourists to the area as possible, thus bringing outside money to the state.

Fortuitously, for his vision, 1932 was the bicentennial of George Washington's birth. The US government agreed with Byrd and viewed the bicentennial as a major source of tourist income. Congress appropriated large sums of money to plan and advertise events to commemorate Washington. Included in the plan was a new four-lane road to be built along the Potomac riverfront from Alexandria to Mount Vernon. Originally called the Mount Vernon Memorial Highway, it opened in 1932 and provided an easy and scenic drive for tourists who wanted to make the pilgrimage to Washington's home.[1]

The newly opened Mount Vernon Memorial Highway (now the George Washington Memorial Parkway) was originally built to provide tourists with a safe and scenic drive to visit Mount Vernon.

Many other events planned for the year attracted thousands of tourists to the area. Their dollars were gratefully received by local businesses. Once that pattern was established, Northern Virginians continued to capitalize on promoting tourism and advertised the region not only for its historic sites but also for its scenery, hunting, and fishing.

While the George Washington bicentennial celebrations and the tourist dollars provided marginal help, the economy was still in terrible straits. Many residents of the region had reached the end of any resources they could tap. The situation was growing more severe with each passing day. People wanted new ideas and hoped that the dire effects of the Depression could be reversed sooner rather than later. Many felt that a change of leadership would bring about better times. So it is no surprise that in the November 1932 presidential election, Franklin D. Roosevelt defeated incumbent Herbert Hoover.

Roosevelt, charismatic and forceful, campaigned on his promise of a "New Deal," proposing novel ideas about how to put the government to work to provide local employment and thereby bring cash back to the people. While he agreed with Hoover that much of the problem was caused by fear of investing or spending, Roosevelt was not going to waste any time begging money hoarders to part with their cash.[2]

Roosevelt's stirring inaugural address, delivered on March 4, 1933, while the country was in the middle of a bank panic, began with this emphatic statement:

> This great nation will endure as it has endured, will revive and will prosper. So, first of all, let me assert my firm belief that the only thing we have to fear is fear itself—nameless, unreasoning, unjustified terror which paralyzes needed efforts to convert retreat into advance.

His brave words were intended to inspire hope and faith in discouraged Americans that better times were coming. But Roosevelt did not mince words or dance around the subject when he followed with this summary of the dire economic situation of the country:

> In such a spirit on my part and on yours we face our common difficulties. They concern, thank God, only material things. Values have shrunken to fantastic levels; taxes have risen; our ability to pay has fallen; government of all kinds is faced by serious curtailment of income; the means of exchange are frozen in the currents of trade; the withered leaves of industrial enterprise lie on every side; farmers find no markets for their produce; the savings of many years in thousands of families are gone. More important, a host of unemployed citizens face the grim problem of existence and an equally great number toil with little return. Only a foolish optimist can deny the dark realities of the moment.[3]

To deal with those "dark realities" and to start the recovery process, Roosevelt immediately sent reform bills to Congress. Introduced by various supporting senators, the bills passed in record time. They included the Emergency Banking Act, which allowed banks to reopen, and the creation of the Federal Deposit Insurance Corporation, which would give the public the confidence to put their money in the banks.[4]

Roosevelt continued his predecessor's relief program for the unemployed but renamed it the Federal Emergency Relief Administration. Many other programs were added, including the National Industrial Recovery Administration, the Agricultural Adjustment Administration (AAA), the Farm Credit Administration, and the Civilian Conservation Corps (CCC). In Roosevelt's first four months in office, the United States government expanded at a rate that was six times faster than normal.[5]

In spite of the speed with which these new agencies were created, it still took time for their benefits to reach the local level. The Fairfax County Board of Supervisors was struggling to fund its services, particularly the public schools. In January 1933, the board speculated that it would have to close schools two weeks early for the summer break.[6]

Every time the board came up with a plan to cut expenses, a citizens' group would fight it. When it proposed raising taxes, everyone complained about that. The Fairfax Grange, a farmer's organization, countered with a suggestion that it cut the salaries of the superintendent and the rural supervisor of public schools by 20 percent. The Fairfax Chamber of Commerce recommended that all county employees have their salaries reduced to the lowest level allowed by state law. Furthermore, it proposed that any job that could be done by another department be transferred and the former position abolished. The board decided to cut all county salaries by 10 percent.[7]

Despite vigorous protests from many groups, it was the teachers who took the biggest hit. First they saw their five days of paid sick leave revoked; then their salaries were reduced. During a Board of Supervisors public hearing on the county budget, Mrs. A. Harmon Roberts of the Mount Vernon District indignantly remarked that the schoolteachers were the only county employees required to have an education to qualify for their job, yet their pay was the lowest. Teachers were paid on average only

$800 per year. Other county employees and officials pulled in annual salaries of $1,200 to $4,500.[8]

Overcrowding added to the woes of the school system. More buildings and teachers were needed. Part of the increase in students was due to families relocating to the area to live with relatives and to look for work. Another factor was families who had taken in poor children who were wards of the District of Columbia court system. Families in need of income were induced to do this because they were paid eighteen dollars per month to house and feed these children. To solve part of the overcrowding problem, the Fairfax County school board put a ban on these children from attending school.

The District of Columbia countered that if the children could not attend school, they would have to be lodged elsewhere. The families who boarded them were reluctant to give them up, and therein started another school battle. In the end, it was agreed that all ninety-six children could remain in place, but the thirty-six who were considered "problem children" could not attend school.[9]

In July 1933, the school board applied to the National Industrial Recovery Administration for $172,000 to build and repair schools. But that application did not get an immediate response. Fortunately, in November 1933, the state allocated $66,000 collected from liquor violation fines to Fairfax County to improve existing schools and build new ones.[10]

At the same time, the school budget had no funds or provisions to provide lunch to children who came to school without anything to eat. That chore was taken up by various citizens' organizations. Once again, in the spirit of neighbors helping each other, women throughout the county organized donations and a schedule to provide daily hot lunches for undernourished children in nineteen county schools. Their mission was to let no child go hungry, even if it meant personal sacrifice for those who prepared the food.[11]

Volunteer Frankie Winston and a friend had prepared soup for the school lunch at Forestville (now Great Falls). Realizing they did not have a ride to the school, they walked more than two miles down Georgetown Pike carrying between them a five-gallon milk can full of soup.[12]

Both Arlington and Fairfax counties had trouble collecting taxes on time. In May 1933, the Fairfax County treasurer issued a strong statement declaring that delinquent taxes that had been due in December of the previous year would have to be paid by May 15. The county policy was that if the taxes were not paid on time, a 5 percent late fee would be added. The treasurer believed that many people used the late fee as a carrying cost and just waited until they were forced to pay. To that end, he declared he would send tax collectors in person to call on those who had not paid their taxes by May 15. By early June, $17,390 in overdue taxes was paid. But the county was still missing $86,219 in uncollected taxes.[13]

Meanwhile, both Arlington and Fairfax counties cracked down on "foreign" car license tags. Owners of cars remaining in either county for more than six weeks were required to buy a county permit. Police officers were instructed to watch diligently for those who tried to avoid the fee.[14]

In addition to county taxes, state taxes added to the taxpayers' burden. In particular disfavor was the high gasoline tax charged by Virginia. Partially to fund the Byrd Road Act, the state had raised its gasoline tax to five cents per gallon. While this might have worked well throughout most of the state, it did not work for Northern Virginia.

The gasoline tax in the District of Columbia was only two cents a gallon, and it was easy for commuters to buy their gasoline in the city. In the beginning, the oil companies supported Northern Virginia retailers by discounting their purchase price. In June 1933, however, the oil companies announced they could no longer absorb this loss. Northern Virginia gas station owners would have to pay the same price as everyone else. In a time when every penny was important to so many people, this policy would have serious ramifications on the well-being of many business owners and their employees.

Citizens were outraged. This was yet one more case in which Richmond failed to understand the needs of the region. A quickly organized group that included former Arlington County commonwealth attorney Crandall Mackey went before Governor Pollard to plead their case, requesting an amendment to the law that would reduce the gasoline tax for the region. Mackey and his fellow citizens argued that 170 gas stations were at risk. If those businesses failed, one thousand men would be unemployed, and it would cost the state about $250,000 in tax revenue.[15]

A bill was introduced in the General Assembly that would establish a ten-mile-deep zone from the border of the District of Columbia, where the state would reimburse two cents per gallon tax to gas station owners. Another zone for five additional miles was attached to the first, where the state would reimburse one cent of the tax. The bill passed by a narrow margin because of strong opposition by representatives from southern Virginia.[16]

By the summer of 1933, Roosevelt's recovery programs were in place and starting to have a positive effect on the region's economy. The CCC provided numerous opportunities for people to be employed on local projects. In Fairfax, the CCC established a reforestation camp on land rented from a private individual. In Arlington, one hundred men were employed to work on county maintenance projects. One of the more controversial projects built by the CCC was a one-hundred-foot-tall fire tower erected on F. E. Stowe's farm at Pender. Everyone agreed the tower was needed to protect against forest fires in the dry season. The controversy started because its location was within a mile of a nudist camp. Since the people manning the tower were supplied with binoculars, there was speculation about what they would be looking for.[17]

Another recovery agency, the Civil Works Administration (CWA), provided more than five hundred job opportunities ranging in length from ten weeks to three months. Focusing on repairs to county infrastructure, projects included roadwork, waterfront cleanup, and sidewalk installation.

Among the CWA projects was the construction of a new Fairfax County jail. The sheriff's department desperately needed a new building.

The new Fairfax County jail.

Its existing jail, more than one hundred years old, contained only sixteen cells. Due to overcrowding, some prisoners were housed in the hallways. In addition, prisoner escapes were a constant problem. The lime-and-sand mortar holding the bricks in place was so old and fragile that inmates could scrape it out with a spoon or even their fingers. Once the bricks were loose, it was easy to create a hole large enough for a man to slip through. The county Board of Supervisors applied to the National Industrial Recovery Administration, which awarded the county $50,000 for a new building with thirty-two cells.[18]

While Roosevelt's new agencies provided money for projects and work for many local citizens, there was another beneficial side effect. As the government expanded, agency by agency, it employed more people who needed homes. Population and job growth in turn stimulated the real estate market. Real estate agents were quick to point out that, for anyone who had any money left to invest, real estate was safer than the stock market.

New homes offered for sale in Lyon Village in Arlington had brisk sales. As government employees gained more confidence that their employment would last, many wanted to take advantage of the cheap prices for homes. Home sales began to pick up throughout the region, even in the farm country. For those who had the resources and confidence in their income, there were bargains to be had. For example, a sixty-acre Virginia farm with a five-room house, electricity, and outbuildings was offered for $5,500.[19]

Some people were still frightened of such a major investment, but the increased population had to have homes. The government stepped in again. A large housing project for federal employees was started at Belle Haven in Alexandria. Ground was broken on April 15, 1933, for the first of twenty-five hundred homes to be built over the next two years. The homes had not even been advertised yet, but through word of mouth, over one thousand people had already applied to purchase one. According to the plan, they could lease the home for fifteen years. At the end of the lease period, the lessee would own the home. The monthly rental prices varied according to the size of the home and ran from $30 to $150. Rent included interest, taxes, and water; the lessee was responsible for all maintenance and repairs. Nothing like this had ever been offered before. People raced to apply even in the midst of uncertain times.[20]

While some parts of the economy were becoming more robust, farmers were still working hard to see any improvement. In 1932, wheat sold for fifty cents a bushel, the crop's lowest price in more than a century. In the spring of 1933, the Fairfax County welfare agent received a small amount of aid from the state to purchase garden seeds to distribute to farmers who could not afford to purchase them. The welfare department also put out a broad appeal to farmers to donate seed potatoes and other seeds for those in need. If a person had a piece of ground to work, they could at least grow a garden and feed themselves and their families.[21]

Roosevelt did not forget the farmers while setting up his relief programs. The AAA was created to aid farmers and to try to force higher prices for their produce by paying farmers to cull herds and to take land out of crop production. This plan backfired with milk producers when the head of the dairy department for the District of Columbia was accused of fixing prices and withholding milk. After a lengthy congressional investigation, milk prices were adjusted to give the farmers more for their product and the processors less. Wheat production came under control, ultimately leading to higher prices. With help from the government and the weather, Virginia farmers were able to increase their income statewide by $12 million over the previous year.[22]

For residents of Northern Virginia, 1933 was a year of change. It began with the bleakest of conditions and with many people wondering how much worse the situation would get. Some who had lived through the very hard times during and after the Civil War feared the current Depression would go on for years to come. By the end of the year, the bad times were far from over, but things had started to improve. Many fears were abated. People faced life with a new sense of resolution. They had reinforced their sense of community as everyone tried to help others. For the first time in three years, hopelessness was replaced by a general aura of hope.

Chapter 29

THE LONG ROAD TO RECOVERY

By early 1934, Northern Virginians had more employment opportunities than they had seen in recent years because President Roosevelt's new federal programs were up and running. In January, the *Washington Post* announced that projects financed through the CWA would provide 712 jobs in Fairfax County alone.

One of those projects, which would provide work for two hundred men, involved construction of six new barracks at the Lorton Reformatory. The prison, which belonged to the District of Columbia, had long been a sore point with Virginians, many of whom questioned why criminals from the District should be imprisoned in their countryside. But no one complained when the expansion project provided more jobs for impoverished local men.[1]

The New Deal was not without its critics. Virginia's two senators, both Democrats, were equally vociferous in their criticism and opposition to Roosevelt's New Deal. Senator Carter Glass, the state's senior senator and the cosponsor of the banking reform Glass–Steagall Act, was adamant that the price paid for quick relief would come back to cause great pain to taxpayers. As reported in the *Washington Post*, he repeatedly warned that *federal aid* was not what the term implied and that "payday" was coming. In an address to the Young Democrats Clubs of Virginia, he asked: "Where does the Federal Government get any money to give away to anybody? Does it pluck money off trees; does it start printing presses?"[2]

Glass stated that many local governments had been fooled into authorizing projects because they were to get "grants" from the federal government. "Grants," he scoffed. "Don't you know who pays for these grants?" His answer: the people who receive them and the people of Virginia who would pay for grants given to other jurisdictions. He went on to point out that Virginia paid more to the federal government than fourteen other states west of the Mississippi combined. "Wait until payday comes," he said. "Wait until the government has to raise your taxes."[3]

Virginia's junior senator, former governor Byrd, was equally opposed to the New Deal. The policies were in direct contrast to everything he believed in and had always promoted in both business and politics. He believed in less government and strict fiscal responsibility. He still adhered to his motto of "pay as you go." He would not support the concept of a continually expanding national government that was racking up a huge amount of debt.

As a lifelong farmer, Byrd was particularly opposed to the AAA, which offered money to farmers to take fields out of production on the theory that a leaner supply of crops would drive their prices higher. He believed wholeheartedly that the law of supply and demand would do a much better job of price regulation than any artificial manipulation of the market. The concept of government control over farm products was simply untenable to him. In a radio address delivered April 22, 1934, and reported in the *Washington Post*, Byrd summed up his position. "Sweeping powers to license the farmers and all who handle food are impractical," he said. "Chaos and confusion to the farming industry will inevitably result." Always a believer in the power of the people and a strong protector of individual rights, he pronounced: "The people must be encouraged to go the way of independence and self-reliance. Business is ready to resume its forward march if the Congress would give assurance of sound legislation."

Expressing his opposition to excessive government intervention, Byrd continued:

> The cost of these enormous bureaucratic machines will become too great to be borne. They are rapidly becoming Frankensteins, the contrivances of ingenious and idealistic political theorists that may grow so powerful as to destroy the very right of the individual to liberty and the pursuit of happiness. The Federal Government has entered the door of every industry, has spied upon the operation of even the small fabricator, has declared that not one additional spindle may be added to a machine without its approval, and it is now proposed to license the farmers of America and the distribution of all food.[4]

Virginia's senators were not alone in their opposition to the New Deal policies. In a speech to the Organized Women Voters of Arlington County, John Locke Green, a Republican candidate for the Eighth Congressional District, made it clear that he believed taxpayers were paying for the programs to employ the unemployed. He thought this was a bad idea, saying, "The great trouble, as I see it, is that we have approximately fifteen hundred college professors in Washington attempting to administer the affairs of the Government. No one ever has been in a position where he had to meet the payroll of even fifteen employees."[5]

No matter which viewpoint one held, conditions in Northern Virginia were slowly starting to improve. In spite of Byrd's opposition to the AAA, 296 Fairfax County farmers were paid a total of $30,918 not to grow wheat in 1934. Farm income was reported at $12 million over the previous year.

Statistics from the Department of Agriculture showed a shortage of cattle, due partially to the drought of 1930 pushing the price for cows higher.[6]

Both the state and the counties were collecting more tax money than in the three previous years, and their various budget cuts were showing results. For example, in Fairfax County, the consolidation of public schools from scattered one- and two-room schoolhouses into larger, more modern buildings was beginning to prove financially effective. From 1929 to 1934, there were enrollment increases of 79 percent in high schools and 13 percent in elementary schools. In spite of the jumps in enrollment, the cost of education had been reduced by an average of twenty-three dollars per student.[7]

While these changes were for the better, both the state and local governments still suffered from a lack of funds. Among other problems, the welfare rolls of both Arlington and Fairfax had increased to the point where the counties' funds were exhausted. This fact was probably driven by slight improvements in the economy as people from distant locations moved to counties where they believed they could find work. In fact, there were many more unemployed people in Fairfax in 1934 than in 1933. As a result, the counties were constantly looking for new revenue sources.[8]

Some favored a sales tax, believing it was the only way to lower real estate taxes. Virginia voters did not agree, and that measure did not pass. Others saw liquor sales as a potential state moneymaker. Now that Prohibition had ended, Virginia granted licenses to private vendors for the sale of beer and wine; however, the state had not established a license for the private sale of distilled spirits. Aside from the loss of potential revenue, it also meant that moonshining and bootlegging continued in Virginia. Local and state governments were still spending money to catch the lawbreakers.

In February 1934, a bill was introduced into the Virginia General Assembly to allow the state to open stores to legally dispense liquor. The proceeds would be divided among the counties, with the goal of lowering the automobile tax from seventy cents to thirty cents per one hundred pounds. As with all measures involving the sale of alcoholic beverages, this one was hotly contested. Many believed that state control was the correct course of action, but quite a number of people held out for private stores and a tax on the sales. The only thing that most agreed on was that restaurants and hotels would not be permitted to sell distilled spirits because of the potential to turn each of them into a barroom.[9]

Eventually, it was agreed that the state would open stores to market liquor in Rosslyn, Clarendon, and Alexandria. Prices would be lower than those in District of Columbia liquor stores and would hopefully draw business away from the city. Of course, the next fight was the exact location of the stores. Almost no one wanted the stores located in their neighborhood for fear that they would attract derelicts and other undesirables. After much debate, store locations were established. The Virginia Alcoholic Beverage Control (ABC) stores opened for business.[10]

The repeal of Prohibition also gave rise to another large business in Fairfax County, when A. Smith Bowman opened a commercial distillery on his Sunset Hills farm near Herndon. The property, with more than four thousand acres, was home to a champion dairy herd. The distillery operation blended well with the dairy business because the corn mash and other by-products left from the whiskey-making operation could be used to feed the cows. Both operations provided employment for numerous locals.[11]

The rise in real estate prices created another positive change. With the expansion of the federal government, new residents gravitated toward Northern Virginia. While many opted to live close to Washington in Arlington and Alexandria, others wanted to live farther away. Some purchased farms as weekend homes, while others became full-time residents of the countryside. No doubt some were partially stimulated by Virginia's campaign to attract tourists to historic sights. Suddenly, old houses, some in derelict condition, were seen as charming and affordable to purchase and rehabilitate.[12]

A primary example of these new buyers was Rixey Smith, Senator Glass's secretary—the equivalent of today's chief of staff—who went in search of a new weekend home in the Great Falls area. Smith had long been a fan of historic houses. He had already owned and renovated one such home in Centreville. Looking for a new project, in 1933, he found the William Gunnell house near the village of Forestville. The house, built circa 1756, had charm, but that was about all. Situated on 159 acres, it had no electricity, indoor plumbing, or central heat. It was suffering from approximately a century of neglect, with a farmyard that extended almost to the walls of the house. But it did have wonderful old windows, doors, floors, woodwork, stone chimneys, and fireplaces. In the backyard, there was a vintage log house of a similar age and decay, along with several sturdy and ancient timber-frame barns.

Smith purchased the property and set about turning it into a country home. He added electricity, plumbing, and bathrooms and a new wing with a master bedroom and bath. He purchased and moved an old log tavern from Ruby, Virginia, which he adjoined to the opposite end of the house, providing a downstairs dining room and an upstairs bedroom. On the back of that structure, he added a new kitchen.

Once the house restoration was underway, Smith turned his attention to the yard, planting boxwood gardens and installing a spring-fed swimming pool. With the addition of a large circular driveway, a formerly run-down home was transformed into a beautiful gentleman's country

The William Gunnell house, c. 1917

estate. And all that rehabilitation work and farming of the land pumped money into the local economy, providing employment for local builders, mechanics, and farm laborers.[13]

The following year, Smith's friends Jack and Ethel Durham also sought a country home. The young couple both worked for the federal government, but they wanted a country lifestyle and were willing to commute to the city for work. After weeks of searching with Smith's help, they came upon an old house in the middle of a field on Towlston Road near Route 7. The house had never been modernized with electricity, plumbing, or heating. In fact, the owner was using it as a hay barn.

After days of negotiation, the owner agreed to sell the building to the Durhams. Therein began the couple's lifelong love affair with their historic house. Due to their youth and limited salaries, it took the Durhams a long time to make the house habitable. And they did not do it on such a grand scale as their friend Smith had. Nonetheless, after several years of hard work and the services of local contractors, they were able to live in the house. They later discovered that the structure had been built in about 1756. Known as Towlston Grange, it was the former home of Bryan Fairfax.[14]

Numerous historic properties that, in better economic times, might have gone under the wrecking ball to make way for more modern

Towlston Grange in 1934 when the Durhams purchased it

structures were saved during the New Deal years. In addition to rebuild projects, new construction provided more local employment. Roosevelt's federal programs had both direct and indirect positive effects on the economy of Northern Virginia. It appears that the indirect effects had much more impact than those that the president had planned.

Chapter 30

RECOVERY PAINS AND EXPANDING BUREAUCRACY

By the end of 1934, it was apparent that the local economy in Northern Virginia was improving, albeit slowly. Despite signs of New Deal improvements, the negative effects of the Great Depression were far from over. Some businesses were too far in debt for small gains to have a positive impact. In January 1935, the Washington & Old Dominion Railroad (W&OD) fell victim to the adverse economic conditions. The railroad company, which was in receivership and owed a huge amount of back taxes, attempted to salvage operations of its main line from Rosslyn to Bluemont by closing the electric trolley line from Thrifton in Arlington to the Great Falls.

Virginia's Corporation Commission had granted permission the previous May for the railroad to abandon its passenger service on the line and continue with only freight hauling. To save money, the company pulled up one set of tracks from its double-track roadbed and cut the number of daily trips. Now it was going to abandon all service for those who had depended on the trolley for affordable transportation and freight service since it opened in 1906. Therein lay the problem. The W&OD

could not make a profit with affordable fares. Despite protests from the community, the company closed the line.[1]

As the Great Falls line was closing, forward-thinking citizens of both Arlington and Fairfax counties organized the Great Falls and Old Dominion Road Association to work on a plan to pave the abandoned rail line. Association members pointed out that the grading and gravel ballast of the railroad bed were a perfect base for an automobile road and all that was needed was pavement. After much debate, the Boards of Supervisors of both counties agreed to pay back taxes owed in their jurisdictions so that a road could be installed.

In Arlington, where part of the right-of-way paralleled Lee Highway, funds would be used to widen that road. The rest of the rail line would be paved after it was transferred into the Virginia secondary road system. Because of a lack of funding, it took several years for the state to complete the job. It was not until the summer of 1938 that money was allocated to pave the last three and a half miles, opening up the new Old Dominion Drive all the way from Cherrydale to the Great Falls.[2]

The delay in completing Old Dominion Drive was no surprise to local citizens. Many miles of roads in Fairfax County were in grim shape. During bad weather, numerous households spent days in isolation. Residents from all over the county alternately begged and demanded that the Board of Supervisors petition the State Highway Commission to repair roads and install new gravel surfaces.

The board duly complied with many of these requests, sending resolutions to State Highway Commissioner Henry G. Shirley. In July 1935, Shirley announced that more than $13.5 million in state and federal funds would be spent on road improvements; however, this plan would create a $1.5 million deficit in the state's road budget because the state would have to provide matching funds of $2.4 million to get the federal grant needed for primary and secondary road construction. Of the total amount, $7 million would be allocated statewide for secondary road projects, including repair and maintenance. The good news was that these projects would provide employment for five thousand local men. Convict road gangs would supply additional labor.[3]

As usual, decisions made in Richmond left many Northern Virginians with the feeling that the needs of their district were not understood. Shortly after Shirley's announcement regarding road funding, the citizens of Great Falls were horrified to find that their road repairs were to be carried out by convicts. A convict road gang was to be transferred from Loudoun County to Great Falls.

This was definitely a case of "be careful what you ask for; you might get it." Residents in the Great Falls area, which contained some of the worst roads in the county, had long clamored for repairs. The decision to move the road gang to Great Falls was no doubt spurred by the area's labor shortage. To make matters worse, the state intended to build a prison road camp on Georgetown Pike to house the convicts.

While Great Falls residents were debating the pros and cons of convict labor, Loudoun County residents were indignant at the thought of losing their road gang. Farmers believed hiring local labor to repair Loudoun's roads would cause a farm labor shortage because the state would offer higher wages than the farmers could afford to pay.

Ignoring all arguments, the state government leased five acres of land on Georgetown Pike near the Difficult Run Bridge and erected a cellblock, an office, a garage, and a mess hall. On August 8, 1935, the state transferred sixty prisoners to the new facility. Camp superintendent F. L. Riordan was quick to reassure local residents that they were not in any danger from their new neighbors, who were serving terms of between one and twenty years. After all, during the three years the camp had been located in Loudoun, only five inmates had escaped. Three had been recaptured. No mention was made of the other two.

In order to minimize the danger of repeat escapes, the prisoners were watched by shotgun-wielding guards who would shoot first and ask questions later. If a prisoner did escape, the guard who let him get away would immediately lose his job. For added security, the prisoners were chained to cellblock walls at night. Residents quickly became familiar with the sight of prisoners working on the roads or marching to the quarry at the Great Falls, where they dug stone and crushed it for gravel.[4]

It was probably a good thing that Great Falls got the prison camp, since Senator Byrd was still fighting against New Deal legislation in Congress. In opposition to Roosevelt's $4,880,999,000 Work Relief program, Byrd proposed a $3,000,000,000 reduction in the allocation. He was quoted in the *Washington Post* as saying, "The plan to revive prosperity by expending borrowed public funds to construct public works is not new and has never been successful in any country."

Byrd went on to point out that Virginia had tried the expenditure method from 1820 to 1861, when it issued state bonds to build canals and railroads. Public works constructed with those bonds had long ago gone out of use through technological advances and destruction during the Civil War, yet Virginia was still paying on those bonds. As reported by the *Washington Post*, he emphatically stated, "I am opposed to mortgaging the future welfare of our children, grandchildren, and even generations to come. The time has come to reduce the spending orgy at Washington and to install economy, efficiency, and simplicity in our public affairs."[5]

No matter how vehemently Byrd argued, Virginians did not want to pass up their share of federal aid programs. The Public Works Administration (PWA) approved fifty-two new projects for a budget of $2,570,413. These projects included the construction of ten new CCC camps, one of which was built at Fort Belvoir. A new Works Progress Administration (WPA) office was opened in Northern Virginia just to administer projects in that area.[6]

A WPA program in Fairfax County employed a worker in each high school and elementary school to serve soup to needy students. The program also hired three visiting housekeepers to travel throughout the county to advise on home management strategies. In addition, state and local governments continued to apply for federal money to finance public works projects.[7]

There was no doubt that the economy of Northern Virginia was improving. Arlington and Fairfax home values were rising, but so were tax assessments. In Fairfax alone, 1935 property assessments increased $155,356 over 1934 assessments. The price of land had not gone up, but the value of improvements had. With more residents meeting their tax obligations, Fairfax County reported a 97 percent collection rate on state income tax. At the same time, Fairfax had the smallest amount of tax-delinquent properties since 1929; however, there were still 329 properties slated to be sold at auction for back taxes.[8]

Thanks to federal funding from New Deal programs, the rise in county revenue programs relieved some of the infrastructure problems. For instance, in September 1935, Fairfax County's public schools experienced their largest jump in enrollment, with 250 more students than the previous year. School buildings were so crowded that, in some cases, auditoriums and hallways were being used as classrooms. For the first time in five years, however, the Fairfax County School Board was able to hire new teachers without having to go through a prolonged search through the county budget for additional funding.[9]

While some segments of the population in Arlington and Fairfax counties experienced improved economic circumstances, most farmers were still struggling to make ends meet. In spite of actions by the AAA to raise prices for farm commodities, it was often the middleman or the ultimate vendor who enjoyed the profits rather than the farmer who actually grew the product. Farming was still very hard work for small gains.

Once again, the AAA programs came under strong criticism from Senator Byrd. As a farmer, he had no patience with government officials who were not experienced farmers trying to manipulate the farm economy. When the secretary of agriculture sought to expand the authority of the AAA, Byrd declared that the government was being conducted "by office holders, exercising more power under a straw hat than did the king of old with a jeweled crown."[10]

As further reported in the *Washington Post*, Byrd went on to say that the AAA was "illustrative of the evil of creating a great bureaucracy that uses some power as a lever to get more power." He predicted that if the agency was not stopped: "Only the person who eats the food will escape this Federal dictatorship. Perhaps later the power of license will be extended to regulate what we shall eat and how much, and save us the trouble of attending to that detail of our daily existence."[11]

Byrd's rhetoric had little effect when the AAA gave Fairfax farmers a raise from twenty-nice cents to thirty-three cents per bushel for the wheat that they did not grow. But the fact that the funds for the increase in price were generated by taxes on the wheat harvested by farmers who did not participate in the government's program did underscore his point about excessive government control.[12]

In spite of Byrd's warnings, at times it was difficult for the farmers to turn down offers of improvements to their lifestyles. Many lived and worked in primitive conditions. While new suburban homes were equipped with indoor plumbing, electricity, and central heating, houses in the rural areas of Fairfax often did not have any of those amenities; therefore, the creation of the Rural Electrification Administration (REA) in May 1935 produced much excitement.[13]

Fairfax farmers held a mass meeting in June to find out how soon the electric lines would arrive in their neighborhoods and how they could connect their properties. The REA would provide the power and run the lines, but each farmer had to pay to wire his own buildings and also pay for the wire and poles to bring the power from the road to his house and barn. The REA would allow the homeowner to pay off his share over a long period of time at a reduced interest rate.[14]

It sounded like a good idea, but Fairfax County Agricultural Agent Derr cautioned people not to rush into wiring their homes until the line was constructed near their property. The distance between farmhouses was a problem. The decision to run a line was based on how many homeowners would agree to connect to the service. Some farms had their own electric generators, so if the cost was too high, farmers would choose not to participate with the REA.

In the end, many were very disappointed by the hollow promise of electrification. After assessing the needs of the rural area of the county, the REA imposed conditions that made the installation of power lines impractical for most areas. The agency required communities to form a cooperative that would employ the necessary people to run the electric company business, purchase equipment, acquire rights of way for lines,

Poster advertising the Rural Electrification Administration

construct the lines, and provide repairs and maintenance. In addition, every mile of line had to generate enough income to pay for itself.

It was impossible for the hardworking farmers to find the time or expertise to comply with these conditions. Their business was farming, not organizing and running an electric company. In the end, after a few months of hope, rural residents realized that electric power would not be available in their homes anytime soon. To many, the New Deal did not seem like quite such a good deal after all.[15]

To others, the New Deal agencies brought relief from their hard struggle for survival. In December 1935, the Fairfax County branch of the PWA announced that new loans were available to assist needy

Poster advertising loans to farmers from the Resettlement Administration

farmers. These loans would allow those who were destitute to purchase seed, fertilizer, work animals, and feed. In a broad sweep designed to help as many as possible, eligibility was extended to farm owners, farm tenants, sharecroppers, and farm laborers.

Applicants had to prove that they had a good reputation and "show evidence of initiative and industry." Those not currently engaged in farming had to prove prior experience. Loans with 5 percent interest rates were payable over a period of three to five years.[16]

Notwithstanding the machinations of the PWA, REA, and MA, farmers began to see some small improvements in their economic conditions. Livestock values in Virginia rose by 13 percent over the previous year. As a result of drought conditions in the western states, the prices of cattle and hogs rose to the highest point in five years. Beef steers went from $7.24 to $13.54 per one hundred pounds, and the price of bacon jumped from $19.65 to $24.87 per one hundred pounds.[17]

It appeared that many of the Fairfax farmers had survived the worst of the Depression. In fact, the 1935 federal census revealed several startling statistics. The number of farms in the county had grown from 1,244 in 1930 to 2,001 in 1935. In that five-year period, the dairy cow population had increased by more than 2,000 head, yielding a 30 percent increase in milk output.

In general, there was a large increase in all livestock, and an additional 1,270 acres were added to planted cropland. But the total value of the farms had decreased since 1930, and so had the size of the farms. In 1930, the average farm size was 99.3 acres, and by 1935, that was reduced to 70.7 acres. With the exception of the fall in land values, these numbers revealed positive economic progress for the farming community.

The reduction in farm size was attributable to the growing popularity of country life among those employed in the city. In that five-year period, numerous military officers, government employees, and those working in private business had migrated to the country. Attracted by cheap land prices and outdoor sports such as fishing, game hunting, and foxhunting, many newcomers had established farms on small sections of older and larger farms. And since they could at best only be part-time farmers, they employed career farmers to work their property.[18]

Equestrian sports were very popular during this era. The busy horse-show season ran from spring until fall throughout all of Fairfax County. In November, the now well-established Fairfax Hunt opened its formal foxhunting season, which lasted through March. Officers from the US Army cavalry stationed at Fort Myer participated in horse shows and foxhunts. In 1935 it was practical and possible to ride a horse from Fort Myer to a show in Fairfax County or to a hunt meet at Sunset Hills Farm.

The growing equestrian activity brought many Washington socialites into the countryside. Some of them purchased their own farms. In 1935 radio personality Arthur Godfrey purchased a farm from the Wheeler family in the Colvin Run neighborhood on Leesburg Pike so he could keep his horses in a location convenient to the Fairfax Hunt Club. Godfrey was soon immersed in the world of horse shows and foxhunting. With his recognizable voice and sense of humor, he was in great demand as the announcer for horse shows.[19]

The migration of city folk to the country began a phase of suburban farming that brought much-needed money into the rural parts of Fairfax County. It also helped to stabilize land prices and later to promote a rise in real estate values. And while the Depression was not over yet, life, in general, looked a lot better.

Chapter 31

BONUS BONDS AND EMERGING HOME AMENITIES

The new year of 1936 opened with a particularly acrimonious congressional debate over the Adjusted Compensation Payment Act bill. Originally passed in 1924, this act provided additional pay for veterans of World War I in the form of service certificates that were not redeemable in full until 1945. Those certificates paid each veteran $1.00 per day for service in the United States and $1.25 per day for overseas service. The bill in question would allow veterans to cash their certificates immediately.

President Franklin D. Roosevelt had prevented this scenario when he vetoed the first bill passed by Congress in 1935. He reasoned that the bill would not qualify as part of the Depression relief program because it was not based on the demonstrated needs of the individuals who would benefit.

In January, a new version of the bill was introduced. It called for the original service certificates to be replaced with Treasury Department bonds in $50.00 denominations. Lesser amounts would be paid by check. The bonds could be cashed at post offices for face value or held at 3 percent interest until 1945. Opponents of the bill predicted the bond payout would create a "road to bankruptcy."[1]

Secretary of the Treasury Henry Morgenthau issued stern warnings that the passage of the bill could cause a $35.5 billion public debt by the end of the next fiscal year. Fearing that the measure would cause a severe fall in the bond market, Morgenthau advised Roosevelt to veto the bill, which the president duly did. But Congress overrode the veto. The bill was passed on January 27, 1936, and it became known as the Bonus Bill.[2]

There was nothing else for President Roosevelt to do but attempt damage control. He delivered an impassioned plea to veterans not to "fritter it away." He urged them instead to use their compensation wisely for home purchases or improvements to existing homes.

At the same time, he cautioned that the bonds would not be available immediately. Issuance of the bonds was an enormous clerical job that would require between twenty-five hundred and three thousand people working for approximately six months. The first step would be to develop an application form for all veterans to complete and submit—another case of expanding government and more piles of paper.[3]

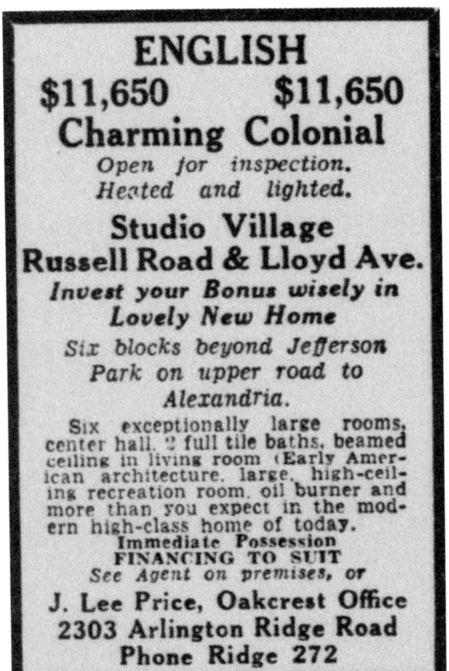

Advertisement in the Evening Star, *1936, encouraging Bonus Bill recipients to invest in real estate*

The controversy over the Bonus Bill came at a particularly bad time for Roosevelt because it was an election year. His opponents were in full swing, attacking his relief programs. Conveniently forgetting his veto, Roosevelt's critics decried the huge amount of money necessary to back the Bonus Bonds, which impinged on funding for the various relief agencies. A March 3, 1936, editorial in the *Washington Post* pointed out that the national debt was well above $31 billion and that it had doubled in the past five years. The writer suggested that new taxes be imposed on the incomes of those in the middle and lower brackets as a way to create support for a stricter government economy.[4]

On the other side, former President Hoover claimed that the excess of spending on the national level had "laid the groundwork for an ever-increasing tax burden." In a speech to the Young Republican League of Colorado, as reported in the *Washington Post*, he said, "Your freedom and your opportunities in life are being mortgaged."[5]

While hot debates were being conducted at the national level, Northern Virginians were working to adjust their own economy. In particular, in the previous year, Fairfax County had collected the most revenue since 1928. Consequently, many citizens believed the county should loosen some of the stringent budget cuts that had been put in place during the lean years.

In January, the Fairfax County Board of Supervisors debated a measure that would put county salaries back to pre-Depression levels. The vote ended in a tie. Annual salaries remained at their same level, ranging from a mere $225 for a jailer to $2,700 for a trial justice. The sheriff was paid $1,200; traffic policemen got $1,500.[6]

On another front, the Board of Supervisors was trying to handle the problem of crowded schools. In 1936, enrollment increased by 222 students. In 1935, the school board had suggested a school-building program that would be financed by the PWA, but the county would have to contribute matching money to qualify for the grant. The only way to generate the matching funds was to authorize a bond issue.

Voters, however, would not support any more public debt, and the issue was defeated. To alleviate school crowding, the county built temporary classroom buildings in the schoolyards. To fund this construction and other expenses, the Board of Supervisors decided to raise taxes. The largest increases were in districts where the most money was being spent.[7]

In spite of the defeat of the bond issue, there were other cases in which the county attempted to work with New Deal program funds. Often, it was a frustrating exercise. When Mrs. James U. Kincheloe donated a forty-acre tract near Clifton for a rural recreation park, it was believed that a WPA grant would provide funds to build the facilities. The plans for the park included building a lake, a playground, a large reception hall, cabins, and athletic fields. The WPA engineers surveyed the property and pronounced it suitable for the proposed use.

The next step was for Fairfax County to agree to pay approximately $4,400 in matching funds. When the Board of Supervisors refused the appropriation, various civic groups raised the money. With the award of a $20,000 WPA grant, citizens were hopeful that the new park would be built quickly, but the project was still stalled. This time it was a labor shortage. Under the terms of the WPA grant, local people had to be hired for the construction. Thirty men were needed to build the park. No one was applying. The fact that men were not rushing to take the offered jobs may have reflected improvements in the local economy.[8]

Senator Byrd tackled the WPA when he fired off his next verbal barrage against excessive government spending and the growing power of its agencies. As the economy showed signs of improvement, he pointed out that instead of cutting back on expenses, the government was proposing to spend even more. He said that the budget for 1937 was to be $1 billion higher than that of 1936. Byrd accused the agencies of mounting higher and higher debt with reckless disregard for actual needs. He believed that people had lost confidence in the "wasteful and corrupt machinery of the WPA and wouldn't take the jobs."[9]

That accusation notwithstanding, the WPA did inaugurate another program that proved to have some lasting benefit for future generations. Under the direction of the University of Virginia, WPA workers were dispatched to collect as much Fairfax County oral history as possible. Moving from one community to the next, they sought the oldest citizens to interview and took detailed notes of their life stories. Since there were Civil War veterans and former slaves still living, the interviewers collected fascinating details of personal narratives that otherwise would have been lost.[10]

While the WPA caused frustrations and delays on projects, the CCC was busy creating a new park at Langley. The land under development was part of the Joseph Leiter estate known as Palisades Farm. This large tract of more than 480 acres stretched from the Georgetown Pike to the Potomac River.

Leiter, an ultrawealthy industrialist from Chicago, also had a large mansion in the District of Columbia. He purchased the land at Langley in 1911 for $50,000 and immediately built an enormous stone, frame, and stucco country home. The three-story house resembled a luxury resort hotel. The construction alone reportedly cost $55,000. It had more than forty rooms—each with its own fireplace—a ballroom, a library, a gun room, and a well-stocked wine cellar in the basement fitted with a steel door. And it had at least seventeen bedrooms, most of which had private bathrooms.

He used the farm as a place to entertain friends and socialites from all over the world. He hosted foxhunts, bird shoots, dinners, dances, and other country weekend entertainments. An army of gardeners kept strolling and bridle paths, lawns, and gardens in pristine condition for the pleasure of Leiter and his guests.[11]

After Leiter died in 1932, it took some years to settle his estate. The situation was complicated by issues with the Internal Revenue Service. Ultimately, Leiter's heirs deeded 176 acres of the Palisades Farm property to the United States government for one dollar to create a new national park. The National Capital Park and Planning Commission developed a plan for the property. A strip close to the Potomac River was allocated for the future construction of the George Washington Memorial Parkway. The rest of the 176 acres was to be developed into hiking and bridle trails, secluded picnic areas, and a playground with a wading stream for

Leiter Mansion on Georgetown Pike, McLean, Virginia

children. The house would be converted into a recreation center. The balance of the land in Palisades Farm was to be sold and subdivided for new homes. These grand plans were to be implemented by the CCC.

Because the property had been vacant for some years, all the once-manicured lawns, strolling paths, and bridle trails were now overgrown with thick strands of briars and vines. It would be no easy job for the CCC. And no one yet knew that the ultimate use of the property would be the site for the George Bush Center for Intelligence.[12]

Spurred by improved economic conditions and a growing demand for homes, real estate sales were on the rise for both new construction and resale homes. Interest rates were still low, at about 5 percent. The growing population of employees for the constantly expanding federal government caused the housing shortage to continue across the Washington metropolitan area.

Because there was still much vacant land within easy commuting distance from the city, many new housing developments were being created throughout Northern Virginia. In anticipation of the distribution of the Bonus Bonds slated for June, builders hurried to get new homes ready. Real estate professionals predicted that bond recipients would follow the president's advice and purchase new homes. In April 1936, the *Washington Post* reported that there were fifteen rapidly expanding new developments in the Virginia suburbs.[13]

Homes in Arlington were being sold faster than they could be built. In the first five months of 1936, new homes totaling $2 million in value had already been built, with an average price of about $6,500 per house. The new development of Aurora Hills quickly sold the first 250 homes and still had room for 150 more. Waverly Hills, near Glebe Road in North Arlington, was also reporting good sales. Fifteen different builders put up eighty new homes in Ashton Heights, near Clarendon. From January through the end of June, Arlington County issued twelve hundred building permits.[14]

Fairfax also reported a great increase in new construction, though prices were slightly lower there due to the longer commute. Permanesque Village in the Beverly Hills section of Alexandria recorded brisk sales. A new home there could be purchased for $5,250, with a monthly payment of principal and interest of $26. A larger upgraded model could be arranged for $7,450, with monthly payments of $35.20. Builders'

Guilford new homes advertisement in the Evening Star *newspaper, 1936*

advertisements claimed "payments cheaper than rent." A bit farther out from the capital, homes in Guilford on Franconia Road were also selling well.[15]

The significant increase in home sales was one indicator of economic recovery for the region. A larger indicator of better times was the style and luxury appointments included in new construction. Buyers focused on larger homes. Whereas a five-room house had been the norm two years earlier, now the demand was for six or more rooms. Brick construction was favored over frame. Slate roofs were deemed a normal feature of any quality construction. Items once considered luxuries were now considered absolute requirements.

Permanesque Homes Village advertised the "New American Carefree Home," boasting features that made it "care free," such as an all-electric kitchen, oil heat, concealed copper radiators, a laundry room, a slate roof, copper gutters and downspouts, casement windows, an automatic water heater, all-brick construction, and aluminum foil insulation. Several designs were offered. Each featured a large living room with a fireplace, a separate dining room, three or more bedrooms, two complete baths finished in ceramic tile, a screened porch, and an attached garage.

Fine interior features and finishes also helped to promote the idea of luxurious living. The kitchen came equipped with a stove, a refrigerator, knotty pine cabinets, and an electric pastry mixer. There was also a natural stone fireplace in the kitchen's cocktail lounge area with a knotty pine mantel. The living and dining rooms featured built-in cupboards and bookcases.[16]

Other builders offered homes with variations on the features found at Permanesque but went one step further and installed forced-air heating and air-conditioning, which was advertised as a new necessity. Advertisements claimed that not only were the hot and humid summers uncomfortable for the home's inhabitants but the weather was positively destructive to furnishings and the structure. Builders were able to reassure the homebuyers that the added expense of air-conditioning would promote comfort and better health. In addition, it would save homeowners money because they would not have to paint and redecorate as often. Rugs, draperies, and furniture would all look better because of proper temperature and moisture control.[17]

While the rising demand for houses and luxury finishes demonstrated one facet of economic recovery, many areas of the local economy were still influenced by the hardships caused by the Depression. The distribution and final dispensation of the Bonus Bonds was illustrative of public opinion regarding the recovery.

Roosevelt was correct about how much labor would be involved in issuing the bonds. In June, post offices had to add extra personnel to handle the deliveries. The bonds were distributed by registered mail, and recipients had to sign for them in person. Then many of the veterans went straight to their local post offices and immediately cashed in their bonds. Of the $1,726,000,000 issued in bonds, $1,096,515,700 had been cashed by the end of July.[18]

Where that money went was a mystery. There was no appreciable increase in any particular retail trade, nor was the money reflected in bank deposits. It appeared that consumer confidence had not really recovered and that the money was being kept in mattresses or other hiding places.

Farmers represented another segment of the population that was having trouble overriding the effects of the Depression. Byrd's arguments against the artificial shortages that resulted when the AAA paid farmers not to grow wheat had proven to be true. Large parts of the United States and Canada were again suffering a severe drought. The wheat and hay crops had failed. Consequently, feed for farm animals rose dramatically in price.

Dairy farming was still the largest industry in Fairfax County. The high price of cattle feed created a hardship for a significant part of the population. The county's 180 dairy farms contributed 10 percent of the county tax revenue and provided employment for 440 families, not including the feed stores and other support businesses.[19]

To make matters worse, the AAA was fixing the price of milk sold in the District of Columbia, which was the market for most of the milk from Fairfax farmers. Throughout the year, farmers fought with the AAA, arguing for a price increase. Finally, on November 1, 1936, after hundreds of hours of farmers' and milk producers' testimonies in federal court, the price of milk was increased one cent per quart, which was passed on to the farmer.[20]

At the close of the year, the economic situation in Northern Virginia revealed a divide. Arlington County, Alexandria, and newly developed parts of Fairfax County were showing great progress toward recovery. The farming community had not advanced nearly as far. Farmers had to be ever vigilant to keep their businesses operating at a small profit or at times just to break even. Commuter residents who lived in new suburban homes were able to enjoy the latest technological advances and luxury items, while many farmers were still wondering if they would ever get electricity and indoor plumbing.

In Fairfax County, the supervisors had to juggle the requests of subdivision residents for sidewalks and street paving with those of rural residents who just wanted their roads graded and the mud holes filled in. And while the economy in general was in better shape than the year before, the effects of the recovery were not shared equally by all areas. It would still take time for most people to regain their consumer confidence.

Chapter 32

SIGNS OF PROSPERITY

Although people were enjoying better circumstances than they had for the previous six years, many residents of Northern Virginia were still very cautious with regard to debt and investments. Many people, unconvinced that the bad times were really over, were still hoarding their cash.

Nonetheless, 1937 opened with positive economic predictions. On January 2, the lead story on the *Washington Post* business page was titled "Prosperity Here At Last, Babson Says." The story reported on the economic forecast for the year as put forth by Roger W. Babson, a noted and respected business theorist. Babson predicted that 1937 would be the first year of real prosperity since 1929. On the positive side, he foresaw a year of genuine business expansion, significant real estate activity, a building boom, and healthy retail trade.

On the downside, he predicted a rise in the cost of living, constant labor troubles, and a shortage of skilled workers. Babson believed the labor shortage would be generally reflected in the forecasted building boom, leading to higher wages and, in turn, higher construction prices.

In spite of the negative elements, Babson's overall prognosis for the national economy was positive. One element omitted from the report was the economic condition of the federal government.[1]

The cost of operating the government during the recovery period had caused a huge rise in the national debt. Roosevelt's New Deal had prompted many positive changes, but at a significant cost. The establishment of so many new agencies had created a rapid expansion of the government. Numerous congressmen expressed uneasiness over the size and expenditures of the government, but they were at a loss as to how to curtail it. While many had a clear idea of the ultimate cost to the taxpayer for these services, they also were reluctant to eliminate them.

The problem the legislators faced was summed up well by John C. Rogers of Alexandria in a letter to the editor of the *Washington Post*. Rogers pointed out that even in good times, half of Virginia's rural population existed under marginal conditions. With the advance of technology each year, more labor-saving devices were introduced that deprived people of jobs. So even in economic recovery, there was still an element of the population that was jobless and homeless. Rogers closed with a statement that defined the puzzle faced by Congress: "Government spending statistics are positively tantalizing when you prove that all of prosperity is due entirely to Government spending, and what do you have when the spending stops—statistics, and the march of hungry men and women."[2]

This problem was by no means isolated to Virginia. As a result, many legislators remained silent on the overriding issue of national debt versus recovery. They concentrated instead on positive economic reforms. Others believed it was crucial to curtail government spending and size before any more damage could be done.

Virginia's Senator Byrd continued in his fight to reform the government's spending habits and to balance the budget. As chairman of the Senate committee appointed to investigate executive agencies, he was appalled at the level of waste and duplication. Even though they were both Democrats, Byrd and Roosevelt disagreed on how best to manage the size and scope of the government.[3]

Byrd was opposed to big government; Roosevelt believed it to be the best policy. But Byrd's vociferous insistence on reform, combined with more moderate voices of other members of Congress, did convince Roosevelt to offer a reorganization plan. This led to a huge clash with Byrd and his committee.

In Byrd's opinion, Roosevelt's plan failed to address the real problems. No concrete solution was offered for the big picture, just a small fix here and there in consolidating some offices and jobs. Byrd wanted to abolish duplication and government waste.

He stated the problem in simple terms in a nationwide radio address—reported in the *Washington Post*—when he said, "We are emerging from the Depression loaded up with the greatest and most costly bureaucracy in all history." Byrd wanted to abolish twenty government boards, bureaus, and agencies that were due to expire in 1937 because they had been established to meet an emergency that was now over. This would, he claimed, "save the taxpayers hundreds of millions of dollars and substitute simplicity for confusion."

In case his listeners did not have a grasp of the size of the government, Byrd described what he called the "Federal jungle." He enumerated the agencies where he found duplication: there were at least fifty legal divisions, along with twenty-four agencies lending government money; three insuring deposits; thirty-four concerned with the acquisition of land; sixteen related to wildlife preservation; ten for government construction; nine involved in credit and finance; and twelve dealing with home and community planning.

"We own or lease office space equivalent to fifty-two Empire State Buildings—all outside of Washington," said Byrd. Unfortunately, he was unable to persuade Congress that his plan was better than Roosevelt's. He lost the first round of his abolition and consolidation fight in mid-January, when the Senate voted 52–22 to extend the Reconstruction Finance Corporation for one year.[4]

While history may have proved the valid points of Byrd's argument, Roosevelt's expanded government certainly had a beneficial effect on the economy of Northern Virginia. The housing shortage caused by the constantly expanding government continued to fuel the real estate market for the entire Washington metropolitan region. Homes were selling as fast as they could be built.

Northern Virginia development was part of that building frenzy; however, the ever-increasing demand and higher labor costs were pushing up new home prices. As a result, many lower-level government employees could not afford to buy and could not find reasonable rental units. Many felt lucky to rent a room in a private home, where they cooked on a hot plate and shared a bathroom down the hall.[5]

Within the housing industry, the champion of the common man was Allie S. Freed, the chairman of the Committee for Economic Recovery. This committee was composed of corporate executives who advised Roosevelt on a comprehensive plan for government, industry, finance, and labor issues.

Freed was as outspoken about the government's failures to stimulate the development of affordable housing and excessive government control as Byrd was on other failings of the government. He also believed strongly that the government's role should stop with stimulation of private enterprise and that for the government to engage in the building process for affordable homes would be prohibitively expensive and wasteful.

In particular, Freed attacked the policies of the Federal Housing Administration (FHA) and its failure to aid a national home-building program. In a speech in Chicago—reported by the *Washington Post*—he vehemently pronounced:

> There is growing up in Washington a carefully conceived, although fortunately, not yet executed plan, whereby the Federal Housing Administration would soon have under its supreme control, the definite power to say what materials shall go into a home, how they shall be applied, where the home shall be located, who shall do the financing, and who shall have the privilege of buying a home in this great country.[6]

Instead of all this government control, he maintained that the mission of the Department of Commerce was "the aid and promotion of home building by private enterprise" and "to aid in providing an ample flow of home mortgage credit."[7]

Freed wholeheartedly believed that building large-scale affordable home projects was "the country's best opportunity to put idle men and idle capital to work." And to prove his point, he set out to develop a credible example that would address the issues of affordable homes, finance, investment, and employment.

He formed Paramount Communities, Inc. His company purchased eighty-five acres in Arlington at the intersection of Glebe Road and Pershing Drive to build a huge complex of rental units. This ambitious and innovative project was named Buckingham Community.[8]

By building a planned apartment community, Freed intended to illustrate a scientific approach to provide affordable and efficient housing for people of moderate annual incomes of $1,500 to $3,000. At the same time, the project was designed to demonstrate that large-scale rental housing could be planned and managed as a sound investment and profitable business.

Freed succeeded in convincing the FHA to insure the initial mortgage of $500,000. Without FHA insurance, it is doubtful that he could have obtained that large a loan. But he was anxious to demonstrate what he perceived as the correct role of the FHA.[9]

The last element of his plan was to provide employment for local men. More than two hundred were employed continuously during the construction of the new community. The first phase called for fifty-four buildings that would provide housing for 510 families. The all-brick buildings would include units only two rooms deep, which would allow for good ventilation and would be planned to maximize floor space. The size of the apartments would run from the smallest of one central room with a kitchen and bath, all the way up to six rooms. Rents would range from $32.50 to $80 per month. All apartments would be constructed with the latest in modern conveniences. The buildings varied in their designs to avoid visual monotony. All were set among open lawns and children's playgrounds.[10]

The first units would be ready for occupancy on July 1, 1937. The project was planned to be completed by October 1. Upon completion of the first phase, the next section would be started. Ultimately, Freed planned to increase the FHA loan to $2 million and to provide housing for two thousand families. Areas designated for commercial and social activities were reserved. Those amenities would be added when the project was completed. Present-day Allie S. Freed Park is named in his honor.[11]

Speed of the construction was another of Freed's innovations, drawn from his experience as president of the Paramount Motors Corporation of New York, which designed and manufactured taxis. He decided to adapt the assembly-line technique used to construct automobiles for home building. But the Buckingham assembly line would be on-site, not in a factory.

As expected, there was a high demand for the apartments. Buckingham offered attractive amenities and reasonably priced modern homes in a rural setting that was close to urban conveniences. People weary of high rents and cramped quarters in the District of Columbia rushed to sign

Buckingham apartments, Arlington, Virginia

Buckingham apartments, Arlington, Virginia

leases. At the end of the year, Paramount Communities had exceeded the original estimate and completed 650 units.[12]

In June, they added the Maisonette, a new design planned for one thousand more housing units. These were built as duplexes with five rooms and a "cellar" suitable for a recreation room. Although rents now ranged from thirty-five to eighty-five dollars a month, the increase in price did not seem to deter applicants. The project had a constant waiting list.[13]

Freed had accomplished his goals and had built an exceptional example to demonstrate how multiple needs could be successfully addressed with one carefully planned construction project. It was to become a national model for other large-scale housing developments. Unfortunately, he did not live to see the project completed. After suffering for two weeks with pneumonia, Freed passed away at age forty-six on January 11, 1938. But his point had been made. By the end of the year, in Northern Virginia alone, the FHA was insuring mortgages on five rental projects and 4,062 single-family homes.[14]

The development of Northern Virginia continued to gain momentum. By October 1937, home building had increased by 60 percent over the previous year. The value of tax assessments for Fairfax County had nearly tripled in the past sixteen years. It had been $6,606,224 in 1920 and was now in excess of $17 million.[15]

But the continued development was not appreciated by all residents. In a letter to the editor of the *Washington Post*, one woman complained bitterly that in the two years she had lived in her new home, the surrounding property had been divided into small, narrow lots that did not afford any privacy. Furthermore, the new homes were "despoiling the natural beauty of the land."[16]

In spite of all the newly gained revenue in the county treasury, Fairfax was applying for a state literary loan to expand schools. Until it found a way to finance more classrooms, the school board had to redistrict students to alleviate crowding in some schools.[17]

As always, development led to infrastructure problems. The increase in county revenue brought in by new development did not begin to cover the costs generated by the increased population.

At the close of the year, the Northern Virginia economy was showing strong growth. Much of the growth, however, was stimulated by the demand for housing. The value of real estate continued to rise. Land development and building were moving forward at a rapid pace, a process that would continue to escalate in the next several years.

Byrd continued to press his reform measures to reduce the size of the government and to curb spending; however, his opponents countered that a rapid reduction in expenditures would be dangerous to the economy. That point certainly made sense to the residents of Northern Virginia. If a large number of government employees suddenly lost their jobs, the local economy would crash right back into a depression. As is often the way with these types of issues, one man's solution translated into creating problems for another. There were no easy answers to be found.

Chapter 33

CONTINUING ON THE PATH TO RECOVERY

The road back to prosperity was certainly not smooth. Possibly stimulated by the call for budget cuts, the PWA was deluged with grant applications from local governments. The *Washington Post* reported that the PWA was driving forward to end the Great Depression by approving construction projects on an average of $43,000,000 a day. And Northern Virginia got its share.

Arlington County received $27,500 for building storm sewers in Virginia Highlands and Ballston. The town of Herndon got a new post office. Fairfax County received funds to purchase a new school site; however, the amount was less than that for previous projects and represented only 10 percent of the county's building budget.[1]

As 1937 passed, the budget-cut battles continued in Congress. Defense concerns were elevated by Hitler's actions in Europe. Many in Congress believed the immediate buildup of US armaments was a necessity. And while those issues were being addressed, there was little progress on reorganizing the government. To Senator Byrd's frustration, he closed

1937 in about the same vein as he had begun it. Interviewed in November, he stated, "I regard economical operation of the government to be of first importance now, especially, in view of the probability of increased armaments."[2]

While Congress wrestled with budget cuts, Northern Virginia's local governments were in better fiscal condition than before the beginning of the Depression. Arlington County's assessments rose to just over $1 million for the first time. Officials were able to collect on 72 percent of the assessments before they were past due. Fairfax County collected enough revenue to spur the Board of Supervisors to consider pay raises for county employees for 1938. The motion did not carry. It was not until 1939 that all county employees got a monthly raise of $5 to $17.[3]

The improved fiscal condition of both counties was fueled by increased employment and new home construction. Fast-paced

Glebewood Village advertisement in the Evening Star *newspaper, 1938*

development in Arlington was creating new homes weekly. At the start of 1938, it was predicted that the building boom would last for at least five years.

In addition to the general housing shortage, this race to build was stimulated by a change in the Federal Housing Administration (FHA) loan program. Originally, FHA loans required a 20 percent down payment. Now the rules changed, offering loans at 90 percent financing for homes priced at less than $6,000. Glebewood Village on North Glebe Road and Lee Highway was a product of the new loan program and was built under the oversight of the FHA construction supervisors.[4]

Each home featured a brick-and-stone exterior, five rooms, a tiled bath, five big closets, a laundry tray in the basement, full-length screens on all windows and doors, and nationally advertised wallpaper. The project was an immediate success. Eighty-five homes sold in the first eighteen weeks. The FHA made homeownership affordable to many who previously could only dream of owning a home. It was one of the most successful of the New Deal agencies.[5]

As predicted, the Arlington building boom continued into 1939. Arlington was the smallest but most heavily populated county in Virginia. From 1930 to 1939, the population doubled to fifty-five thousand, which equated to fifteen hundred people per square mile. The building frenzy also spread throughout the City of Alexandria. Newly constructed commuter highway systems and the Memorial Bridge provided easy access into the city and encouraged those employed in the District to move across the river to Virginia.[6]

Many residents of Fairfax who were watching the building activity in the neighboring areas were anxious to bring that income to their county. There were some new homes being built, but not on the scale seen in Arlington and Alexandria. Fairfax, for the most part, did not have the wonderful major highway systems that made Arlington and Alexandria attractive to commuters. In fact, many of its roads were in poor condition, which added more time to the longer-distance commute.

The Fairfax Chamber of Commerce petitioned the Board of Supervisors to promote development of the county. The Chamber of Commerce started an advertising campaign that proclaimed the advantages of living in "historic and progressive Fairfax." The county was billed as a "Modern County with a historical setting" in a *Washington Post* story. The writer painted a picture of the glories of its history and homes, such as Mount Vernon, that would make the reader want to join in this elegant lifestyle of country estates. The Board of Supervisors invited homebuyers, farmers, and investors to come and see for themselves. With a population of just over thirty thousand scattered over its 407 square miles, Fairfax County

Hickory Hill advertisement in the Evening Star *newspaper, 1940. Later, it became the home of Robert and Ethel Kennedy.*

was still mainly agrarian. With more than half of its area covered in forest, it was a blank slate for development.[7]

Despite the efforts to draw development to Fairfax, the reality was far from a building boom. Except for the areas close to Arlington and Alexandria, most people moved to the county for the very things covered in the *Washington Post* story. It was an era when many were attracted to the bucolic life of a gentleman farmer. And, if they could afford them, historic properties were certainly at the top of their wish list.

In 1940, Cornwell Farm in Great Falls was offered for sale with two hundred acres and a sixteen-room house complete with all the modern conveniences, servants' quarters, and a bell system to call servants to specific rooms. The farm included a modern caretaker's house, a barn, and a tenant house. The following year, historic Hickory Hill in McLean—eventually home to John and Jacqueline Kennedy and later to Robert and Ethel Kennedy—went on the market. Completely restored and renovated with all the modern conveniences, Hickory Hill was offered at $47,950.[8]

At the same time, Hollin Hall, south of Alexandria, was offered for sale. The six-hundred-acre property, once owned by George Mason, was a large dairy farm. The original house had been destroyed by fire, but that did not prevent its owners from regarding the property as historic. Graced by a large brick mansion built in 1920, the estate included acres of formal gardens, a guesthouse, a greenhouse, a swimming pool, a spinning house from the Mason era, a large dairy barn, and many farm buildings. It had languished on the market since 1936, with no one able to afford property of that size.

Finally, in 1941, Roosevelt advisor Merle Thorpe, Jr. purchased the main house and sixty acres. N. C. Hines & Sons, auctioneers and Realtors, disposed of the balance of the property by offering it at auction after subdividing the land into five- and ten-acre parcels. They retained one hundred acres for the dairy farm. Hoping to capitalize on the history of the estate, real estate brokers advertised it with slogans such as "History

Hollin Hall advertisement in the Evening Star *newspaper, 1941*

and Romance Live within this Beautiful Spot" and "Build Your Country Home on Ground Hallowed by History." For those who were unable to afford a large estate, there were numerous five- and six-room homes on the five- and ten-acre parcels offered for prices ranging from $2,990 to $3,990. Because many government workers had grown up on farms or had come from small towns, these more modest properties appealed to them. They could have room for a garden, chickens, and even a cow or horses.[9]

While the Fairfax County real estate market was not as strong as Arlington's, it was picking up momentum. By June 1940, a *Washington Post* headline announced, "Building Hits All Time Peak In Fairfax." New developments such as Annandale Acres, Pinecrest, Fairlawn, Plymouth Haven, and Tremont Gardens were selling rapidly. Tremont Gardens offered five-room bungalows, or Cape Cod models, in the $4,000 price range on large lots near Falls Church. In addition to offering lower prices for new construction, Fairfax had the advantage of lower real estate taxes than Arlington. Assessments on real and personal property were based on only one-third of the market value, and the tax rate was $1.74 per $100 value.[10]

Advertising campaigns to attract builders and homebuyers to Fairfax were successful. By July 1941, the county clerk reported that 3,484 deeds had been recorded in the previous six months at a value totaling $4,850,614. And that was just the beginning of the conversion of Fairfax from an agrarian to a suburban county. As usual, the increase in population led to overcrowded schools and a shortage of teachers, school buses, and bus drivers. To solve the school bus problem on some routes, the county contracted with private drivers who owned their own buses.[11]

Throughout 1940 and 1941, Congress continued to debate the best way to cut the national debt. World War II had broken out in Europe in September 1939. There was much pressure for the United States to aid England and France. But first, many agreed, it was crucial to build up national defenses. In January 1941, President Roosevelt asked Congress for $10.8 billion for armaments. Budgets for nondefense items—including the WPA, the PWA, and the CCC—were cut.[12]

To pay for strengthening national defense, in April 1941, taxes were raised and new taxes were added. First, there was a one-cent-per-gallon tax on gasoline. The excise tax on automobiles jumped from 3 percent to 5 percent. Next, Roosevelt proposed a rise in income tax from 4 percent to 6 percent. The tax hike was aimed at the middle-income bracket, with annual earnings of $5,000 to $50,000. By August, Treasury Secretary Morgenthau was urging even more dramatic changes. He wanted to broaden the tax base to include millions of new taxpayers by lowering the exemptions to $750 for single people and $1,500 for married couples. He also wanted to raise estate and gift taxes.[13]

Unfortunately, recovery from the Depression was corroborating the earlier predictions of senators Glass and Byrd: payday had come, and the future of the next generation had been well and truly mortgaged.

Byrd was elected chairman of a new fourteen-man joint committee to investigate methods to bring about more economical use of governments funds. Byrd, true to style, was quoted in the *Washington Post* as stating, "It is vital to our future security that nonessential Federal spending be cut to the bone." Even though he was a strong proponent of strengthening the national defense, he believed that "our financial security is just as important to our democracy as our defense security."[14]

In spite of all the new development, Fairfax County was still primarily agrarian, with 60 percent of the land in working farms. Dairying was the main farm industry, with poultry running a close second. Others raised market gardens, beef, orchards, corn, wheat, and hay.

In May 1941, Fairfax was suffering from a six-month drought that had reduced corn planting by 50 percent, and 30 percent of all the farmland had not been plowed. The pastures were burning up, and cattle had to be fed hay. Everyone remembered the devastating drought in 1930 and feared the worst as temperatures soared day after day into the mid-nineties. Milk production declined, causing farmers to worry about a loss of income.[15]

Some rain fell in June, preventing a total crop loss and resulting in surprisingly good early harvests. But the extreme heat and drought conditions returned in July and continued well into the fall. September was the driest month since 1884. Daily high temperatures were still reaching into the nineties in October. Rainfall was 8.35 inches below normal. The weather finally cooled down at the end of October, which helped pastures, but the lack of moisture played havoc with the planting of fall crops. Milk

Horses pulling a hay wagon during the harvest on a farm in Vienna, Virginia, c. 1940

production picked up with the revived pastures, and farmers were able to avoid a crippling drop in income.

As 1941 drew to a close, the economy of Northern Virginia was doing well. While not everyone had recovered completely from the ill effects of the Depression, most people were living in better conditions. The economy had steadily improved for the last several years, and life had returned to a normal pace.

But that change was not to be enjoyed for long. On December 7, 1941, the Japanese attacked the American naval fleet at Pearl Harbor, and the United States went to war.

Chapter 34

GROWTH SPURRED BY ENTRY INTO WAR

At Roosevelt's request, Congress declared war on Japan on December 8 and on Germany on December 11, 1941, and the United States geared up for combat. All branches of the military expanded immediately. Many new government agencies were created overnight to manage matters of national defense and to support the armed forces.

The population of Washington and its suburbs exploded as people rushed to take wartime jobs. And as usual, the economy of Northern Virginia benefited from the region's proximity to the nation's capital.

Builders and developers in Arlington had been productive during 1941, erecting new construction valued at $15,453,040. And that was only in the private sector. Many new government buildings were also being added to the county's landscape, including the Pentagon.[1]

Started on September 11, 1941, after a sharp debate in Congress, the five-sided, five-story building was being built to house the War Department. After war was declared, contractors raced to complete the building. Approximately 13,000 men were employed on the project. By May 1942,

The Pentagon under construction, 1941

500,000 square feet of the new building were ready for occupation. With its finished size of more than 6.5 million square feet, it became the world's largest office building when it was completed in 1943.[2]

All across Northern Virginia, builders were racing to take advantage of the heightened housing shortage created by the influx of about 5,000 war workers per month. The housing shortage was so acute that people were lucky to find a room to rent. There were almost no apartments or single-family homes available. Prices were rising for both sales and rentals.[3]

To correct that type of war profiteering, in April 1942, the Office of Price Administration instituted rent control. Originally, director Leon Henderson planned to restrict prices to the level of March 1, 1942. But he found that the increases in rents were so "exorbitant" that he had to go back further. Henderson ordered that, as of July 1, 1942, all rents had to be rolled back to the price charged in January 1941.[4]

Nonetheless, the building frenzy continued. At the end of 1942, Arlington County had 548 new single-family homes and 3,103 new apartments. Alexandria had 305 new single-family homes and 2,486 new apartments. Fairfax County had 821 new single-family homes but only eighty new apartments. In spite of all the new homes, there was still a housing shortage. In Arlington County alone, the population jumped from 56,500 in 1940 to 100,000 in 1943.[5]

In January 1942, Congress launched the $100 million Defense Housing Program to provide 14,500 single-family homes, 7,500 apartments, and 1,500 dormitory units in Washington and its suburbs to house war workers. Under this program, the Alley Dwelling Authority (ADA) purchased 155 acres in Fairfax near Alexandria and Belle Haven to construct temporary wartime housing. The houses were to be demountable. This meant that they could be taken apart and moved to another location. The government preferred to rent these structures rather than sell them because the law required that they be removed within one year of the close of the war. In cases where they were sold, the purchasers got separate titles to the land so they could rebuild with more permanent structures.[6]

The largest Defense Housing Program project for war workers in Northern Virginia was Fairlington, which opened in April 1943. Built on 323 acres straddling the Fairfax-Arlington county border, the development consisted of 321 buildings. This project was the exact opposite of

Arlington subdivision under construction, 1942

the demountable temporary structures. Its construction cost the government $14,440,000.

The Williamsburg colonial-style brick buildings were trimmed with native stone and topped with slate roofs. The community consisted of rental units in two- and three-story apartment buildings and two-story duplex houses. Each duplex model had a full basement; a living room, dining room, and kitchen on the main floor; and two or three bedrooms on the top floor.

The apartments were all on one floor, with one or two bedrooms and a private basement storage area. Hot water heat was provided by thirty-four coal-fired furnaces. Rents ranged from $58.50 to $89.50 per month, which included heat, water, and electricity. Strict rules determined who was allowed to rent the units. The National Housing Agency required each applicant to have moved into the Washington metropolitan area within the last twelve months from another part of the country.[7]

During 1943, the rate of private building in Northern Virginia had declined. This was due to two factors. Both building materials and labor were in short supply because of the war. To supplement the housing provided by private builders, the government built trailer camps, apartments, and single-family homes. In Arlington, projects built by the Federal Housing Administration included apartment projects at Lee Gardens, Parkland

Fairlington, c. 1943

Trailer camp housing provided for war workers' families near Alexandria, c. 1942

Gardens, Wakefield Manor, Filmore Gardens, Markwood Hall, and a detached-home development, Columbia Forest. Federal regulations required that the dwellings be rented to war workers for a minimum of four months. After that, single-family homes could be sold to the tenants at fair market value, not to exceed $6,000.[8]

These federal housing projects did not address the needs of one significant group of war workers: young single women. Thousands of these women had difficulty finding a room to live in because most landlords preferred to rent to men.

To satisfy this housing need, the federal government built dormitories in many locations, including a large complex called Arlington Farms. Located on part of the original Custis-Lee estate near the Pentagon, Arlington Farms was a large complex of dormitory buildings that contained 7,220 rooms. A woman could rent a single room for $24.50 a month or share with a roommate for $16.50 per month. The cheaper price was the most popular because the average annual salary for women was $1,440, and many were sending money to their families back home. The dormitories included a cafeteria service, social halls, and laundry facilities. Special bus service provided transportation to and from the women's workplaces, but they had to pay their own fares. The buildings were

Arlington Farms dormitories for women war workers, c. 1943

constructed in record time. The first residents moved in on March 1, 1943.[9]

Fairfax was also experiencing growing pains as it struggled with new development in what was still an agrarian county. The county's dairy and poultry farms continued to rank among the top in the state. While the rise in population was not as great as that in Arlington, the population did increase from 40,929 in 1940 to approximately 60,000 in 1943.[10]

The strain of providing services and infrastructure to accommodate the extra citizens presented daily problems for county officials. One of the most immediate problems caused by the influx of war workers and their families was overcrowding in the schools. There were simply not enough teachers or classrooms to accommodate all the children from the families lodged in temporary housing. To make matters worse, the pay scale for teachers in Fairfax was far below that in the District of Columbia, Alexandria, and Arlington County. In April 1943, the Board of Supervisors increased all teachers' pay by $300 a year. The following year, they increased it by another $100, but the salaries were still not competitive.[11]

The same was true for many county government workers and law enforcement officers. In 1945 Fairfax sheriff Eppa P. Kirby requested a pay raise for himself and for his deputy, clerk, jailer, and cook, plus funds to hire another deputy. When his request was denied, he sued the Board of Supervisors. They quickly reached a compromise and approved raises of $300 per year for the deputy, $240 for the clerk, and funds to hire an additional deputy. But the salaries of Kirby, the jailer, and the jail's cook remained static.[12]

Trying to balance new development while protecting the interests of the farmers was a challenge for the Board of Supervisors. In 1942, Congress approved funds to build a large new office building for the Public Roads Administration—now the Federal Highway Administration—at Langley. The great irony attached to this decision was the poor quality and narrow width of the Georgetown Pike, the road that accessed the site. It did not provide an easy commute for the people who worked at the site planning and maintaining the nation's highways. And it was difficult for anyone to find a home near that location because it was mainly an area of farms with very limited development.[13]

New building in Fairfax County decreased slightly in 1943, but more permit requests were submitted in 1944. Developers were attracted to the county in spite of its poor roads because the land was cheaper than that in areas close to the District of Columbia. Also, unlike Arlington, there were very few zoning regulations. This was a problem the Board of Supervisors decided to address.

A new, stricter zoning ordinance was proposed to replace the one passed in 1941. It would require subdivision developers to have their plans approved by the county Planning Commission. Furthermore, any projects where the size of the lot was ten thousand square feet or less would require the developer to install paved roads, sidewalks, curbs, gutters, public water, and sewers. It appears the supervisors were tired of trying to find funds to provide the infrastructure after the developers took their profits and moved on to their next projects. The developers sent up a howl of protest that the proposed ordinance would drive their costs up and that they would not be able to work in the county.

At the subsequent official hearing, many arguments, both pro and con, were offered. Those same words have been heard many times in the years since. Former state senator John W. Rust argued that the new ordinance would slow down development and hurt property values. W. S. Hoge from the Alexandria, Arlington, and Fairfax Real Estate Board testified that the real estate professionals agreed on the need for some sort of ordinance, but this one was too drastic and would prohibit development. The supervisors certainly did not want to drive away development because they believed the added tax revenue would be good for the county. The matter was deferred for two weeks for further study.

In those two weeks, both sides ramped up their arguments. The citizens' associations returned to the hearings strongly in favor of the new ordinance. They believed the developers should pay for the infrastructure so that citizens would not have rising taxes to cover those costs. Meanwhile, an amendment to the original ordinance requiring the minimum lot size in agricultural districts to be five acres brought new waves of protest from owners of large properties and from farmers, developers, and others. The matter was once again deferred. This issue, combined with others, caused new construction starts in the county to drop for that year.[14]

Cars stored for the duration of World War II on a farm near Vienna, Virginia.

It is not surprising that the farmers took such a strong stand on the zoning ordinance issues. While all citizens in the entire region were suffering from the deprivations and shortages caused by World War II, the farmers had a particularly bad time. From the start of the war, almost everything had been rationed or was not available. Gasoline, some kinds of food, other fuel, and clothes were hard to get. Rubber tires were almost impossible to find; their purchase was very restricted. This caused some farmers' fields to be turned into temporary parking lots where cars were stored for "the duration."[15]

The amount of suffering from the shortages was a trade-off depending on what someone wanted. Those who lived in the city and suburbs had public transportation but were rarely able to get certain types of food. Many planted small victory gardens in their backyards to supplement their rationed diet. The country residents could eat what they raised on their farms and had more choices in food but had a difficult time leaving their own home or community. Everyone felt the pinch when trying to buy new clothes and shoes.

From the beginning to the end of the war years, there were two main problems that plagued farmers: a severe shortage of labor and extreme weather conditions. In May 1942, a freak storm dropped hail the size of baseballs on much of Fairfax County. The hailstones flattened crops and killed thousands of chickens, causing financial hardship to the farmers. A 1943 drought caused crop losses worth millions of dollars and killed off cattle pastures. As a result, the cows had to be fed winter feed. To make matters worse, no replacement feed was available. Milk production in the region dropped by four thousand gallons per day, and farm incomes seriously declined.[16]

By August, many farmers were very discouraged. No significant amount of rain had fallen for seventy-five days. The corn crop was down from the previous year by 86 percent; only one railroad carload of the relief feed promised by the federal government had been delivered. Farmers were paying $54 a ton for the same quality of hay that they had purchased for $28 a ton the year before. Those who had truck gardens to grow vegetables for sale in the city markets were also suffering serious crop losses of at least 50 percent. The tomato crop had declined by 78 percent. At the end of the year, total crop loss in the Washington metropolitan region amounted to $12 million.[17]

Added to the farmers' weather woes was an extreme shortage of labor. With almost all the young men in the armed forces, it was very difficult to find enough help to get crops planted and harvested. In spite of the huge loss of crops, there was still not enough available labor to harvest what was left. Consequently, the United States Employment Service, a federal agency, worked with the state and county agricultural agents to recruit and place labor where it was needed.

The agency advertised for two thousand workers for two months to harvest tomatoes, peaches, and apples. Any federal employees who wanted to earn extra money during their vacation weeks were welcome to apply for the jobs, which paid sixty cents an hour. Even with this appeal, there was still a labor shortage. When the apple crop was ready for harvest in the fall, the Fairfax County School Board decided that high school students could be excused from their classes every other day for up to twenty days to work in the orchards.[18]

The farmers' problems continued into 1944. Some farmers solved their labor issues in creative ways. In one case, the work was performed by neighboring teenagers who were supervised by elderly and retired farmers. In another case, a group of federal workers from Washington formed a "troubleshooting" society to help farmers in Fairfax. The members of this group agreed to work on weekends at the Rhineharts' dairy farm in McLean. Thanks to their labors, the spring corn crop got planted. Unfortunately, all that work produced very little as drought conditions continued throughout the region. By July 1944, rainfall was 5.45 inches less than the year before. Even suburban victory gardens were dying from the heat and lack of water.[19]

In 1945, the drought ended, but the farmers' weather problems did not. That year, there was too much rain. Crops rotted in the fields and gardens. The labor shortage was partially alleviated by two hundred German prisoners of war who had been brought into the county to work on the farms. But that was still not enough labor. The county government had to petition the State Highway Department to borrow some of their road-maintenance convicts to help with the corn harvest.[20]

The damage done to all the farms significantly impacted a large part of Northern Virginia. Even with the development that had occurred in the previous twenty years, much of the region was still farmland. In 1945, Arlington County had almost 1,000 acres of farmland divided among fifty different owners. Fairfax County had almost doubled its total number of farms since 1940. It now had 2,411 farms with a total of 146,258 acres of cropland and pasture. That total included almost 5,000 acres that had been added to the actively farmed land in the county since 1935.[21]

Chapter 35

THE POSTWAR DEVELOPMENT FRENZY

The close of the war in 1945 did not end the housing shortage in the Washington metropolitan area, which would continue to have an effect on the conversion of farmland to suburbs.

While some soldiers and war workers returned to their home states throughout the next year, others settled in the area because of job opportunities. Returning servicemen were aided in finding employment by the United States Employment Service, which had a Northern Virginia office. Another choice was the on-the-job training program administered by the Veterans Administration. Under that program, veterans hired for new jobs by an approved business were entitled to monthly subsistence allotments, with seventy-five dollars granted to single men and ninety dollars to those with families. One hundred businesses in Northern Virginia were approved for the program by March 1946.[1]

As more people returned from overseas and settled in the area, the housing shortage became more severe. The problem was most acute for couples who had married during the war and had not yet established a home. One veteran decided to turn a chicken house on his mother's Tysons Corner property into a home. His wife and child had lived with his mother while he was away. When he returned, the couple was unable to find a home of their own. So the resourceful veteran cleaned out the chicken house, installed insulation, hooked up water and electricity, and used wallboard to divide the structure into five rooms. The finished product boasted new windows, a bathroom, a coal stove for heat, and a kerosene stove for cooking.[2]

While people were scrambling to find homes, the US government decided to get out of the housing business and sell the apartment complexes that had been built to house war workers. On January 7, 1946, the Defense Homes Corporation (DHC), which had built and managed the units, advertised for bids for six different complexes, including Fairlington.[3]

This task turned out to be more difficult than anticipated. In the first round for Fairlington, out of eighty bids, fifty-eight were rejected as "foolish" because they were very low. The project had 3,442 units and had cost the government $32 million to build. All bids for Fairlington were again rejected in the second round of bidding. Low bids continued to be submitted throughout the year. It was not until June 1947 that an offer was accepted. Two Texans, Leo F. Corrigan and Leland Fikes, formed the Fair-mac Corporation and were successful with their bid of $43,600,000 for Fairlington in Virginia, McLean Gardens in Washington, DC, and a 180-unit property in Bremerton, Washington. It was agreed that the DHC would retain a twenty-eight-year mortgage at a rate of 2.5 percent.[4]

The new owners were immediately beset by the tenants for better services. Fairlington was home to almost thirteen thousand residents. Many were young families with school-age children. They wanted a new school, playgrounds, and a library. To facilitate these plans, the Fair-mac Corporation decided to raise the rents. Depending on the type of unit, when leases were renewed the rents would increase by between 9 and 14 percent. The two-year leases guaranteed a stabilized rent. Tenants who declined to sign the lease could remain on a month-to-month agreement.

Meanwhile, private builders were constructing new homes at a rapid rate. It was definitely a seller's market. Houses were sold as fast as they could be built. In a three-year period ending in March 1946, the population of Arlington had increased by another 20,000 people. It was the fastest-growing county in the country. Approximately 109,000 people lived in apartments and approximately 105,000 in single-family homes. Those in single-family homes included many people who were only renting a room from the homeowner.[5]

This population explosion created great problems for county officials, who scrambled to provide desperately needed infrastructure. The biggest issue was sewage disposal. More than half of the sewage generated in Arlington and Alexandria was being dumped, untreated, into the Potomac River. This unsanitary situation caused great protest from environmentalists and the District of Columbia government. Trash disposal was another problem. When a 5 percent rise in property taxes in 1945 failed to generate the necessary funds for sewage treatment and trash incinerators, the Arlington Board of Supervisors ordered a reassessment of all properties in 1946.[6]

The Fairfax County government was also suffering from problems related to the expanding population. In 1946, the county's population was approximately seventy-four thousand—almost double that of 1940. In addition to overcrowded schools and a lack of schoolteachers, the county still battled with the age-old problem of poor secondary roads, many of which were gravel. During seasons of wet weather, there were many places where automobiles could not travel. To add to the trouble, Fairfax roads and highways carried the highest traffic count in the state, with an average of 434,660 vehicle miles per day.

Road problems did not stop the Fairfax County Board of Zoning Appeals from approving new building projects. In December 1946, the board listened to an appeal for more homes for veterans when developers proposed to build two large apartment complexes near Falls Church. They ignored vigorous opposition from the residents in the area and approved the plans. The same thing happened again and again. Apartments were constructed near Bailey's Crossroads and Belle Haven.[7]

In spite of infrastructure problems, the Board of Supervisors was anxious to encourage development. Developers and builders, lured by cheap land prices, a low property tax rate, and several good highways, began the trend that would finish changing Fairfax from an agrarian county into a commuter suburb.[8]

Postwar housing projects centered near existing roads, such as Mount Vernon Memorial Highway, Lee Boulevard, Little River Turnpike, and Leesburg Pike, offered new single-family homes selling in the range of $12,000 to $18,000. For those who could afford more, prices went up to as much as $45,000. Properties in Langley Forest, a new development near McLean, were being marketed as "Small Estates" of one to five acres for approximately $1,500 per acre.

In the interior of Fairfax County, Stephen Yeonas of Yeonas Realty was building in the town of Vienna. He started with the Vienna Woods subdivision in 1951. Most of the homes were three-bedroom, full-basement brick ramblers priced at $16,250. Special features included quarter-acre lots, town water and sewer, and paved streets. Air-conditioning was an option for an extra price.[9]

The area was not as readily accessible as those near larger highways—I-66 would not be built until 1964. Advertised directions instructed potential purchasers to drive west on Arlington Boulevard to five miles past Seven Corners, and then turn right onto Cedar Lane and continue across Lee Highway to turn left onto Park Street. Nonetheless, these homes sold very well.

As reported in the *Washington Post*, when Yeonas opened his next subdivision of West Vienna Woods in 1953, he was referred to as the "honorary mayor" by the mayor and town council, who credited him with putting Vienna "on the map"—which he did. In addition to home construction, he developed a ten-store shopping center to serve all the residents of the town.[10]

Beyond a doubt, the biggest catalyst to development was the construction of the Henry G. Shirley Memorial Highway, named for the Virginia

Advertisement from the Evening Star *newspaper, 1952*

Department of Highways' commissioner, who died in 1941 right after he had approved the start of construction of present-day I-395 and I-95. The route was planned as a four-lane, limited-access, concrete superhighway to run from the Pentagon in Arlington to Woodbridge in Prince William County.[11]

Because of the road's great military value, the federal government financed most of it. Upon completion, it was expected to be one of the most heavily traveled routes on the Eastern Seaboard south of Washington. The first section, from the Pentagon to the Arlington-Fairfax county line, opened in 1944. Given that this was Virginia's first limited-access highway, it seems odd that there was no opening ceremony. Workers just removed the barriers and allowed drivers to start using the road. This lack of ceremony may have been because the country was at war.

After the first section of Shirley Highway opened, construction continued at a slow pace during the war years. But far-thinking developers were undeterred. They bought land in the areas that the road would access and prepared to launch Fairfax County's postwar development frenzy. In 1940 Fairfax County had issued only 1,125 building permits. In 1946 the number had risen to 3,051. It increased every year after that. The largest development to date was planned by Edward R. Carr.[12]

Shirley Highway under construction, c.1943

In 1947, Carr got approval for a rezoning to develop a subdivision of 20,000 homes at the small crossroads farm village of Springfield, which was near the new highway. While the Board of Supervisors was willing to grant the zoning change to build homes, they refused to allow any commercial development, preferring to leave the highway open for high speeds. They used Route 1 in the southern part of the county as their example. It had become "cluttered" with businesses, which had slowed the pace of the traffic. The Shirley Highway was still under construction in that area and was scheduled to be completed by 1949. Since there was no readily available limited-access highway for them to observe, the board failed to realize that businesses would not slow down the traffic. Thus, the commuter suburb of Springfield was launched.

As developers raced to buy farmland near the new highway, they were forced to confront the lack of water, sewer, and gas lines. But the availability of land allowed them to solve the problem by allocating larger lots for each home to accommodate wells and septic systems. In 1949, half-acre to one-acre lots were marketed for $500 to $1,500. They could be purchased for a down payment of $50. The balance was payable at $15 per month. Homes were selling for $10,000 to $14,000, truly a bargain rate for a new home. Closer-in properties at Pinecrest near Columbia Pike were selling for $15,000 to $30,000.

Because Carr's subdivision did provide public utilities, the lots were smaller. Construction of the utility lines delayed the start of home building until 1952; however, the builders quickly caught up and built 385 houses that year. Seventy-seven percent were sold to government workers. The most popular model was a brick rambler with three bedrooms and a full basement, priced at $18,000. At the same time, another company was promoting prefabricated homes in the subdivision of Springfield Forest. It offered 115 different designs, with prices starting at $12,950 and promised delivery in thirty days.

The Shirley Highway to Springfield opened on September 6, 1949, in the same way the Pentagon section had: work crews just removed the barriers. Commuters were ecstatic. While the road had been constructed for vehicles to travel at speeds of up to seventy miles per hour, the speed was limited to zones of forty and fifty miles per hour. A reporter for the *Washington Post* summed it up in a piece titled "Shirley Highway Gets You There In A Breeze," writing: "Completion of the new artery is expected to open up thousands of acres of nearby Virginia farmland for real estate development. Southeastern Fairfax County can be reached in 20 minutes."[13]

He was certainly right about the development; however, the twenty-minute commute would be short-lived, as the road became overloaded. Shirley Highway had to be widened for the first time in 1951, a solution that would need to be repeated in years to come.

At the same time that Shirley Highway was being opened, members of Congress were working on another high-speed road plan. Aviation advances during and after World War II gave rise to deep concerns about the safety of the government in Washington. Many believed that the government was too vulnerable to an attack by enemy aircraft. Existing highways such as Route 7 and Route 50 in Virginia had been improved, as had several in Maryland, to facilitate an emergency evacuation of the capital. In addition to aiding commuters to the Pentagon, Shirley Highway was also part of the emergency plan. But many in Congress felt these arteries should be connected by a ring road that ran all the way around Washington.[14]

In 1951 the Senate Public Works Committee asked the Truman administration to develop a plan for a new circumferential, limited-access, high-speed highway. The committee wanted to disperse different branches of the government to suburban locations to reduce the attractiveness of the capital city as an enemy target. They believed that a "belt" road would provide a good emergency route, a practical connection between distant government buildings, and an efficient commuter route for government employees. As a bonus, they were sure that such a highway would be a major factor in solving the Washington traffic problem.[15]

As with most things in Congress, the debate on the new highway took a long time. There were some who favored one circumferential route and others who felt that there should be an inner belt road and an outer belt road. The National Capital Park and Planning Commission had planned an inner belt road before World War II; however, due to postwar building and a dramatic increase in property prices, that plan had to be scrapped as too expensive.

When the first bills were introduced in the Senate in 1951, the price to be allocated for development of the road was $28 million. Less than a year later, the price had climbed to $36 million. It was not until September 28, 1955, that the project was finally approved by the federal government. Then there were more delays as it went through the approval process in all the Virginia and Maryland jurisdictions where it would be located. The first section opened on December 21, 1961. The Capital Beltway (I-495) was finally finished in August 1964.[16]

As time went on, the development of Northern Virginia continued, sometimes at a frenzied pace, and at other times it temporarily slowed. With the spread of the population and the rising amount of commuter traffic, planners advocated the addition of new superhighways to the landscape. By the early 1970s, there was very little vacant land in Arlington. New building was done as in-fill development on vacant lots or the razing of older structures. New developments in Fairfax County continued to flow westward.[17]

The largest development of all was cultivated by Robert E. Simon. Following the same philosophy as Dr. Max Wiehle from the previous century, Simon purchased the 6,750-acre Sunset Hills farm in 1961. His goal was to build a new town where people could live, work, and play. This massive project took some years to initiate, but once work started, it took off. Today, Reston is home to approximately sixty-five thousand people and the workplace of about sixty thousand people.[18]

As the tide of development rolled westward, Fairfax County farmers either retired or relocated. Their farms produced one final crop—houses.

The last working dairy farm in Fairfax County, belonging to the Spalding family in Great Falls, closed in 1991. Several areas in the county, such as Great Falls, Clifton, Mason Neck, and parts of Vienna and Oakton, have preserved a semirural way of life, but most farming is for pleasure. One can always plant a vegetable garden. It's one good use for the land.[19]

Over the course of nearly four centuries, the Northern Virginia landscape has seen many alterations. What started as an unmapped and often hostile territory, claimed by people who never saw it, became a place where everything is neatly divided and accounted for. The price of real estate has shifted many times, according to supply and demand, as has the common perception of its value. One constant is people's desire to own their own home.[20]

EPILOGUE

The rampant development of Northern Virginia that started after the close of World War II has continued into the present day. And while the transition from an agrarian culture to suburban communities has been accomplished, the current status is far from the end result. We don't know what that end result will look like nor can anyone accurately predict it.

Real estate values have always been closely tied to the fluctuations of the general economy. When the economy goes into a recession, the price of real estate usually falls. Upon recovery from the recession, real estate values rise. Northern Virginia values have always eventually climbed higher than the peak price before the recession—it just takes time. Does that make local real estate a good investment? Yes. It has been proven over the course of almost four centuries that careful investment in the real estate of Northern Virginia is a good long-term investment.

But one should pay attention to the lessons that can be learned from our predecessors. They enjoyed the good times and suffered, sometimes brutally, during the bad times. Many of them were resourceful and resilient enough to make the most out of both economic situations. They left to us a legacy of lessons that they learned. Lessons that should be taken seriously.

That legacy is a major reason to study history. In the words of Homer Bast, professor of history at Roanoke College: "Those who ignore the past are doomed to relive it."

His message was more succinct and to the point than that of the philosopher George Santyana, whom he was paraphrasing. And he made believers out of many of his students.

Lessons from Northern Virginia's past show that one should invest and save money wisely, but not hoard it in a mattress or a safe-deposit box. Alternatively, an economy based on large amounts of credit may not always be a healthy economy. During times of recession or depression, both debtors and creditors alike can suffer the ill effects from too much outstanding debt.

Another crucial point is that the additional taxes garnered by the counties from new development do not immediately provide enough income to pay for the cost of the infrastructure required by the increase in population. And last, national or worldwide events, such as wars and pandemics, can generate economic repercussions. Those are just a few outstanding examples among many.

As we reflect on the lessons to be learned from the actions of our predecessors, it is crucial to suspend judgment until all the facts are studied. To truly learn from their actions, it is critically necessary to understand their circumstances. Learning about their actions after the fact does not always give us the capability to fairly judge. One must remember we did not live in their times nor experience their situations.

Finally, life is not static. Change is inevitable. There will always be good times and bad times, with no way of predicting the length of either. History is full of examples of extraordinary human resilience that carried people through the bad times. And the innovators among them created the good times. For better or worse, it is what happened.

ENDNOTES

CHAPTER 1

1 Fairfax Harrison, *Landmarks of Old Prince William: Volumes I* (Baltimore: Gateway Press, 1987), 19–21.

2 Beth Mitchell, *Beginning at a White Oak Patents and Northern Neck Grants of Fairfax County* (Fairfax County Administrative Services, 1977), 3.

3 Nan Netherton, Donald Sweig, Janice Artemel, Patricia Hickin, and Patrick Reed, *Fairfax County, Virginia: A History* (Fairfax, Virginia: Fairfax County Board of Supervisors, 1978), 12 (hereafter cited as Fairfax County, preceded by the author of that section, for example: Sweig, *Fairfax County*).

4 Mitchell, *Beginning at a White Oak*, 6.

5 Mitchell, *Beginning at a White Oak*, 3; The Diary, Correspondence, and Papers of Robert "King" Carter of Virginia 1701–1732, transcribed, edited, and annotated by Edmund Berkeley Jr.

6 Sweig, *Fairfax County*, 6; Carter Papers.

7 Mitchell, *Beginning at a White Oak*, 6; Fairfax County Circuit Court Archives have many chancery suits over boundary disputes.

8 Sweig, *Fairfax County*, 6.

CHAPTER 2

1 Iain Gately, *Tobacco: A Cultural History of How an Exotic Plant Seduced Civilization* (London: Simon & Schuster, 2001), 70–72; Sweig, *Fairfax County*, 22–23.
2 Harrison, *Landmarks*, 77.
3 Beth Austin, "1619: Virginia's First Africans," Hampton History Museum, 2019.
4 Fairfax County Circuit Court Archives deed books have recorded Three Lives Leases.
5 Sweig, *Fairfax County*, 23–24.
6 Louis Jordan, "The Comparative Value of Money between Britain and the Colonies," University of Notre Dame; John J. McCusker, Money and Exchange in Europe and America, 1600–1775: A Handbook (Chapel Hill, NC: University of North Carolina Press, 1978).

CHAPTER 3

1 Maxine Williams, "Myth and Reality: Alexandria, Virginia, 1745–1820" (PhD diss., Lehigh University, 2000), 16.
2 Harrison, *Landmarks*, 405; Williams, "Myth and Reality," 19.
3 Harrison, *Landmarks*, 405; Williams, "Myth and Reality," 19.
4 Harrison, *Landmarks*, 407; Williams, "Myth and Reality," 24–25.
5 Sweig, *Fairfax County*, 56; Williams, "Myth and Reality," 25.
6 "Carlyle House Historic Park," Nova Parks, https://www.novaparks.com/parks/carlyle-house-historic-park/history.
7 Harrison, *Landmarks*, 407; "Myth and Reality," 26.
8 Edith Moore Sprouse, *Colchester Colonial Port on the Potomac* (Fairfax, VA: Fairfax County of Comprehensive Planning, 1975), 16–2.
9 Sprouse, *Colchester*, 41–42.
10 Tanya Edwards Beauchamp, "The Georgetown Historic District," Georgetown Heritage Trust, 1998; Richard K MacMaster, "Georgetown and the Tobacco Trade, 1751–1783," *Records of the Columbia Historical Society, Washington, DC*, 66/68, 1966, 9–10; "Georgetown Historic Waterfront: A Review of Canal and Riverside Architecture," United States Commission of Fine Arts and Office of Archeology and Historic Preservation, National Park Service, Department of the Interior, 1968.

CHAPTER 4

1 Sweig, *Fairfax County*, 82.
2 Fairfax County Circuit Court Archives deed books, recorded farm leases.

3 A. Glenn Crothers, "Agricultural Improvement and Technological Innovation in a Slave Society: The Case of Early National Northern Virginia," *Agricultural History* 75, no. 2 (2001): 138.
4 Carter Papers; Letters, George Washington to Robert Cary and Company, Fred W. Smith National Library for the Study of George Washington at Mount Vernon.
5 J. H. Soltow, "Scottish Traders In Virginia 1750–1775," *Economic History Review* 12, no.1 (1959): 84; Peter Victor Bergstrom, "Markets and Merchants: Economic Diversification In Colonial Virginia, 1700–1775," (PhD diss., University of New Hampshire, 1980), 164.
6 Carter Papers; Washington to Cary.
7 Washington to Cary.
8 Washington to Cary; Carter Papers.
9 Carter Papers; Bergstrom, "Markets and Merchants," 165.
10 Washington to Cary.
11 Soltow, "Scottish Traders," 84.
12 T. M. Devine, "Glasgow Merchants and the Collapse of the Tobacco Trade, 1775–1783," *Scottish Historical Review* 52, no. 153 (1973): 58–59.
13 Sprouse, *Colchester*, 48; Jordan, "Comparative Value"; McCusker, "Money."
14 Sprouse, *Colchester*, 41, 51; Soltow, "Scottish Traders," 85.
15 Sprouse, *Colchester*, 45, 46.
16 Sprouse, *Colchester*, 41.
17 Soltow, "Scottish Traders," 84; Renee Costello, "The Biography of the Snow Jeanie: A Merchant Vessel in the Pre-Revolution Tobacco Trade, an Undergraduate Research Scholars Thesis" (Texas A&M University, May 2015), 24.

CHAPTER 5

1 Thomas H. Ellis, "The Ohio Company," *William and Mary Quarterly* 5, no. 2 (189): 129–131; MacMasters, "Georgetown," 25.
2 Sweig, *Fairfax County*, 84.
3 Sweig, *Fairfax County*, 90.
4 Sprouse, *Colchester*, 66.
5 "The Fairfax Resolves, July 18,1774," Education@Library of Virginia, (http://edu.lva.virginia.gov/); Sweig, *Fairfax County*, 95; Donald M. Sweig,"A Newfound Washington Letter of 1774 and the Fairfax Resolves," *William and Mary Quarterly* 40, no. 2 (April 1983): 283–291.

6 Sweig, *Fairfax County*, 96–108.
7 Devine, "Glasgow Merchants," 50–74.
8 Sprouse, *Colchester*, 66–71; Costello, "Snow Jeanie," 24.
9 The personal and family correspondence of Colonel John Carlyle of Alexandria, Virginia, annotated by J. F. Carlyle, http://www.novaparks.com.
10 Sprouse, *Colchester*, 69.
11 Sweig, "A Newfound Washington Letter."
12 Devine, "Glasgow Merchants," 50–74.
13 Devine, "Glasgow Merchants," 50–74; MacMasters, "Georgetown."
14 Sprouse, *Colchester*, 71.
15 Larry G. Bowman, "The Scarcity of Salt in Virginia during the American Revolution," *Virginia Magazine of History and Biography* 77, no. 4 (1969): 464–472.

CHAPTER 6

1 Williams, "Myth and Reality," 38; Harrison, *Landmarks*, 408–409.
2 Williams, "Myth and Reality," 35; newspaper advertisements, *National Intelligencer.*
3 Sprouse, *Colchester*, 92–94, 104–105.
4 Sweig, *Fairfax County*, 127; Sweig, *Fairfax County*, 12; Williams, "Myth and Reality," 28–39; Sprouse, *Colchester*, 94.
5 Williams, "Myth and Reality," 55–56; newspaper advertisements, *National Intelligencer.*
6 Williams, "Myth and Reality," 39.
7 Harrison, *Landmarks*, 401; Charles Preston Poland Jr., *From Frontier to Suburbia* (Marceline, MO: Walsworth Publishing Company, 1976), 26–27.
8 Warren R., Hofstra and Robert D. Mitchell, "Town and Country in Backcountry Virginia: Winchester and the Shenandoah Valley, 1730–1800," *Journal of Southern History* 59, no. 4 (1993): 619–646.
9 Williams, "Myth and Reality," 41.
10 Crothers, "Agricultural Improvement," 139.
11 Williams, "Myth and Reality," 50.
12 Worthington C. Ford et al., "Diary of Mrs. William Thornton, 1800–1863," *Records of the Columbia Historical Society, Washington, DC* 10 (1907): 88–226.

CHAPTER 7

1 Robert J Kapsch, *The Potomac Canal: George Washington and the Waterway West* (Morgantown, WV: West Virginia University Press, 2007), 11–15.
2 Kapsch, *Potomac Canal*, 21, 42; Artemel, *Fairfax County*, 203.
3 Kapsch, *Potomac Canal*, 45–46; Artemel, *Fairfax County*, 205.
4 Corra Bacon-Foster, "Early Chapters in the Development of the Potomac Route to the West," *Records of the Columbia Historical Society, Washington, DC* 15 (1912): 96–322; Artemel, Fairfax County, 153; Kapsch, *Potomac Canal*, 208–239.
5 Bacon-Foster, "Early Chapters," 163; Artemel, *Fairfax County*, 205.
6 Bacon-Foster, "Early Chapters," 164.
7 Bacon-Foster, "Early Chapters," 164.
8 George Washington Diaries.
9 Bacon-Foster, "Early Chapters," 185.
10 Kapsch, *Potomac Canal*, 90; Bacon-Foster, "Early Chapters," 185, 189.
11 Bacon-Foster, "Early Chapters," 191.
12 Kapsch, *Potomac Canal*, 253–258; Bacon-Foster, "Early Chapters," 282.
13 Kapsch, *Potomac Canal*, 259; Bacon-Foster, "Early Chapters," 183; Hugh T. Taggart, "Old Georgetown," *Records of the Columbia Historical Society, Washington, DC* 11 (1908): 120–224.
14 Bacon-Foster, "Early Chapters," 191.
15 Artemel, *Fairfax County*, 206.
16 Artemel, *Fairfax County*, 206; Bacon-Foster, "Early Chapters," 191.
17 Artemel, *Fairfax County*, 206.
18 Kapsch, *Potomac Canal*, 271–283.
19 Kapsch, *Potomac Canal*, 288–301.

CHAPTER 8

1 Harrison, *Landmarks*, 411.
2 Fairfax Harrison, "With Braddock's Army: Mrs. Browne's Diary in Virginia and Maryland," *Virginia Magazine of History and Biography* 32, no. 4 (October 1924): 305–320.
3 Willian Waller Hening, Statutes at Large, Vol.VI Laws of Virginia 1748 Chap. XXVIII, An Act concerning Highways, Mill Dams, and Bridges, 65–69, transcribed by Freddie L. Spradlin.
4 Sweig, *Fairfax County*, 79–80.
5 Sweig, *Fairfax County*, 122–123.

6 Tanya Edwards Beauchamp, "Georgetown Pike in Arlington and Fairfax Counties," National Register Nomination, 1996.
7 Sweig, *Fairfax County*, 146–149.
8 Beauchamp, "Georgetown Pike."
9 Harrison, *Landmarks*, 564.
10 Beauchamp, "Georgetown Pike."

CHAPTER 9

1 Bacon-Foster, "Early Chapters," 195.
2 Artemel, *Fairfax County*, 156–166.
3 "Thorntown Diary."
4 "Thorntown Diary"; advertisements, *Alexandria Gazette* & Daily Advertiser, Alexandria, VA, Library of Congress; *Phenix Gazette*, Alexandria, Virginia, Library of Congress; *National Intelligencer*, Washington, DC, Library of Congress.
5 Advertisements, *Alexandria Gazette & Daily Advertiser*, Alexandria, VA, Library of Congress; *Phenix Gazette*, Alexandria, VA, Library of Congress.
6 Artemel, *Fairfax County*, 161–170.
7 Artemel, *Fairfax County*, 161–170.
8 Will of Ann Gunnell 1822 Fairfax Circuit Court Archives Will Book M1, 383. Note: This is just an example. There are numerous wills from this era that leave clothing.
9 Will of Henry Gunnell 1822 Fairfax Circuit Court Archives Will Book M1, 301.
10 Andrew Levy, *The First Emancipator: The Forgotten Story of Robert Carter* (New York: Random House, 2005).
11 Artemel, *Fairfax County*, 154.
12 Donald Sweig, ed., *Registrations of Free Negroes Commencing September Court 1822 Book 2 and Register of Fee Blacks 1835 Book 3* (Fairfax, VA: Research Historian Office of Comprehensive Planning, 1977), 1–6. Note: Many Fairfax wills provide additional items for people the deceased were freeing from slavery.
13 Sweig, *Registrations of Free Negroes*, 1–6; Artemel, *Fairfax County*, 154–155.
14 Fairfax Circuit Court Archives Cff62A 1837, *Oscar Gunnell Mix vs. George Gunnell*, executor; William A. Gordon, "Recollections of a Boyhood in Georgetown," *Records of the Columbia Historical Society, Washington, DC* 20 (1917): 122–123. Note: While this was written about

families in Georgetown, the sentiment it provides reflects those in many other oral histories.

15 Isabel Howell, "John Armfield, Slave-Trader," *Tennessee Historical Quarterly* 2, no. 1, (1943): 3–29; Thornton Diary; "Slavery and the Slave Trade in the District of Columbia," *Negro History Bulletin* 14, no.1 (October 1950): 7–8.

16 Artemel, *Fairfax County*, 157.

17 Fairfax Circuit Court Archives Cff62B 1839, *Guardian of Emily Mix vs. Admins of Dr. William H. Gunnell, etc.*

18 Artemel, *Fairfax County*, 174–177; Williams, "Myth and Reality," 61, 76.

19 Fairfax County Circuit Court Archives have numerous chancery cases involving personal notes and include the original notes.

20 Artemel, Fairfax County, 152–170; advertisements, *Alexandria Gazette & Daily Advertiser*, Alexandria, VA, Library of Congress; *Phenix Gazette*, Alexandria, VA, Library of Congress; *National Intelligencer*, Washington, DC, Library of Congress.

21 Arthur G. Peterson, "The Alexandria Market Prior to the Civil War," *William and Mary Quarterly* 12, no. 2 (April 1932): 104–114.

22 Williams, "Myth and Reality," 74.

23 Williams, "Myth and Reality," 85; Artemel, Fairfax County, 224–231.

24 *National Intelligencer and Washington Advertiser*, "Awful Fire At Alexandria," January 20, 1829.

25 Artemel, *Fairfax County*, 242.

26 "The Alexandria Market," 109–111; Artemel, Fairfax County, 209; Williams, "Myth and Reality," 78.

27 Williams, "Myth and Reality," 78.

28 Sweig, *Fairfax County*, 253.

CHAPTER 10

1 Poland Jr., *From Frontier to Suburbia.*

2 Frank W. Gapp, "Jones and Melville Encounter in the Pacific 1843," *Yearbook: The Historical Society of Fairfax County, Virginia* 25 (1995–1996): 5.

3 Gapp, "Jones and Melville," 30.

4 Hickin, *Fairfax County*, 251–260.

5 Hickin, *Fairfax County*, 254–255.

6 Hickin, *Fairfax County*, 254–255; Susan Hellman and Maddy McCoy, "Soil Tilled by Free Men: The Formation of a Free Black Community in

Fairfax County, Virginia," *Virginia Magazine of History and Biography* 125, no.1 (2017): 38–67.

7 Hickin, *Fairfax County*, 258–259; Hellman and McCoy, "Soil Tilled."

8 Hickin, *Fairfax County*, 268; Artemel, *Fairfax County*, 154.

9 Hickin, *Fairfax County*, 275–277.

10 Hickin, *Fairfax County*, 267.

CHAPTER 11

1 Hellman and McCoy, "Soil Tilled"; Samuel Sharper, Southern Claims Commission Claim no. 16700 December 4, 1876, National Archives; Nathaniel Gaskins, Southern Claims Commission Claim no. 41753, October 14, 1876, National Archives; Henry Escridge, Southern Claims Commission Claim no.48711, July 6, 1878, National Archives; William Ashton, Southern Claims Commission Claim no. 20471, February 25, 1873, National Archives; Ferdinand Seals, Southern Claims Commission Claim no. 13071, December 4, 1876, National Archives; Noel G. Harrison. "Atop an Anvil: The Civilians' War in Fairfax and Alexandria Counties, April 1861–April 1862," *Virginia Magazine of History and Biography* 106, no. 2 (1998): 133–164. Note: The National Archives has many Southern Claims Commission files for Alexandria and Fairfax Counties. The ones cited here are just a small sample.

2 Ashton Claim; Harrison, "Atop an Anvil," 139; Salona Fairfax County, Virginia. Ellen Anderson, Fairfax County Office of Comprehensive Planning, February 1979; Alice M. Coates, "The Civil War Experiences of a Northern Family Settled in Virginia," Diaries of Charles and Phebe Sutton, Historical Society of Fairfax County, Virginia, Inc., 8 (1962–1963): 45–62; Ralph LeRoy Miliken, "Then We Came to California: A Biography of Sarah Summers Clarke—written in the first person," Historical Society of Fairfax County, Virginia, Inc., 8 (1962–1963): 1–44; John Chichester Mackall, "McLean, Fairfax County Virginia," Historical Society of Fairfax County, Virginia, Inc., 4 (1955): 5; Martha C. Ball, Claim no. 21061, December 1887, Southern Claims Commission, National Archives.

3 Harrison, "Atop an Anvil," 139–141; The War of the Rebellion: Official Records, vol. 1 Alexandria County 1861 Fairfax County Library, Virginia Room,123–125; Benjamin Franklin Cooling. "Defending Washington during the Civil War." *Records of the Columbia Historical Society, Washington, DC*, 71/72 (1971): 314–337; Charles O. Paullin,

"Alexandria County in 1861," *Records of the Columbia Historical Society, Washington, DC* 28 (1926): 107–31.

4 Charles Preston Poland Jr., Dunbarton Dranesville, Virginia (Fairfax, VA: Fairfax County Office of Comprehensive Planning, 1974), 41–43; Miliken, "A Biography of Sarah Summers Clarke"; Southern Claims Commission files.

5 Harrison, "Atop an Anvil," 161; Coates Diaries, 53–54; Southern Claims Commission files.

6 Don DeBats and Margaret-Ann Williams, "Emma Green: The Making of a Southern Identity," http://sociallogic.iath.virginia.edu/emmagreen.

7 Paulin, "Alexandria County"; Cooling, "Defending Washington," 320; Miliken, "A Biography of Sarah Summers Clarke," 21–23.

8 Anderson, *Salona*, 28–33.

9 Harrison, "Atop an Anvil," 143–144; Sharper Claim; Escridge Claim; Seals Claim; Mary W. Jones, Southern Claims Commission Claim no. 21622, March 3, 1873, National Archives.

10 Miliken, "A Biography of Sarah Summers Clarke," 1–44; Harrison, "Atop an Anvil," 143; Coates Diaries, 51; Jones Claim; Hickin, *Fairfax County*, 321–325.

11 Harrison, "Atop an Anvil," 149, 154; Coates Diaries, 52–53; Poland, Dunbarton, 33–44; Ann Coleman, Claim 9989, Southern Claims Commission, National Archives.

12 Sharper Claim; Miliken, "A Biography of Sarah Summers Clarke," 21; Escridge Claim; Virginia Carter Castleman, *Reminiscences of an Oldest Inhabitant: A Nineteenth-Century Chronicle* (Herndon, VA: Herndon Historical Society, 1976), 16.

13 Jones Claim.

14 Harrison, "Atop an Anvil," 154–155.

15 Harrison, "Atop an Anvil," 133.

16 Miliken, "A Biography of Sarah Summers Clarke"; Jones Claim; Sharper Claim; Ashton Claim; Escridge Claim; Thomas Carper Southern Claims Commission Claim no. 15734, April 7, 1875, National Archives; Richard Follin Southern Claims Commission Claim no.15327, December 30, 1875, National Archives.

17 Heidler, David Stephen; Heidler, Jeanne T.; Coles, David J., eds., "Arlington," *Encyclopedia of the American Civil War: A Political, Social, and Military History, Volume 1* (New York: W. W. Norton & Co., 2000); Arlington House, National Register of Historic Places Inventory Nomination Form, United States Department of the Interior National Park Service, 1940.

18 Miliken, "A Biography of Sarah Summers Clarke," 1–44; Jones Claim; William Selwyn Ball, "Reminiscences of an Old Rebel," Fairfax County Library, Virginia Room.

19 Ball "Reminiscences"; Hickin, Fairfax County, 371.

20 Arlington House National Register.

CHAPTER 12

1 Melvin Lee Steadman Jr., *Falls Church by Fence and Fireside* (Annandale, VA: Turnpike Press, 1964), 71–72; Ball, "Reminiscences"; Mackall, "McLean," 5; Castleman, *Reminiscences*, 31, 33; Connie Pendleton Stuntz and Mayo Sturdevant Stuntz, *This Was Vienna* (1987), 135.

2 Hickin, *Fairfax County*, 373–375; multiple news articles from *Alexandria Gazette*, *Evening Star*.

3 Hickin, *Fairfax County*, 372–373.

4 Connie Pendleton Stuntz and Mayo Sturdevant Stuntz, *This Was Tysons Corner* (1990); Joseph Trammell, Personal Interview, 1995; Hazel Thompson, Personal Interviews, 1985–1995.

5 Richard J. Faulkner, Claim no. 21774, December 20, 1875, Southern Claims Commission 1871–1880: Virginia, National Archives and Records Administration, Washington, DC, 20005; Seals Claim; Escridge Claim; Ashton Claim; Mackall, "McLean," 2–5.

6 D'Anne A. Evans, Kevin Conley Ruffner, Kathi Ann Brown, and Michael F. Johnson, *Stone Ground: A History of Union Mills* (Fairfax, VA: Fairfax County History Commission, 2003), 89–90; Ames W. Williams, *The Washington & Old Dominion Railroad* (Arlington, VA: Arlington Historical Society, 1989), 25–27; Herbert H. Harwood Jr., *Rails to the Blue Ridge: The Washington and Old Dominion Railroad, 1847–1968*, Third Edition (Fairfax Station, Virginia: Northern Virginia Regional Park Authority), 19–23; Nan Netherton, Donald Sweig, Janice Artemel, Patricia Hickin, Patrick Reed, *Fairfax County, Virginia: A History* (Fairfax, VA: Fairfax County Board of Supervisors, 1978), 460–461.

7 Hickin, *Fairfax County*, 386.

8 Reed, *Fairfax County*, 407.

9 Reed, *Fairfax County*, 409; Stuntz, *Vienna*, 189.

10 Stuntz, *Vienna*, 88,129, 189.

11 Reed, *Fairfax County*, 395.

12 Reed, *Fairfax County*, 460–462.

13 Reed, *Fairfax County*, 460–462; Steadman, *Falls Church*, 80–81.

14 Mackall, "McLean," 5–6; Stuntz, *Tysons*, 17, 23.

15 Stuntz, *Tysons*, 17, 19.

CHAPTER 13

1 Hazel Thompson, personal interviews, 1985–1995; Marion Reid, personal interviews, 1985–2000; *Washington Post*, "Save The Palisades," August 18, 1907, R4.
2 Robert S. Gamble, Sully (Chantilly, VA: Sully Foundation, Limited, 1973), 115–121; Reed, *Fairfax County*, 408–411.
3 Reed, *Fairfax County*, 408–411.
4 Castleman, *Reminiscences*, 33; *Washington Post*, classified advertisement, June 26, 1904, A4.
5 Brown and Johnson, *Stone Ground*, 94–95; Reed, *Fairfax County*, 409.
6 Brown and Johnson, *Stone Ground*, 92–98.
7 Reed, *Fairfax County*, 409.
8 Reed, *Fairfax County*, 432; Stuntz, *Vienna*, 170, 184.
9 Reed, *Fairfax County*, 415–416.
10 Hazel Thompson, personal interviews, 1985–1995; Marion Reid, personal interviews, 1985–2000; Stuntz, *Vienna*, 73.
11 *Washington Post*, "Homes for Summer," May 7, 1905, B6.

CHAPTER 14

1 Stuntz, *Tysons*, 17, 19. Note: The Edmund Flagg diary quoted here gives the time it took to ride or drive a horse and buggy from one location to another.
2 Reed, *Fairfax County*, 461–463; *Fairfax Herald*, March 18, 1892, "Prospect Hill"; John E. Merriken and LeRoy O. King Jr., *Old Dominion Trolley Too* (Dallas, TX, 1987), 3.
3 Reed, *Fairfax County*, 461–463.
4 Reed, *Fairfax County*, 465–466.
5 Reed, *Fairfax County*, 465–466.
6 Map of Wiehle, Fairfax County, Virginia 1892, surveyed and drawn by Joseph Berry.
7 *Fairfax Herald*, April 5, 1889, March 18, 1892, 3, May 13, 1892, August 25, 1893.
8 *Washington Post*, "Resorts," April 23, 1898; A. Smith Bowman Jr., " A History of Sunset Hills Farm," Historical Society of Fairfax County, Virginia, Inc., 6 (1958–1959): 41; Marion Reid, personal interviews, 1985–2000; Hazel Thompson, personal interviews, 1985–1995.
9 Reed, *Fairfax County*, 465–466; *Fairfax Herald*, March 1, 1901.

10 Merriken and King, *Old Dominion*, 1.
11 Merriken and King, *Old Dominion*, 5.
12 Merriken and King, *Old Dominion*, 5; Reed, *Fairfax County*, 474–479.
13 Reed, Fairfax County, 479; Tanya Beauchamp and Karen Washburn, National Park Service, oral history for "DC Public Schools Project," Martin Luther King Library, Washington, DC; "Alexandria News In Brief," *Washington Post*, July 17, 1915, 8; Nelson Reeves, "Recollections of Arlington's Last Dairy Farmer," *Arlington Historical Magazine* 5, no. 3 (October 1975): 35.
14 "The Depression of 1893," http://projects.vassar.edu/1896/depression.html; David O. Whitten, Auburn University, "The Depression of 1893," http://encyclopedia/article/whitten.panic.1893.

CHAPTER 15

1 "Enforcing the Smoke Law," *Washington Post*, August 3, 1899, 1B.
2 *Fairfax Herald*, January 8, 1892, 3; "Railroad Bill Introduced," *Fairfax Herald*, January 29, 1892, 2; "Prospect Hill," *Fairfax Herald*, March 18, 1892, 2.
3 Harwood, *Rails to the Blue Ridge*, 31; "A Railroad to Arlington," *Washington Post*, January 5, 1891, 2; "On to Arlington," *Washington Post*, May 30, 1891, 6; "Another Cable Line," *Washington Post*, January 10, 1891, 2.
4 Steadman, *Falls Church*, 192; *Fairfax Herald*, March 11, 1892, 3.
5 Great Falls and *Old Dominion* Railroad Minute Book, 1898, Mackall family collection; July Court Minutes, 1900, Mackall family collection.
6 "To Cross Aqueduct Bridge," *Evening Star*, January 31, 1903, 18; "President Signs Bridge Bill," *Evening Star*, February 1, 1903.
7 "M'Lean to Control Great Falls Road," *Washington Times*, March 11, 1903, 1.
8 "Line to the Great Falls," *Washington Post*, March 20, 1903, 5; "Financial Gossip of Washington," *Washington Post*, May 16, 1903, 16; "Sees the City Expand," *Washington Post*, May 24, 1903, E2.
9 "Line to Great Falls," *Washington Post*, March 20, 1903, 5.
10 "Cars in Operation on Road to Great Falls," *Washington Times*, March 9, 1906; "Time Schedule Great Falls and *Old Dominion* Railroad Company," *Washington Post*, March 12, 1906; "Great Falls by Trolley through Cars Today," *Washington Post*, July 4, 1906, 2; "Great Falls Opening," *Washington Post*, July 5, 1906, 11.
11 "One Third of a Pint," *Washington Post*, October 18, 1903, E2.

12 Classified ads, *Washington Post*, January 7, 1900; Classified ads, *Washington Post*, October 10, 1902, 15.
13 Classified ads, *Washington Post*, May 17, 1905; Classified ads, *Washington Post*, October 1, 1905, A3.
14 "Real Estate Market," *Washington Post*, June 11, 1906, T4; "Arlington's Rolling Landscape and the Opportunities There," *Washington Post*, April 1, 1906, R2.
15 "Publicity Urged for City Boom," *Washington Post*, August 7, 1906, 2.
16 "Real Estate Market," *Washington Post*, June 11, 1905, T4; "Arlington's Rolling Landscape and the Opportunities There," *Washington Post*, April 1, 1906, R2.
17 Ingleside subdivision map, 1905, author's private collection.
18 "Frankline Park," *Washington Herald*, April 25, 1909, 3; "Franklin Park: The Crown Of Virginia Hills," *Washington Herald*, May 16, 1909, 2.
19 "Along The Great Falls and *Old Dominion* Railway Line," *Washington Times*, May 6, 1906, 9.

CHAPTER 16

1 Mackall, "McLean," 12–13; Henry C. Mackall III, personal interview; "Seek Homes In Virginia," *Washington Post*, May 20, 1907, R2; "Railway Aids Suburb," *Washington Post*, July 7, 1907; "Develop Virginia Suburbs," *Washington Post*, September 29, 1907, 23.
2 Reed, *Fairfax County*, 489.
3 Reed, *Fairfax County*, 489.
4 Reed, *Fairfax County*, 479.
5 Stuntz, *Vienna*, 170, 184.
6 Milburn Sanders, personal interviews, 1977–2005; Marion Reid, personal interviews, 1985–2000; Alice Utterback, personal interview, 1985–1986.
7 Milburn Sanders, personal interviews, 1977–2005; Marion Reid, personal interviews, 1985–2000; Alice Utterback, personal interview, 1985–1986.
8 Harwood, *Rails to the Blue Ridge*, 63; Manning Gasch, personal interviews, 1978–1985; Oliver Gasch, personal interviews, 1995; flyer from Herman Gasch, author's personal collection; Ruth C. DeBevoise, "Reminiscences of the Ballston Area," *Arlington Historial Magazine* 5, no. 2 (1974): 47.
9 Harwood, *Rails to the Blue Ridge*, 57–58.
10 Harwood, *Rails to the Blue Ridge*, 57–58; Manning Gasch, personal interviews, 1978–1985; Oliver Gasch, personal interviews, 1995; flyer from Herman Gasch, author's personal collection.

11 Manning Gasch, personal interviews, 1978–1985; Oliver Gasch, personal interviews, 1995; flyer from Herman Gasch, author's personal collection.

12 "Automobile First Seen in Fairfax Village," *Fairfax Herald*, July 13, 1900, 3; "Motor Carriage Here," *Washington Post*, April 3, 1897, 11.

13 https://detroithistorical.org; https://corporate.ford.com/articles/history/the-model-t.html.

14 Carolynn Cornwell Miller, personal interview; unidentified newspaper clipping with photograph of Daniel Cornwell in his Stanley Steamer, courtesy of Carolynn Miller.

15 "Discuss Great Falls Line," *Washington Post*, March 11, 1904, 9; Harwood, *Rails to the Blue Ridge*, 43–46.

16 Mackall, "McLean," 12–13.

CHAPTER 17

1 Mackall, "McLean," 6.

2 Marion Reid, personal interviews, 1985–2000; Hazel Thompson, personal interviews, 1985–1995; Anne Cornwell Starke, personal interview, 1989; Oliver Gasch, personal interviews, 1995; Milburn Sanders, personal interviews, 1977–2005.

3 Marion Reid, personal interviews, 1985–2000; Hazel Thompson, personal interviews, 1985–1995; Anne Cornwell Starke, personal interview, 1989; Oliver Gasch, personal interviews, 1995; Milburn Sanders, personal interviews, 1977–2005.

4 Mackall, "McLean," 6; "Revolution on Farm," *Washington Post*, September 11, 1904, A7.

5 "The Ford Tractor," *Washington Post*, January 7, 1917, R2; multiple newspaper advertisements.

6 "The Potash Embargo," *Washington Post*, February 24, 1915, 6; "How to Fight High Prices," *Washington Post*, November 1, 1916, 6; "Prices Up 35 Per Cent," *Washington Post*, September 24, 1916, A7; "The Cost of Living," *Washington Post*, November 20, 1916, 4; "The High Cost of Living," *Washington Post*, January 4, 1917, 4; "U.S. to Scan Milk Costs," *Washington Post*, September 14, 1916, 3; "Asks High-Cost Inquiry," *Washington Post*, December 24, 1916, ES1.

7 "Farm Credit by Coup," *Washington Post*, February 26, 1915; "Farm Credit Bill Is Passed," *Washington Post*, May 16, 1916, 2.

CHAPTER 18

1 "War Is Enriching the City," *Washington Post*, May 6, 1917, 2.
2 "Record Realty Sales," *Washington Post*, June 3, 1917, 2; "War Boom Is Making Capital Hum," *Washington Post*, June 11, 1919, 7; "Prosperity Flooding Capital," *Washington Post*, June 24, 1917, E3.
3 "Record Realty Sales," *Washington Post*, January 13, 1918, R8; "Record Realty '148 Sales Closed,'" *Washington Post*, June 24, 1918, R6.
4 "Reserve Camp a 'City,'" *Washington Post*, May 1, 1917, 3.
5 Lila Spitz, "'More Tons, Less Huns': World War I Shipbuilding in Alexandria/ 12/23/2016/in Virginia"; "Shipyard Prospect Elates Alexandria," *Washington Post*, December 6, 1917, 9; "5,000,000 in Payroll," *Washington Post*, December 12, 1917, 12; "Land for Ship Plant," *Washington Post*, December 19, 1917, 8; "Virginia Shipbuilding Corporation," US National Park Service.
6 Spitz, "More Tons."
7 Spitz, "More Tons."
8 "Seek Food for Capital," *Washington Post*, May 6, 1917, 9.
9 "Forming Women's Land Army," *Washington Post*, March 17, 1917, 2; "Women Discuss War Work," *Washington Post*, April 6, 1918, 7.
10 "High Food Cost Unjust," *Washington Post*, April 21, 1917, 9.
11 "Help by Food Dealers," *Washington Post*, May 11, 1917, 12; "Aided by Food Dealers," *Washington Post*, May 25, 1917, 5.
12 "Prices Show Decline," *Washington Post*, December 9, 1917, 8.
13 "Boys Busy in Garden," *Washington Post*, May 13, 1917, 4; "Boy Scouts Ready to Farm," *Washington Post*, May 13, 1918, 9.
14 "Spuds Flood the City," *Washington Post*, August 6, 1917, 12.

CHAPTER 19

1 "Camp Work A Model," *Washington Post*, January 1, 1918, 7; no title, *Evening Star*, March 13, 1918, image 1.
2 "Mr. Baker Suggests Institution for Military Engineer Course," *Evening Star*, May 15, 1918, 9; "Camp Works," *Washington Post*, February 19, 1918, 5.
3 "Cold within 1 of Zero," *Washington Post*, December 30, 1917, 2; "Snow Storm Binds Alexandria in Grip," *Washington Post*, January 29, 1918, 9.
4 "Rushing Work on Camp Humphreys," *Washington Post*, April 7, 1918, E2.

5 "New Camp Takes Form," *Washington Post*, May 10, 1918, 5; "Camp Humphreys Railroad in Operation," *Washington Post*, June 11, 1918, 4; "$420,000 for Line Four Miles Long," *Washington Post*, August 9, 1918, 5; "Building Tracks," *Evening Star*, February 11, 1918, image 3; "Plans Railway Extensions," *Evening Star*, April 29, 1918, 7.

6 "To Make Camp Trips," *Evening Star*, March 25, 1918, 14; "300 Laborers Rushed to Belvoir," *Washington Post*, March 31, 1918, 13; "Rushing Work On Camp," *Washington Post*, April 7, 1918, E2.

7 No title, *Alexandria Gazette*, March 13, 1918, image 1; "Stenographers, Typists, Bookkeepers, and Timekeepers," *Evening Star*, February 2, 1918, image 13; "Wanted: 1,000 Laborers," *Evening Star*, February 7, 1918, 17; "Wanted at Camp Humphreys," *Evening Star*, February 9, 1918, image 13; "Ten White Cooks," *Evening Star*, 12.

8 No title, *Alexandria Gazette*, March 13, 1918, image 1.

9 "Army Trucks Spoil Fairfax Highways," *Washington Post*, February 14, 1918, 10.

10 "Fine Riding in Virginia," *Washington Post*, May 14, 1918, A5; "Begin Humphreys Road," *Washington Post*, June 4, 1918, 5.

11 "Rushing Work on Camp," *Washington Post*, April 7, 1918, E2.

12 "Camp Humphreys Formally Opened," *Washington Post*, May 5, 1918, 11.

13 "17,000 at Humphreys," *Washington Post*, June 8, 1918, 8.

14 "Will House 30,000 Men," *Washington Post*, July 7, 1918, 17; "40,000 for Humphreys," *Washington Post*, July 14, 1918; "Gets $53,695.40 for Camp Site," *Washington Post*, October 2, 1918, 3; "Kutz Head of Camps," *Washington Post*, October 27, 1918, 2; "Plan New Army Roads," *Washington Post*, November 1, 1918, 6; "Great Camp Built in Forest within Space of Four Months," *Evening Star*, July 1, 1918, 10; "Camp Humphreys Likely Permanent," *Evening Star*, July 16, 1918, image 5.

15 "Ft. Humphreys to Be Renamed," *Evening Star*, February 16, 1935.

CHAPTER 20

1 "Coldest Blast of Winter Due in DC," *Evening Star*, January 13, 1918, 1; "Allies Needs Put US Flour Users on One-Half Basis," *Evening Star*, March 24, 1918, 20.

2 "Asked to Pledge for Food Saving," *Evening Star*, November 20, 1917; "Porkless Day Is Asked," *Washington Post*, December 14, 1917, 2.

3 "Price Order Soon on Coal at Retail," *Evening Star*, September 6, 1917, 11; "Shortage of Hard Coal Grips Capital," *Evening Star*, October 4, 1917, 9; "DC Fights Losing Battle with Cold in Coalless Homes," *Evening Star*, December 30, 1917, 1; "DC Coal Up 50 Cents," *Washington Post*, December 1, 1917, 5; "Great Falls and Vicinity," *Washington Post*, December 6, 1917, ES-3.

4 "Asks Compromise on Coal Contract," *Evening Star*, October 3, 1917, 1; "Wages of Coal Miners Amicably Readjusted," *Evening Star*, October 6, 1917, 2; "Asks Compromise on Coal Contract," *Evening Star*, October 3, 1917, 1; "Hard Coal Miners Given Wage Raise," *Washington Post*, November 18, 1917, 18; "Crisis in Fuel Is Here," *Washington Post*, September 12, 1918; "Some Plain Coal Facts," *Alexandria Gazette*, January 3, 1918, image 1.

5 "Electric Roads Asked to Save," *Washington Post*, December 9, 1917, E4; "Wants Skip Stop Plan Universal," *Evening Star*, September 3, 1918, 20.

6 "Alexandria Stops Hoarding of Coal," *Alexandria Gazette*, December 5, 1917, 12; "Alexandria City and Suburbs," *Alexandria Gazette*, December 8, 1917, 1; "Alexandria Hit Hard," *Washington Post*, January 17, 1918, 10.

7 "DC Coal Up 50 Cents," *Washington Post*, December 1, 1917, 5; "Alexandrians Get Coal in Small Lots," *Washington Post*, January 1, 1918, 5.

8 "Washington Short on Kerosene Now," *Washington Post*, January 9, 1918, 2.

9 "Closing General in Alexandria," *Washington Post*, January 22, 1918, 4; "Save Coal Again Today," *Washington Post*, January 28, 1918, 2.

10 "No Coal Shortage Says Dr. Garfield," *Evening Star*, October 5, 1917, 2; "Soft Coal for Boilers," *Washington Post*, December 26, 1917, 2.

11 "Small Coal Men Hurt," *Washington Post*, December 9, 1917, 3; "Millions Idle as Cities Obey Edict To Save US Fuel," *Evening Star*, January 18, 1918, 1; "Text of the Order Issued by Garfield Which Halts the Nation's Business," *Alexandria Gazette*, January 18, 1918, 1.

12 "Record Realty Sales," *Washington Post*, January 13, 1918, R8; "Numerous Realty Sales Reported," *Washington Post*, June 8, 1918, R3; "Want Small Homes," *Washington Post*, September 16, 1917, R2; "Sale of Houses Continues Great," *Washington Post*, October 13, 1918, R2.

13 "Home Registration," *Alexandria Gazette*, October 30, 1918, 1; "Classified Ads," *Evening Star*, November 3, 1918, 10; "Official," *Evening Star*, November 7, 1918, 4.

14 "US Needs Girls and Boys to Work," *Washington Post*, January 2, 1918, ES10.

15 Milburn Sanders, personal interviews, 1977–2005; Marion Reid, personal interviews, 1985–2000; Wade Jackson, interviewed by Janet Hofer, June 8, 1984, Great Falls Historical Society Oral History Project; Paul Cornwell, interviewed by Ruth Hill, Great Falls Historical Society Oral History Project; Alice Virginia Jenkins, personal interviews, 1977–2000.

16 "For the War Garden," *Evening Star*, March 24, 1918, 8; "Prices Here Highest," *Washington Post*, July 23, 1918, 12.

17 "Sugar Ration Planned," *Alexandria Gazette*, April 27, 1918, 5; "Face Sugar Famine," *Alexandria Gazette*, June 24, 1918, 1; "Huge Crops Indicates," *Alexandria Gazette*, August 9, 1918, 1; "To Ration Sugar Beginning July1," *Evening Star*, June 24, 1918, 1; "Losses in Sugar Huge," *Washington Post*, June 9, 1918, 3; "Use Pork; Save Beef, Food Officers Warn," *Washington Post*, June 13, 1918, 2; "City on Sugar Ration July 1," *Washington Post*, June 25, 1918, 9.

18 "City Is Visited by Wave of Heat," *Evening Star*, June 2, 1918, 2; "The Prevailing Hot Wave," *Alexandria Gazette*, August 7, 1918, 2; "Apples Bake on Trees in Virginia," *Washington Post*, August 8, 1918, 3.

19 "Stringent Order Hits Alexandria," *Evening Star*, July 7, 1918, 2; "Alexandria Begins Sanitary Crusade," *Evening Star*, July 8, 1918; "Typhoid Experts at Alexandria," *Evening Star*, July 9, 1918, 2; "Typhoid Fever," *Alexandria Gazette*, July 9, 1918, 1.

CHAPTER 21

1 "Influenza Kills Here," *Washington Post*, September 22, 1918, 3; "The Influenza," *Fairfax Herald*, October 11, 1918, 3.

2 Influenza Encyclopedia, "The American Influenza Epidemic of 1918–1919: Washington, DC," University of Michigan Center for the History of Medicine and Michigan Publishing, University of Michigan Library, https://www.influenzaarchive.org/cities/city-washingtondc.html; "The Influenza Pandemic of 1918," https://virus.stanford.edu/uda/; "Deaths Reported," *Evening Star*, October 8, 1918, 17; "Uncle Sam's Advice on Flu," *Fairfax Herald*, October 18, 1918, 1; "Youth Was Mark for Flu," *Alexandria Gazette*, January 22, 1919, 1.

3 "The Influenza," *Fairfax Herald*, October 1, 1918, 3; "To Check Spanish Flu," *Alexandria Gazette*, October 4, 1918, 1; "Temporary Hospital," *Alexandria Gazette*, October 12, 1918, 1; "Situation Is Serious," *Alexandria Gazette*, October 12, 1918, 1; "Flu Wipes Out Family," *Alexandria Gazette*, September 14, 1919, 1; "Influenza Nurses Badly Needed," *Evening Star*, October 8, 1918,16; " Influenza Unabated," *Alexandria*

Gazette, October 14, 1918, 1; "The Flu in Virginia," *Alexandria Gazette*, October 15, 1918, 4; "Maryland and the Virginias," *Washington Post*, November 5, 1918, 7.

4 Milburn Sanders, personal interviews, 1977–2005; Marion Reid, personal interviews, 1985–2000; Hazel Thompson, personal interviews, 1985–1995.

5 "Death Rate Is Lower," *Alexandria Gazette*, October 17, 1918, 1; "Decided Improvement," *Alexandria Gazette*, October 28, 1918, 1; "Flu Conditions Improve," *Fairfax Herald*, October 25, 1918, 3; "Influenza Increasing," *Fairfax Herald*, December 13, 1918, 3; "Reappearance of Flu," *Alexandria Gazette*, December 10, 1918, 2.

6 Reed, *Fairfax County*, 499.

7 Milburn Sanders, personal interviews, 1977–2005; Marion Reid, personal interviews, 1985–2000; Hazel Thompson, personal interviews, 1985–1995.

8 "Want $1 a Day Raise," *Washington Post*, May 31, 1919, 12; Reed, Fairfax County, 506–508.

9 "War Time Fuel Rates Placed in Force Again by Garfield's Orders," *Washington Post*, December 9, 1919, 1.

10 "City Short of Homes," *Washington Post*, January 25, 1919, 14; "Waiting to Buy Here," *Washington Post*, February 9, 1919, R2; "Want Legislation for Amortization," *Washington Post*, March 16, 1919, R1; "Many to Buy Homes," *Washington Post*, March 23, 1919, RE1; "Predict a Big Revival," *Washington Post*, April 13, 1919, R1; "Newly Married Demand Kitchens," *Washington Post*, May 11, 1919, R3.

11 "Want $1 A Day Raise," *Washington Post*, May 31, 1919, 12; classified ads, *Washington Post*, March–June 1919; classified ads, *Evening Star*, March–June 1919.

12 "Milk Lower in May," *Washington Post*, April 14, 1919, 2; "Milk Prices Cut by Some Dealers," *Washington Post*, May 26, 1919, 2; "Housewives on Food," *Washington Post*, August 19, 1919, 7; "Increase Shown in Food Prices Here," *Evening Star*, January 3, 1919, 1; "Largest Increase in Food Price Here," *Evening Star*, November 23, 1919, 1; "Living Cost Rises 88 Percent Here," *Evening Star*, December 17, 1919,1; "Living Expenses Are Still Soaring," *Evening Star*, September 13, 1920, 12.

13 "Fast Run to Market," *Washington Post*, March 9, 1919, A8; "Farmers Buy Trucks," *Washington Post*, June 1, 1919, A13; "More Farmers Buying Tractors," *Washington Post*, July 18, 1919, 6; "Value of the Farm," *Washington Post*, August 19, 1919, AU9; Reed, Fairfax County, 513–515.

14 “Milk Producers to Discuss Price,” *Washington Post*, A5; “ Country Butter at 22 to 25 Cents,” *Washington Post*, December 14, 1920, 9; “Says Rise in Prices Vital to Farmers,” *Washington Post*, April 3, 1921.
15 “The Farmer and the Square Deal,” *Washington Post*, August 17, 1923, 6.
16 Reed, *Fairfax County*, 514–519.
17 Reed, *Fairfax County*, 418; Milburn Sanders, personal interviews, 1977–2005; Marion Reid, personal interviews, 1985–2000; Hazel Thompson, personal interviews, 1985–1995.

CHAPTER 22

1 Oliver Gasch, personal interviews, 1995; Manning Gasch, personal interviews, 1978–1985; Reed, Fairfax County, 521–532; “Farmers Seek Good Roads,” *Washington Post*, January 1, 1920, 2; “Asks for Lower Car Fare,” *Washington Post*, September 23, 1913, 7; “Second Commuter Sues,” *Washington Post*, August 17, 1916, 10. Note: There are numerous articles in all local newspapers related to this subject. These are just examples.
2 Milburn Sanders, “Thirteen Dry Years In Forestville,” Reflections Great Falls Historical Society, 1984–1985, 5–7.
3 Sanders, “Thirteen Dry Years”; *History of the Fairfax County Police Department, 1921–1990*, Hsitory4All, Inc. July 2010, 3.
4 Sanders, “Thirteen Dry Years”; “Six Held as Sheriff Begins Liquor Drive in Arlington County,” *Washington Post*, January 3, 1924, 3; “Still Owner Fined and Sent to Jail,” *Washington Post*, August 25, 1925, 2. Note: All local newspapers had notices of arrests of Liquor Law violators in almost every issue. These are just examples.
5 Sanders, “Thirteen Dry Years.”
6 “Charming Homelike Country Place in Fairfax County, Virginia,” *Evening Star*, April 25, 1925,18; “Gilt Edge Investment,” *Alexandria Gazette*, October 20, 1920, 3; “For Sale—Farm 100 Acres,” *Alexandria Gazette*, March 22, 1923.
7 Reed, *Fairfax County*, 521–532.
8 Ruth P. Rose, “The Role of Frank Lyon and His Associates in the Early Development of Arlington County,” *Arlington Historical Society Magazine* 5, no. 4 (October 1976): 55–56; “Lyon Park Sales $100,000 This Year,” *Washington Post*, July 24, 1921, 38.

9 "Frank Lyon Realty Pioneer," *Washington Post*, December 1, 1955, 26; "Frank Lyon Developer of Lyon Park in 1930s," *Evening Star*, December 1, 1955, A-32; Rose, "Frank Lyon," 55–56.

10 "Live in Lyon Park," *Evening Star*, August 12, 1021, 16.

11 "Lyon Park," *Evening Star*, September 24, 1921, 2; "150 Lots," *Evening Star*, May 1, 1922, 17.

12 "Buys 80 Building Lots in Lyon Park," *Washington Post*, October 30, 1921, 48; "Lyon Park Sales $100,000 This Year," *Washington Post*, July 24, 1921, 38.

13 "Reports Virginia Sales of $75,000 Last Week," *Washington Post*, March 12, 1922, 45; "Opens Virginia House Branch of Business," *Evening Star*, January 21, 1922, 14.

14 "Second Mortgage Is Safe If Properly Made, Says Expert," *Washington Post*, August 15, 1925, R1.

CHAPTER 23

1 "Ruby Lee Minor," *Alexandria Gazette*, March 31, 1922, e7; "Virginia Needs Improved Roads to Develop Wealth," *Washington Post*, July 15, 1925, SM8; "Highway-to-Bridge Group Begins Work on New Boulevard," *Washington Post*, July 2, 1926, 2.

2 "Arlington County Realty Sales Show Big Risc in Value," *Washington Post*, August 6, 1925, R1.

3 "Arlington County Chamber Is Busy," *Evening Star*, July 24, 1920, 6; "Key Bridge Ready on New Years Day," *Washington Post*, June 4, 1922, 43; "Sees Arlington Co. as Suburb to City," *Washington Post*, June 4, 1922, 42.

4 "400 Lots in Alcova Heights Go Rapidly," *Washington Post*, April 1, 1923, 44; "Alcova Heights," *Washington Post*, April 1, 1923.

5 "War Department Aids Highway Plan," *Evening Star*, March 27, 1931, 15; "Bridge to Arlington to Cost $13,750,000 Asked as Memorial," *Washington Post*, April 10, 1924, 12; "Senate Passes 136 Bills in Cleaning Up Calendar," *Washington Post*, December 31, 1924, 1; "The Memorial Bridge," *Washington Post*, February 21, 1925, 6; "First Work Is Begun on Memorial Bridge," *Washington Post*, March 12, 1925, 5.

6 "Demand Increases for Real Estate in Arlington County," *Washington Post*, March 29, 1925, 45.

7 "Lee Heights Prices to be Advanced 25 Per Cent Sept. 15," *Washington Post*, September 6, 1925, R2; "Lee Heights Sales Of Homes Reach $45,000 in 10 Days," *Washington Post*, September 13, 1925, 35.

8 "New Lee Heights Addition Planned as Home Section," *Washington Post*, July 4, 1926, R2; "87 New Home Sites in Lee Heights, Virginia Offered for Sale," *Washington Post*, July 11, 1920, R1.

9 "Sales Totaling $80,000 Made in Lee Heights," *Washington Post*, August 8, 1926, R5.

10 "Historic Virginia House Sold to State Senator," *Washington Post*, August 22, 1926, R1.

11 "Tripp Farm to Be Made into Home Sites Soon," *Washington Post*, May 15, 1927, R5; "Greenway Downs," *Washington Post*, June 26, 1927, R4.

12 "Sunset Farm for Sale by Ruby Lee Minar, Inc.," *Washington Post*, August 8, 1927, R4; "Great Stock Farm Near Herndon Sold by Heirs of Doctor," *Washington Post*, October 9, 1927, R3; *The History of the Fairfax Hunt, 1929–1972*, 1–5.

13 "Arlington Building Boom Is Predicted in Suburban Sites," *Washington Post*, December 20, 1925, 15.

14 "County Heads Study Water Supply Plan in Arlington County," *Washington Post*, June 7, 1924; "Arlington County Makes Application for Water Supply," *Washington Post*, September 5, 1925, M9; "Lee Heights School Will Be Dedicated Tuesday," *Washington Post*, April 26, 1925, 12; "New $35,000 School Will Be Ready Soon," *Washington Post*, September 13, 1925, 35; "Bridge, Water System, Good Roads Promised," *Washington Post*, December 20, 1926, 15; "Future of Nearby Virginia Declared Greatest in Nation," *Washington Post*, June 26, 1927, R7.

15 "Arlington County Group to Discuss Development Plan," *Washington Post*, July 21, 1925, 5; "Realtors in Virginia Decry Land Booms," *Washington Post*, September 23, 1927, R3; "Arlington County Zoning Approved," *Washington Post*, February 13, 1929, 3.

CHAPTER 24

1 Reed, *Fairfax County*, 530–534; J. H. Shepherd, Letter to the Editor, *Washington Post*, October 11, 1925; "Loans to Farmers," *Washington Post*, May 1, 1926, 6; "Helping the Farmers," *Washington Post*, June 12, 1936, 6; "Potomac Bank Reduces Its Farm Loan Interest," *Washington Post*, March 1, 1928, 14; Milburn Sanders, personal interviews, 1977–2005; Hazel Thompson, personal interviews, 1985–1995.

2 Milburn Sanders, personal interviews, 1977–2005; Hazel Thompson, personal interviews, 1985–1995; "The Tariff on Milk and Cream," *Washington Post*, February 19, 1926, 6.

3 Reed, Fairfax County, 533–534; "Milk Products Control Bill Passed by House," *Washington Post*, February 16, 1925, 4; "Cattle Inspection," *Washington Post*, July 4, 1927, 4.
4 Threat of Dairies to Stop City Milk Regarded as Bluff," *Washington Post*, June 28, 1927, 20.
5 "Lee Heights School Structure Will Be Dedicated Tuesday," *Washington Post*, April 26, 1925, 12; "New Rosslyn Bank Expected to Open on or about May 10," *Washington Post*, August 25, 1925, 2; "Contract Is Given for Dairy Plant in Arlington County," *Washington Post*, August 24, 1925; Rose, "Frank Lyon," 57.
6 Reed, *Fairfax County*, 533–534; "News of the Latest Happenings," *Washington Post*, February 25, 1928.
7 Nathaniel Mason Pawlett, "Historic Roads of Virginia," Virginia Highway & Transportation Research Council, Charlottesville, Virginia, October 1977.
8 "Road Bond Defeated," *Fairfax Herald*, November 19, 1923, 3.
9 "Virginia Auto Tag Stand May Lead to General Arrests," *Washington Post*, October 5, 1927, 2. Ronald L. Heinemann, *Harry Byrd* of Virginia (Charlottesville, VA: University Press of Virginia, 1996), 1–3.
10 Ronald L. Heinemann, *Harry Byrd of Virginia* (Charlottesville, VA: University Press of Virginia, 1996), 1–3.
11 Heinemann, *Harry Byrd*, 1–9.
12 Heinemann, *Harry Byrd*, 5–9
13 Heinemann, *Harry Byrd*, 19–31.
14 Heinemann, *Harry Byrd*, 19–31.
15 Heinemann, *Harry Byrd*, 32–56; "At Inaugural as Governor Urges Efficient Economy," *Washington Post*, February 2, 1926, 1.
16 "Governor Byrd Demands Equalized Tax for Farm and Industry," *Washington Post*, February 3, 1926, 2.
17 "Urges 28 Bureaus in Virginia Dropped by Legislative Acts," *Washington Post*, February 13, 1917, 12.
18 "Arlington County Car Owners Roiled By 1927 Tag Prices," *Washington Post*, December 5, 1926, p. M1.
19 "Byrd Road Law Effective July 1," *Herndon Observer*, July 7, 1932, 1; "Byrd Road Law Wins Sweeping Victory," *Herndon Observer*, August 11, 1932, 1.
20 "Dairying Industry Booms in Virginia," *Washington Post*, August 28, 1929, 20; "Dairy Production Leads in Fairfax," *Washington Post*, December 15, 1929, M18.

CHAPTER 25

1 Milburn Sanders, personal interviews, 1977–2005; Hazel Thompson, personal interviews, 1985–1995; Oliver Gasch, personal interviews, 1995; Jack Durham, personal interview, 1979.

2 "Fairfax Chamber Urges Road Work," *Washington Post*, January 16, 1930, 20; "New Pay Raise Urged by Teachers," *Washington Post*, January 18, 1930, 20.

3 "Supervisors Study Budget in Fairfax," *Washington Post*, March 14, 1930, 20; "Some Cuts Made," *Fairfax Herald*, March 7, 1930, 1; "Tax Rate Reduced," *Fairfax Herald*, April 4, 1930, 1.

4 "Diversified Crops Aid Virginia Farmers," *Washington Post*, January 17, 1930, 20; Sweig, *Fairfax County*, 554–555.

5 "Mercury Sinks to 7' Rise Expected Today," *Washington Post*, February 17, 1930, 1.

6 "Light Peach, Apple Crops in Prospect," *Washington Post*, June 14, 1930, 20; "Rain Badly Needed," *Fairfax Herald*, May 16, 1930, 1.

7 "One Succumbs as Heat Wave Reaches Peak," *Washington Post*, July 30, 1930, 1; "Four Persons Heat Victims before Rains," *Washington Post*, July 23, 1930, 1; "Mercury in Capital Climbs to All Time Mark, Reaching 105.6," *Washington Post*, July 21, 1930, 1; "Hoover Acts to Aid States Hit By Drought; Capital Reaches 103; Cooler Today," *Washington Post*, August 16, 1930, 1; "Temperature Passes 100 Mark for Tenth Time in 21 Days," *Washington Post*, August 9, 1930, 1.

8 "Farmers in Virginia Face Crop Failure," *Washington Post*, July 25, 1930, 10.

9 "Survey in Fairfax Shows Crops Hurt," *Washington Post*, August 15, 1930, 2; "Serious Solution, Drought Is Causing Heavy Financial Loss in County," *Fairfax Herald*, August 8, 1930, 1; "Face Disaster," *Fairfax Herald*, August 8, 1930, 1; "Emergency Feeding," *Fairfax Herald*, August 15, 1930, 1.

10 "Virginia Drought Costs $80,000,000," *Washington Post*, August 18, 1930, 3; "Prospects Gloomy for Virginia Apples," *Washington Post*, August 21, 1930, 18; "Tragic Winter Faces Farm Community in Virginia—No Vegetables, Corn, or Meat," *Washington Post*, Letter to the Editor from Mrs. Leslie H. Gray, August 23, 1930, 6.

11 "Hoover Acts to Aid States Hit by Drought; Capital Reaches 103; Cooler Today," *Washington Post*, August 16, 1930, 1; Heinemann, *Harry Byrd*, 117–118; "Drought Relief," *Fairfax Herald*, August 22, 1930, 1.

12 "Heads of 12 States Most Affected Called to White House," *Washington Post*, August 8, 1930, 1; "Byrd Says Drought Aid Far Inadequate,"

Washington Post, October 18, 1930, 22; "Fairfax Drought Costs $1,000,000," *Washington Post*, October 30, 1930, 22.

13 "Hoover Acts to Aid States Hit by Drought; Capital Reaches 103; Cooler Today," *Washington Post*, August 16, 1930, 1.

14 "Virginia Drought Cost $80,000,000," *Washington Post*, August 18, 1930, 3; Heinemann, *Harry Byrd*, 116.

15 "Congress Tied in Deadlock on Drought Help," *Washington Post*, December 17, 1930, 1.

16 "Fairfax Drought Costs $1,000,000," *Washington Post*, October 30, 1930, 22; "Money Available," *Fairfax Herald*, September 5, 1930, 1; "Drought Loans," *Fairfax Herald*, September 12, 1930, 1.

17 "Byrd Says Drought Aid Far Inadequate," *Washington Post*, October 18, 1930.

18 Heinemann, *Harry Byrd*, 116.

19 "Byrd Says Drought Aid Far Inadequate," *Washington Post*, October 18, 1930; "Drought Relief," *Fairfax Herald*, October 10, 1930, 1.

20 "Rain Aids Vegetation Fails to End Drought," *Washington Post*, November 18, 1930, 3; "Farm Loans for Fall Seeding," *Herndon Observer*, September 13, 1930, 1; Heinemann, *Harry Byrd*, 117–118.

21 Letter to the Editor from F. L. Ward, "Farmers in Dire Need," *Washington Post*, December 18, 1930, 6.

22 "Congress Tied in Deadlock on Drought Help," *Washington Post*, December 17, 1930, 1; "Hoover Signs Draught Loan Appropriation," *Washington Post*, January 16, 1931, 1.

23 "Falls Church Gets Three Water Tanks," *Washington Post*, September 9, 1930, 22; "Drought May Shut Fairfax Schools," *Washington Post*, September 6, 1930, 3; "Drought Increases Heating Problems," *Washington Post*, October 20, 1930, 5.

24 "Lack of Pressure Aids $25,000 Blaze," *Washington Post*, December 5, 1930, 4.

25 "Mercury Tumbling to 15 Smashes 58 Year Record," *Washington Post*, November 29, 1930, 1.; "Fairfax Farmers Fear 1931 Failure," *Evening Star*, December 28, 1930, B-2.

26 "Rain Here Called $1,000,000 Relief," *Washington Post*, May 9, 1931, 16.

CHAPTER 26

1 Netherton, Fairfax County, 571–574; "Fairfax County to Close Several Schools," *Washington Post*, June 6, 1930, 18; "Fairfax Schools' Bills to Be Paid," *Washington Post*, April 8, 1931.

2 "Arlington to Open School Bids Today," *Washington Post*, July 10, 1930; "Arlington County Leads in Schools," *Washington Post*, August 19, 1930, 18; Elizabeth Cannon Kimball et al., "Washington and Lee High School: The Early Years, 1924–1939," *Arlington Historical Magazine* 5, no. 2 (October 1974): 12.

3 "Fairfax Tax Board Will Resume Work," *Washington Post*, December 20, 1930, 3.

4 "Alexandria to Get List of Late Taxes," *Washington Post*, June 16, 1930, 16.

5 "Arlington County Tax Suits Filed," *Washington Post*, August 9, 1930, 16.

6 "Electricity Rates Cut in Arlington," *Washington Post*, August 15, 1930, 5.

7 "Arlington Alters Tax Assessments," *Washington Post*, October 18, 1930, 22; "Assessment Rate Cut in Alexandria," *Washington Post*, December 27, 1930, 3; "County Valuations Raised by $510,760.00," *Washington Post*, February 8, 1931, M3.

8 Multiple classified and display advertisements, *Washington Post*; "Arlington County Leads in Schools," *Washington Post*, August 19, 1930, 18.

9 "Golf Big Feature at Strathmeade," *Washington Post*, December 21, 1930, R1; "Paving Order Let for Strathmeade," *Washington Post*, April 19, 1931, R1; "Real Estate Plot to Be Sold in Debt," *Washington Post*, August 12, 1932, 10; "Tract in Fairfax Sold for $100,000," *Washington Post*, September 19, 1932, 2.

10 "Devonshire Gardens Is Subdivision Name," *Washington Post*, May 13, 1928, R1; "Grunwell Estate to Become Village," *Washington Post*, December 9, 1928, RE3; "Arlington Trust's Head Is Reelected," *Washington Post*, January 17, 1930, 3; "Country Club Hills," *Washington Post*, January 5, 1930, A3.

11 "Building of Homes Held National Duty," *Washington Post*, May 3, 1931, R5.

12 "Old House Problem Studied In Article," *Washington Post*, December 15, 1931, R1.

13 "Tax on Income Cut by Fairfax Drought," *Washington Post*, September 21, 1931, 11; "Assessment Reduced," *Fairfax Herald*, January 20, 1931, 1.

14 Letters between John Laylin and Grote Hutcheson, private collection of Laura Laylin Nichols; Lucy Housel, personal interview, 1985; Ethel Durham, personal interview, 1979; Jack Durham, personal interview, 1979; Edith Spaulding, personal interview, 2010.

15 *The History of the Fairfax Hunt, 1929–1972*, 7–8.

16 Laylin letters; Lucy Housel, personal interview, 1985; Jack Durham, personal interview, 1979; Ethel Durham, personal interview, 1979; Lavinia Lambert, personal interview, 2000.

17 "Catherine Filene Shouse," Wolftrap National Park for the Performing Arts, National Park Service; "I Bought a Mink Coat and Had a Feeling That the World Was Endless in Depth," *Washington Post*, October 28, 1979, K1; Jack Durham, personal interview, 1979; Ethel Durham, personal interview, 1979.

CHAPTER 27

1 Hazel Thompson, personal interviews, 1985–1995.

2 "Hoover Pleads for Success in Hoarding Drive," *Washington Post*, March 7, 1932, 1.

3 "Hoover Pleads for Success in Hoarding Drive," *Washington Post*, March 7, 1932, 1.

4 "Hoover Pleads for Success in Hoarding Drive," *Washington Post*, March 7, 1932, 1.

5 "Arlington Official Urges Tax Payment," *Washington Post*, March 26, 1932, 7; "Lower Tax Rates Are Set in Fairfax," *Washington Post*, April 7, 1932, 13.

6 "$3,000,000 Savings on Byrd Plan Seen," *Washington Post*, March 16, 1932, 4; "Pollard Signs Byrd Road Plan Measure," *Washington Post*, April 1, 1932, 4; "Byrd Road Law Effective July 1," *Herndon Observer*, July 7, 1932, 1; Netherton, *Fairfax County*, 594.

7 "Road Control Plan Opposed in Fairfax," *Washington Post*, March 2, 1932, 13; "Budget Is Adopted by Fairfax Board," *Washington Post*, March 17, 1932, 13; "Lower Tax Rates Are Set in Fairfax," *Washington Post*, April 7, 1932, 13; "Arlington Citizens Form Road Group," *Washington Post*, July 27, 1932; "To Vote on Road Law," *Herndon Observer*, July 28, 1932, 1; "Election Next Tuesday Byrd Road Law," *Herndon Observer*, August 4, 1932, 1.

8 "Board in Arlington Attacks Byrd's Act," *Washington Post*, April 30, 1932, 5; "Byrd Act Rejection Urged at Ballston," *Washington Post*, June 29, 1932, 10.

9 "Convicts May Work on Arlington Roads," *Washington Post*, July 10, 1932, M17; "Road Plan Debated at Fairfax Meeting," *Washington Post*, July 29, 1932, 9.

10 "Board to Open Road Work Bids Tonight," *Washington Post*, June 13, 1932, 5.

11 "Byrd Road Law Wins Sweeping Victory," *Herndon Observer*, August 11, 1932, 1.

12 "Colvin Run Horse Show Brings Many," *Washington Post*, August 28, 1932, M10; "Fairfax to Receive $150,585 for Roads," *Washington Post*, September 10, 1932, 10; "Fairfax Road Work Starts Tomorrow," *Washington Post*, September 11, 1932, 4.

13 "Car Line Service to Be Abandoned," *Washington Post*, July 31, 1932, 2; Netherton, Fairfax County, 599.

14 "Home Loan Bank Board to Meet at Once," *Washington Post*, August 3, 1932, 7; "Home Loan Bank Law Is Explained," *Washington Post*, September 11, 1932, R1; "Home Loan System Will Affect Realty," *Washington Post*, October 2, 1932, R2.

15 "Realty Men Urge Foreclosure Halt," *Washington Post*, April 24, 1932, 14; "Appraisers' Group to Protect Public," *Washington Post*, July 24, 1932, R3.

16 "Individual Incomes Falls Seven Billion," *Washington Post*, November 30, 1931, 5.

17 "Mrs. Fain Attacks Bootlegger Law," *Washington Post*, May 3, 1932, 13.

18 "3,844 Years Arrests under Virginia Dry Act," *Washington Post*, January 1, 1931, 2; "Liquor Cases Fill Docket in Fairfax," *Washington Post*, September 22, 1931, 11.

19 "Alexandria Police Nab 3,827 Persons," *Washington Post*, January 3, 1931, 18.

20 "Arlington Liquor Fines in Month Total $455.00," *Washington Post*, July 6, 1932, 14.

21 "Fairfax to Ask Recovery Fund For Jail," *Washington Post*, August 15, 1933, 4; "Fairfax Plans to Raze Jail 100 Years Old," *Washington Post*, August 22, 1933, 10; "Fairfax Jail Loan Granted," *Washington Post*, September 30, 1933, 21; "Utah's Formal Ballot Closes US Dry Rule," *Washington Post*, December 6, 1933, 1.

22 "Fairfax Business Taxes Show Drop," *Washington Post*, February 11, 1933, 17; "Charitable Work," *Fairfax Herald*, December 16, 1932, 1.

23 "Fairfax County Paper Joins Barter System," *Washington Post*, March 11, 1933, 10.

24 Milburn Sanders, personal interviews, 1977–2005.

CHAPTER 28

1 Capital Trade Sees Promise in 32's Smile," *Washington Post*, January 1, 1932, 1; "Bicentennial Held Prosperity Source," *Washington Post*, February 18, 1932, 18; "Mount Vernon Highway," *Washington Post*, February 15, 1932, 6.

2 "Gold Embargo Discussed as Possible First Step," *Washington Post*, March 5, 1933, 1.

3 "Text of New President's Address at Inauguration," *Washington Post*, March 5, 1933, 2.

4 "Plans Drawn by Roosevelt in Bank Crisis," *Washington Post*, March 4, 1933, 8; "7 Regulations Are Issued to Assist Bank Users," *Washington Post*, March 7, 1933, 1; "Bank Crisis Met," *Washington Post*, March 10, 1933, 6; "Text of Bank Measure Passed by Congress," *Washington Post*, March 10, 1933, 5; "Text of Talk," *Washington Post*, March 13, 1933, 1; "Senate Enacts Plans to Prevent Finance Emergencies," *Washington Post*, May 26, 1933, 1.

5 "Our Growing Government," *Washington Post*, July 16, 1933, 6.

6 "Fairfax Educators Discuss Economies," *Washington Post*, January 6, 1933, 9; "Tentative Budget Ready for Fairfax," *Washington Post*, February 2, 1933, 7; "School Board," *Fairfax Herald*, January 13, 1933, 1.

7 "Fairfax Tax Rate Slash Is Proposed," *Fairfax Herald*, February 24, 1933, 10; "Grange Is against Fairfax Tax Raise," *Fairfax Herald*, March 3, 1933, 19; "Fairfax Chamber Urges Cut in County Salaries," *Fairfax Herald*, March 8, 1933, 4; "Fairfax Taxpayers Urge Budget Slash," *Fairfax Herald*, May 31, 1933, 12; "Meeting Depression," *Fairfax Herald*, January 6, 1933, 1.

8 "Fairfax Education Budget $198,954.20," *Washington Post*, February 15, 1933, 4; "Tax Rate Revealed in Fairfax County," *Washington Post*, April 6, 1933, 10; "Fairfax School Slash Is Held Averted," *Washington Post*, August 21, 1933, 5.

9 "Needy Pupils Will Eat Free Meals Daily," *Washington Post*, October 6, 1933, 24; "Fairfax's Bar to DC Welfare Wards Is Lifted," *Washington Post*, November 7, 1933, 4.

10 "County Seeks $172,000 for New Schools," *Washington Post*, July 28, 1933, 4; "$66,000 Rum Fines Will Aid County Schools," *Washington Post*, November 28, 1933, 8.

11 "A Fine Work," *Fairfax Herald*, February 3, 1933, 1; "Hot Lunches," *Washington Post*, February 6, 1933, 4.
12 Marion Reid, personal interviews, 1985–2000.
13 "Tax Must Be Paid Now Says Official," *Washington Post*, May 2, 1933, 4; "Penalties Begin Friday On Uncollected Taxes," *Washington Post*, June 11, 1933, 10.
14 "Fairfax Rounds Up Foreign Auto Tags," *Washington Post*, June 20, 1933, 3.
15 "Gasoline Prices Go Up outside Of DC," *Washington Post*, June 3, 1933, 1; "Gasoline Tax Stirs Fairfax and Arlington," *Washington Post*, August 28, 1933, 11.
16 "Virginia Ends District's Gas Competition by New Law," *Washington Post*, September 3, 1933, 1.
17 "32 Camps Nearby in New Jobs Plan," *Washington Post*, June 3, 1933, 17; "100 More Get Federal Jobs in Arlington," *Washington Post*, September 29, 1933, 5; "Many Register," *Fairfax Observer*, October 20, 1933, 1; "State to Build 100-Ft. Tower Near Fairfax Nudist Colony," *Washington Post*, November 2, 1933, 17.
18 "Fairfax to Ask Recovery Fund for Jail," *Washington Post*, August 15, 1933, 4; "Fairfax Plans to Raze Jail 100 Years Old," *Washington Post*, August 23, 1933, 10; "Virginia Work Program Given New Impetus," *Washington Post*, November 30, 1933, 27; "Work for 360 Carried On in New CWA Projects," *Washington Post*, December 16, 1933; "Fairfax Given $42,735 More for CWA Jobs," *Washington Post*, December 16, 1933.
19 "Lyon Village Home Sale Pace Is Brisk," *Washington Post*, May 1, 1932, R2; "More Homes Plan of Lyon Projects," *Washington Post*, April 9, 1933, R1; classified ad, *Washington Post*, September 11, 1934, 24.
20 "Big Home Project Work Opens Today," *Washington Post*, April 15, 1933, 5; "US Employee Housing Projects Under Way," *Washington Post*, July 25, 1933, 11.
21 Netherton, *Fairfax County*, 553–554; "Fairfax Seeds Bought to Distribute to Needy," *Washington Post*, April 2, 1933, R6; "Charitable Work," *Fairfax Herald*, December 1932, 1.
22 Netherton, *Fairfax County*, 554.

CHAPTER 29

1 "CWA to Build Six Barracks At Reformatory," *Washington Post*, December 31, 1933, 9.

2 "Glass Scores Federal Aid as Wasteful," *Washington Post*, July 29, 1934, 1.

3 "Glass Scores Federal Aid as Wasteful," *Washington Post*, July 29, 1934, 1.

4 "New Deal Way to Prosperity Flayed by Byrd," *Washington Post*, April 23, 1934, 2; "Byrd Calls AAA Changes Doom of Farmers," *Washington Post*, May 23, 1934, 4; Heinemann, *Harry Byrd*, 165–170.

5 "Woes of Nation Far from Over, Says Candidate," *Washington Post*, September 27, 1934, 5.

6 "Nearby Wheat Farmers Paid $30,918 by US," *Washington Post*, January 3, 1934, 19; "Virginia Farm Income Rises," *Washington Post*, September 2, 1934, 5; "Virginia Farm Incomes Rise 12 Million Over '33" *Washington Post*, October 10, 1934, 18; "Drought Seen Boosting Price of US Cattle," *Washington Post*, December 15, 1934, 17.

7 "Fairfax Pupils Totaled 5,915 in Fiscal Year," *Washington Post*, August 20, 1934; "Fairfax County Income Taxes Show Increase," *Washington Post*, August 21, 1934, 5; "Fairfax Pupils Increase While Cost Decreases," *Washington Post*, October 16, 1934, 12.

8 "Federal Funds for Arlington Poor Expected," *Washington Post*, April 22, 1934, 6; "Fairfax County Child Clothing Appeal Issued," *Washington Post*, September 3, 1934, 5; "Sunrise in the Suburbs," *Washington Post*, September 29, 1934, 4; "Welfare Plans Protested by Fairfax County," *Washington Post*, October 4, 1934, 6; "County Appeals for Additional Welfare Funds," *Washington Post*, November 23, 1934, 10; "Fairfax Seeks Larger Fund to Aid Relief," *Washington Post*, December 13, 1934, 10.

9 "Fight Forecast on Virginia's Rum Sale Plan," *Washington Post*, January 1, 1934, 5; "Joint Liquor Hearings Open at Richmond," *Washington Post*, January 19, 1934, 3; "District Faces Virginia Liquor Store Threat," *Washington Post*, February 25, 1934, 12; "Arlington Dry Forces Form for Battle," *Washington Post*, February 26, 1934, 13; "Liquor Is Legal as Perry Signs Virginia Bill," *Washington Post*, March 8, 1934, 4.

10 "Virginia Senate Passes Liquor Control Bill," *Washington Post*, February 2, 1934, 14; "Virginia ABC Board Opens Headquarters," *Washington Post*, March 23, 1934, 6.

11 National Register of Historic Places Registration Form 029-5014, A. Smith Bowman Distillery, October 18, 1999.

12 "Land on Potomac River Is Desired," *Washington Post*, July 3, 1932, R2; "Being Modernized," *Fairfax Herald*, April 7, 1933, 1.

13 Durham letters, William Gunnell house historic documents, author's private collection.

14 Ethel Durham, personal interview, 1979; Jack Durham, personal interview, 1979; Durham letters.

CHAPTER 30

1 "Railroad Plans to Abolish Line to Great Falls," *Washington Post*, January 27, 1935, 4; Harwood, *Rails to the Blue Ridge*, 75–77; Marion Reid, personal interviews, 1985–2000; Manning Gasch, personal interviews, 1978–1985; Oliver Gasch, personal interviews, 1995.

2 Harwood, *Rails to the Blue Ridge*, 77–78; "Fairfax Board Arranges Deal for Rail Route," *Washington Post*, April 28, 1936, 6; Marion Reid, personal interviews, 1985–2000; Manning Gasch, personal interviews, 1978–1985; Oliver Gasch, personal interviews, 1995; "Want a Road," *Fairfax Herald*, August 7, 1936, 1; "Road Meeting," *Fairfax Herald*, September 4, 1936, 1.

3 "Vast Road Program Likely in Virginia," *Washington Post*, February 28, 1935, 3; "Fairfax Wants Road Improvements at Great Falls," *Washington Post*, July 4, 1935, 4; "Road Moneys Are Allotted by Virginia," *Washington Post*, July 24, 1935, 15.

4 "Loudoun Citizens Fight Convict Camp Removal," *Washington Post*, August 4, 1935, 12; "Armed Men Guard 60 Prisoners at Great Falls Camp," *Washington Post*, August 9, 1935, 7; Carl Schmitz, personal interview, 2006; Gary Schmitz, personal interview, 2006; Emily Ring, personal interview, 2006.

5 "Byrd Launches Second Attack on Works Bill," *Washington Post*, February 28, 1935, 7.

6 "Virginia to Add Ten CCC Camps for New Quota," *Washington Post*, May 3, 1935, 21.

7 "Fairfax County WPS Program Is Inaugurated," *Washington Post*, December 11, 1935, 11.

8 "Fairfax Taxes 97 Percent Collected Report Shows," *Washington Post*, July 3, 1935, 12; "Assessed Value of Fairfax Land Rises Slightly," *Washington Post*, July 8, 1935, 3.

9 "Fairfax Schools Taxed by Enrollment," *Washington Post*, September 22, 1935, 13.

10 "New Deal Way to Prosperity Flayed by Byrd," *Washington Post*, April 23, 1935, 2; Heinemann, *Harry Byrd*, 171–175.

11 "Byrd Voices Hope for Less Spending," *Evening Star*, September 8, 1935, 9.
12 "Fairfax Wheat Likely to Draw 33 Cent Bonus," *Washington Post*, August 3, 1935, 5.
13 "Mass Meeting to Hear Pleas for Power Line," *Washington Post*, June 28, 1935; Milburn Sanders, personal interviews, 1977–2005; Ellen Sanders, personal interviews, 1977–2005; Marion Reid, personal interviews, 1985–2000; Bessie Brown, personal interview, 1989; Alice Utterback, personal interview, 1985–1986; Lucy Housel, personal interview, 1985.
14 "Mass Meeting to Hear Pleas for Power Line," *Washington Post*, June 28, 1935, 9.
15 "Electric Light for All Fairfax Called Remote," *Washington Post*, August 1, 1935, 19; Netherton, Fairfax County, 608–609.
16 "FRA Plans Farm Loans in Virginia," *Washington Post*, October 7, 1935, 9; "Fairfax County PWA to Assist Needy Farmers," *Washington Post*, December 25, 1935, 5.
17 "Virginia Cattle Holding Gain In Past Year," *Washington Post*, February 19, 1935, 25; "Beef, Pork Prices Jump in Virginia," *Washington Post*, May 13, 1935, 11; "High Meat Prices to Aid Cattlemen," *Washington Post*, May 28, 1935, 20; "Virginia Hogs at Highest Price in Last 5 Years," *Washington Post*, August 9, 1935, 4.
18 "Fairfax County Farms Gaining Census Shows," *Washington Post*, December 3, 1935, 11.
19 "Storm Spreads Damage, Ends DC Heat Wave," *Washington Post*, June 15, 1935, 1; "Fairfax School Costs Mount for Year, Capital Outlay Up—Colvin Run Show Set," *Washington Post*, August 18, 1935, 9; "Major Carson Horses in Spotlight," *Washington Post*, April 19, 1936, X2.

CHAPTER 31

1 "Split Imperils Plan to Speed New Bonus Bill," *Washington Post*, January 4, 1936, 5; "Bonus Clears First Hurdle, Speeds Ahead," *Washington Post*, January 7, 1936, 1; "House Chiefs Push for Vote on Bonus Bill," *Washington Post*, January 8, 1936, 1; "Bonus Accord by Senators Today Hinted," *Washington Post*, January 13, 1936, 1.
2 "Senate Group Backs Bonus, Deaf to Debt Rise Warning," *Washington Post*, January 15, 1936, 1; "Bonus by Bond Issue Forecast Even over Veto," *Washington Post*, January 18, 1936, 2; "Senate Votes Bonus 74–16 Show Power to Block Veto," *Washington Post*, January 21, 1936; "Bond

Bonus Voted; Is Sent to Roosevelt," *Washington Post*, January 23, 1936, 1; "Politics and People," *Washington Post*, January 25, 1936, 2; "The Road to Bankruptcy," *Washington Post*, January 25, 1936, 6.

3 "Roosevelt Asks Veterans to Use Bonus Wisely," *Washington Post*, January 28, 1936, 7.

4 "The Financial Crisis," *Washington Post*, March 3, 1936, 6.

5 "Taxes Threaten Liberty, Fail to Provide Jobs, Hoover Says," *Washington Post*, March 8, 1936, 1.

6 "Tie Votes Halt Salary Shifts for Fairfax," *Washington Post*, January 7, 1936, 21.

7 "Fairfax Plans Frame Schools for Overflow," *Washington Post*, February 7, 1936, 6; "Fairfax Study of Budget Plan Due Wednesday," *Washington Post*, March 30, 1936, 30; "Schools Growing," *Fairfax Herald*, November 6, 1936, 1.

8 "Dearth of Labor Delays Fairfax Works Project," *Washington Post*, March 31, 1936, 11; "Fairfax Drive for Recreation Center Planned," *Washington Post*, April 27, 1936, X3; "Fairfax County Gives $2,300 for New Park," *Washington Post*, June 14, 1936, M13; "Fairfax Co. Park Funds Awarded," *Washington Post*, July 1, 1936, X28.

9 "The Road to Disintegration," *Washington Post*, June 3, 1936, X6.

10 "WPA Orders Study of Fairfax History," *Washington Post*, February 3, 1936, 5.

11 "Leiter Buys Big Tract," *Washington Post*, July 23, 1911, 2; "Trail Gang of Efficient Bandits Who Rifled $300,000 Wine Vault," *Washington Post*, October 10, 1921, 1; "Vast Leiter Estate Is Divided to Give US a New National Park," *Washington Post*, August 28, 1936, B2.

12 "CCC Will Start Work on Leiter Estate Park," *Washington Post*, August 17, 1936, X4; "CCC to Convert Leiter Estate," New York Times, August 18, 1936, 15.

13 "Building Shows Important Gain in Arlington," *Washington Post*, May 3, 1936, R13; "Nearby Virginia's Building Increases," *Washington Post*, May 3, 1936, R13; "Building Boom in Virginia Led by Alexandria," *Washington Post*, May 10, 1936, R10.

14 "Virginia Ideal Site for Homes of Capitolians," *Washington Post*, April 19, 1936, R10; "Hills Homes, Residence Site Has 250 Homes," *Washington Post*; "Waverly Hills Development Attracts Many," *Washington Post*, June 7, 1936, R14; "Virginia Area Held Desirable Home Location," *Washington Post*, April 26, 1936, R10; "2-Million Mark Set Since Jan.1 In Arlington," *Washington Post*, May 17, 1936, R18; "Nearby Virginia Is Scene of New Homes Project," *Washington Post*, May 31, 1936, R10.

15 "Guilford Plan Allows Owner a Wide Choice," *Washington Post*, March 8, 1936, R4; "Guilford Land Model Homes Is to Open Today," *Washington Post*, March 8, 1936, R5; "Buyers View Permanesque Home Exhibit," *Washington Post*, March 15, 1936, R6; "Many Visit Virginia House By Guilford Co.," *Washington Post*, April 5, 1936, R4; "Fairfax Issues 47 Construction Permits in July," *Washington Post*, August 11, 1936, X6; "Northern Virginia Bureau Charts City's Growth," *Washington Post*, September 20, 1936, R3; "Many Deeds Recorded," *Fairfax Herald*, June 12, 1936.

16 "Permanesque Homes Village Growing Fast," *Fairfax Herald*, April 12, 1936, R1; "Trend Toward Larger Homes Survey Shows," *Fairfax Herald*, June 28, 1936, R11.

17 "Home Luxury Ideas Undergo Rapid Change," *Fairfax Herald*, July 12, 1936, R4.

18 "1,302 Bonuses Are Distributed at Alexandria," *Fairfax Herald*, June 16, 1936, 7; "$1,726,000,000 in Bonus Paid Effect in Doubt," *Fairfax Herald*, June 31, 1936, X1; "Bonus Bonds," *Fairfax Herald*, June 19, 1936, 1; "Redeeming Bonds," *Fairfax Herald*, June 26, 1936, 1.

19 "No Rain in Sight for at Least 36 Hours, Assert Weather Experts," *Washington Post*, July 7, 1936, X1; "Drought Relief Topic of Parley By Virginians," *Washington Post*, July 7, 1936, X3; "Dairy Farming in County Gains C of C Is Told," *Washington Post*, September 10, 1936, X24.

20 "Uniform Price Plan for Capital Milk Assailed," *Washington Post*, July 22, 1936, X6; "Milk Price War in Capital Area Seen at Hearing," *Washington Post*, July 25, 1936, X3; "Virginia's Milk Act Is Attacked before 3 Judges," *Washington Post*, July 31, 1936, X9; "Distributors Oppose Rise in Milk Prices," *Washington Post*, August 5, 1936, X15; "Milk Prices Must Go Up Farmers Say," *Washington Post*, August 11, 1936, X15; "Injunction Suit Planned to Balk AAA Milk Pact," *Washington Post*, September 2, 1936, X10; "Milk Increase of Cent a Quart Effective Today," *Washington Post*, November 1, 1936, M1.

CHAPTER 32

1 "Prosperity Here at Last," *Washington Post*, January 2, 1937, 2.

2 "The Propertyless," *Washington Post*, January 6, 1937, B7.

3 "Byrd-Roosevelt Reorganization Clash Is Hinted," *Washington Post*, January 12, 1937, 1; "Reorganization Unit of Senate Splits on Plans," *Washington Post*, February 7, 1937, 3.

4 "Byrd Demands Merging of US Loans Agencies," *Washington Post*, January 2, 1937, 1; "Hostility Appears as His Message Is Completed; Hill Stunned by Brownlow Report Indorsement," *Washington Post*, January 13, 1937, 1; "Byrd-Roosevelt Showdown Set for Hill Today," *Washington Post,* January 15, 1937, 1; "Byrd's Economy Program Upset by Senate, 52–22," *Washington Post,* January 16, 1937, 1; "Senate to Push Roosevelt Plan Despite Byrd," *Washington Post,* January 17, 1937, 1; "The News of the Week Passes in Brief Review," *Washington P*ost, January 17, 1937, B3; "Byrd Pictures Mounting Costs in Government," *Washington Post,* April 19, 1937, 1.

5 "Construction Showing Gain in Local Area," *Washington Post*, January 31, 1937, R8; "Modern Homes Are Featured at Beverly Hills," *Washington Post*, June 6, 1937, R4; "Local Building Is Up 68 Pct., Report Shows," *Washington Post*, July 25, 1937, R4; "Home Building Registers Gain in Washington," *Washington Post*, October 31, 1937, R9; Ethel Durham, personal interview, 1979; Jack Durham, personal interview, 1979.

6 "Recovery Chief Assails Federal Aid Plan," *Washington Post*, February 21, 1936, 2.

7 "Recovery Chief Assails Federal Aid Plan," *Washington Post*, February 21, 1936, 2.

8 "New Va. Project Result of US Home Shortage," *Washington Post*, May 16, 1937, R1.

9 "220 Employed on Community Development," *Washington Post*, January 13, 1937, R4.

10 "New Va. Project Result of US Home Shortage," *Washington Post*, May 16, 1937, R1; "Public Pleased with Features at Buckingham," *Washington Post*, May 23, 1937, R1.

11 "Public Pleased with Features at Buckingham," *Washington Post*, May 23, 1937, R1.

12 "Plans Enlarged in Buckingham Homes Project," *Washington Post*, June 6, 1937, R5; "Assembly Line Technique Used at Buckingham," *Washington Post*, January 7, 1938, R5

13 "Assembly Line Technique Used at Buckingham," *Washington Post*, January 7, 1938, R5.

14 "Allie S. Freed Dies; Leader in US Industry," *Washington Post*, January 12, 1938, 16; "FHA Insuring 8,247 Loans in DC, VA, MD," *Washington Post*, September 5, 1937, R1.

15 "Home Building Registers Gain in Washington,"*Washington Post*, October 31, 1937, R9.

16 "Ethel B. Morse, Letter to the Editor," *Washington Post*, June 15, 1937, 10.

17 "Fairfax Seeks $39,000 to Aid School System," *Washington Post*, April 16, 1937, 26.

CHAPTER 33

1 "King to Urge Dredging for WPA Politics," *Washington Post*, May 21, 1938, X1; "Fairfax School Building Is Set to Start Soon," *Washington Post*, July 6, 1938, 13; "$43,000,000 a Day," *Washington Post*, July 15, 1938, X4; "PWA Approval of Arlington Sewers Sought," *Washington Post*, September 9, 1938, X3; "Fairfax Votes to Purchase School Site," *Washington Post*, October 29, 1938, X26; "PWA Disbursements," *Fairfax Herald*, February 18, 1938, 1.

2 "Byrd Denounces New Deal Waste," *Fairfax Herald*, November 11, 1937, 1; "Attack Opens on Bill to Put Civil Service under 1 Man," *Fairfax Herald*, February 25, 1938, X1.

3 "Official Tie-Breaker Ponders Long before He Votes," *Fairfax Herald*, March 10, 1938, M1; "Arlington Tax of Over Million 72 Percent Collected," *Fairfax Herald*, December 8, 1938, 16; "Fairfax Gives Employes More Pay for 1939," *Fairfax Herald*, January 5, 1939, 4; "Fix Salaries," *Fairfax Herald*, January 7, 1938, 1.

4 "Development at Arlington FHA Financed," *Fairfax Herald*, May 8, 1938, R9; "Sale of Homes Reflects 'Boom' in Nearby VA," *Fairfax Herald*, July 10, 1938, R2.

5 "Population Is 1,500 to Square Mile: Thriving Area Has Rapid Growth in Past 9 Years," *Fairfax Herald*, September 24, 1939, R9.

6 "Alexandria Construction Totals $53,417," *Fairfax Herald*, September 25, 1939, 13; "53 Building Permits Issued in Fairfax," *Fairfax Herald*, October 1, 1939, 2; "County CofC Is Eagor to Cooperate: Historic Area Boasts of Population of More than 30,000," *Fairfax Herald*, November 26, 1939, R8.

7 "Fairfax Offers Historic Homes and Estates," *Fairfax Herald*, June 30, 1940; "Yen for Soil Draws Many from Capital," *Fairfax Herald*, July 14, 1940, 7; "Low Tax Rate Helps Fairfax to Expand," *Fairfax Herald*, June 30, 1940, R12; "Good Highways Speed Traffic to Washington," *Fairfax Herald*, June 30, 1940, R15; "Historic Old Hickory Hill Now for Sale," *Fairfax Herald*, June 15, 1941, R2.

8 "Agriculture Still Leads in Fairfax," *Fairfax Herald*, June 30, 1940, R10; "Hollin Hall, Show Place of Virginia to Be Sold at Auction," *Fairfax*

Herald, June 22, 1941, R6; "Merle Thorp Buys Hollin Hall and Part of Mason Estate," *Fairfax Herald*, July 14, 1941, 11.

9 "Building Hits All-Time Peak in Fairfax," *Fairfax Herald*, June 30, 1940, R10; "Five-Room Bungalow Situated on Large Lot, Air Conditioned," *Fairfax Herald*, June 30, 1940, R12; "Low Tax Rate Helps Fairfax to Expand," *Fairfax Herald*, June 30, 1940, R12; "Fairfax Shows Substantial Gains Also," *Fairfax Herald*, September 29, 1940, R6; "Section Among Area Leaders in Building," *Fairfax Herald*, October 13, 1940, 51.

10 "Fairfax Building for Six Months Totals $4,850,614," *Fairfax Herald*, July 2, 1941, 5; "Fairfax School Attendance Up 1,200 in 5 Years," *Fairfax Herald*, July 18, 1940, 13; "Fairfax Fears Overcrowding of Schools, Teacher Shortage," *Fairfax Herald*, September 3, 1940, 13.

11 "$10,811,000,000 Asked for Arms; Roosevelt Calls for Utmost Effort," *Fairfax Herald*, January 9, 1941, 1.

12 "Cent Rise Due in Federal Tax on Gasoline," *Fairfax Herald*, April 19, 1941, 1.

13 "Economy Unit Formed; Byrd Is Chairman," *Fairfax Herald*, October 30, 1941, 1; Heinemann, *Harry Byrd*, 218–222.

14 "Agriculture Still Leads in Fairfax," *Washington Post*, June30, 1940, R10; "Drought Area Gloomy; Clear Skies Forecast," *Washington Post*, May 25, 1941, 8.

15 "VA Harvest Acreage Dips 2 Percent in Year," *Washington Post*, July 12, 1941, 11; "Driest Month in 57 Years Was September," *Washington Post*, October 1, 941, 17; "Shower Breaks Drought and Heat of 92 Degrees," *Washington Post*, October 2, 1941, 21; "Humid Heat Reaches 94; No Respite Is in Sight," *Washington Post*, October 7, 1941, 1; "Milk Scarcity Looms Here As Result Of Drought," *Washington Post*, October 9, 1941, 1; "Cool Weather Eases Milk Shortage Fear," *Washington Post*, October 10, 1941, 1.

CHAPTER 34

1 "$198,161,037 Gain Recorded in Metropolitan Area Building," *Washington Post*, January 1, 1942, F8.

2 David Brinkley, *Washington Goes to War* (New York: Alfred A. Knopf, 1988), 72–75.

3 Brinkley, *Washington*, 107; "New Alexandria Low-Cost Housing Project Is Opened," *Washington Post*, February 9, 1941, 21.

4 "Suburban Rent Ceiling Due July 1," *Washington Post*, June 23, 1942, 17; "Rent Freeze Will Cover Over 400,000," *Washington Post*, June 24, 1942, 21; "DC Suburb Rent Control Effective Tomorrow," *Washington Post*, June 30, 1942, 12; "Rents in DC Suburbs Cut to '41 Level," *Washington Post*, August 29, 1942, 1.

5 "$65,599,646 Spent on 1942 Homebuilding," *Washington Post*, November 22, 1942, R1; "Historic Arlington Is Hive of Wartime Housing," *Washington Post*, April 18, 1943, R4; Brinkley, *Washington*, 107.

6 Brinkley, *Washington*, 238; "4198,161,037 Gain Recorded in Metropolitan Area Building," *Washington Post*, January 2, 1942, F8.

7 "Housing Seen for Members of Congress," *Washington Post*, January 30, 1943, 36; "Fairlington to Be Ready about April 1," *Washington Post*, February 21, 1943, R1; "Agency Lists War Workers Rates," *Washington Post*, February 25, 1943, 11; "1000 War Worker Family Settles Down in Fairlington," *Washington Post*, August 29, 1943, M10; Brinkley, *Washington*, 237.

8 "New Building for 8 Months Shows Decline," *Washington Post*, September 21, 1943, R4; "11-Month Total Construction off 26 Million," *Washington Post*, December 19, 1943, R5; "DC Building Figures Show Drop for 1943," *Washington Post*, January 16, 1944, R4.

9 "House Votes 29 1/2 Million for Housing," *Washington Post*, April 30, 1942, 25; "Arlington Housing Project Awards $4,268,000 Contracts," *Washington Post*, September 21, 1942, 9; "Residence Hall Ready for First 200 Occupants," *Washington Post*, February 20, 1943, 31; "Government Girls Occupy New Dorm," *Washington Post*, April 2, 1943, B1; Brinkley, *Washington*, 108.

10 "Fairfax Has Substantial Construction Schedule," *Washington Post*, May 2, 1943, R4; Netherton, *Fairfax County*, 560.

11 "Pay Increase of $300 Year Pledged by Board for All Teachers in Fairfax County Schools," *Washington Post*, April 7, 1943, 15; "Fairfax Raises Pay $100 Each for Teachers," *Washington Post*, April 7, 1944, 4; "School Opens Next Week," *Fairfax Herald*, September 1, 1944, 1.

12 "Court to Hear Pay Appeal of Fairfax Sheriff," *Washington Post*, February 4, 1945, M4; "Sheriff's Pay Compromise Is Reached," *Washington Post*, February 18, 1945, M2.

13 "Funds Asked for Projects in DC Area," *Washington Post*, March 6, 1942, 21.

14 Netherton, *Fairfax County*, 560; "Zoning Ordinance Passed," *Fairfax Herald*, March 7, 1941, 1; "Area Building Volume Shows 1943 Decline," *Washington Post*, March 21, 1943, R1; "Hearing Is Set on Ordinance for

Fairfax," *Washington Post*, November 12, 1944, M5; "Fairfax Defers Subdivision Control Action," *Washington Post*, November 17, 1944, 8; "Fairfax Citizens Groups Approve Zoning Ordinances," *Washington Post*, November 30, 1944, 5; "Fairfax Zoning Ordinance Up Tomorrow," *Washington Post*, December 3, 1944, M4; "Fairfax Board Defers Zoning Act Revision," *Washington Post*, December 6, 1944, 4; "Fairfax Zoning Ordinance Up for Rehearing," *Washington Post*, December 12, 1944, 9; "Revision Hearings Delayed on Fairfax Zoning Ordinance," *Washington Post*, December 13, 1944, 5; "Hearing on Zoning Ordinance," *Fairfax Herald*, December 1, 1944, 1; "Opposed Zoning Ordinance," *Fairfax Herald*, December 8, 1944, 1; "Oppose Zoning Ordinance," *Fairfax Herald*, December 29, 1944, 1.

15 Ross and Nan Netherton, *Fairfax County in Virginia* (Norfolk and Virginia Beach, VA: Donning Company Publishers, 1986), 114.

16 Netherton, *Fairfax County*, 560; "Huge Hailstones Kill Poultry, Ruin Crops in Fairfax," *Washington Post*, May 5, 1942, 1; "Drought Acute in Maryland and Virginia," *Washington Post*, August 7, 1943, 1; "County Agent Report," *Fairfax Herald*, September 15, 1944, 1.

17 "All Will Be Lost Unless Heavy Rain Comes within 2 Days," *Washington Post*, August 19, 1943, 1; "Drought Brings Crop Loss of 1 1/2 Million to Nearby Farms," *Washington Post*, August 11, 1943, 11; "Nearby Farmers Map Appeal to WFA for Drought Relief," *Washington Post*, August 17, 1943, 1; "Drought Area Farmers Try to Sell Stock," *Washington Post*, August 20, 1943, B1.

18 "20 Needed in Fairfax," *Washington Post*, June 1, 1944, 7.

19 "Girls Have Fun and Corn Gets Planted," *Washington Post*, June 6, 1944, B6; "1944 Crop in Nearby States Estimated Below Last Years," *Washington Post*, July 31, 1944, 1.

20 "Fairfax Crops Suffer Severe Loss From Rain," *Washington Post*, July 29, 1945, M4; "Fairfax County to Seek Convict Labor on Farms," *Washington Post*, September 13, 1945, 4.

21 "Fairfax Farms Nearly Double Total in 1940," *Washington Post*, August 10, 1945, 5; "Northern VA Farm Census Is Completed," *Washington Post*, August 12, 1945, M3.

CHAPTER 35

1 "100 in VA Ask to Employ GIs for Training," *Washington Post*, March 18, 1946, 5.

2 “A Red Brick Bungalow by Summer,” *Washington Post*, March 1, 1946, 2.

3 “Bids to Be Opened Today on 6 US Housing Projects,” *Washington Post*, January 7, 1946, 12; “DHC Rejects 58 of Housing Bids as Foolish,” *Washington Post*, January 8, 1946, 1; “All Fairlington Bids Rejected Board Reveals,” *Washington Post*, February 13, 1946, 1; “Veteran’s Bid for Fairlington Is Rejected,” *Washington Post*, September 25, 1946, 6; “Public Housing Sale Clinched,” *Washington Post*, June 17, 1947, B3.

4 “Fairlington Now Looking to Tomorrow,” *Washington Post*, August 1, 1947, 16; “Fairlington Tenants Asked to Take Rent Hike,” *Washington Post*, November 22, 1947, 7.

5 “Arlington Rides Crest of Capital Overflow,” *Washington Post*, August 4, 1946, B1.

6 “Assessors Start Field Survey in Arlington,” *Washington Post*, February 28, 1946, 7.

7 “Population Growth in Nearby VA,” *Washington Post*, August 4, 1946, B1; “Shortage of Teachers Plagues Fairfax County Public Schools,” *Washington Post*, January 3, 1946, 4.

8 “Property Owners Protest Poor Fairfax Roads,” *Washington Post*, April 11, 1946, 14; “Fairfax Board Approves Two Housing Plans,” *Washington Post*, December 31, 1946, 7.

9 “Fast Road Net, Cheap Land Lure Builders to Fairfax County,” *Washington Post*, June 22, 1947, R1.

10 “Area-Wide Exhibition Rapidly Taking Shape Now,” *Washington Post*, July 22, 1951, R1.

11 “Ribbon Cutting Time in Vienna,” *Washington Post*, July 26, 1953, R1.

12 Netherton, Fairfax County, 595–596; “Henry G. Shirley Memorial Highway,” *Roads to the Future*, http://www.roadstothefuture.com/Shirley_Highway.html#Pentagon_Road_System.

13 “2,055,000 Bid Offered on VA Road Work,” *Washington Post*, June 22, 1946, 3; “Fairfax Acts Show Speed of Its Growth,” *Washington Post*, September 18, 1947, 15; “Paving Begun on Shirley Expressway,” *Washington Post*, February 7, 1947, M19.

14 “Vast Shirley Highway Area Awaits Development,” *Washington Post*, November 13, 1949, R1.

15 “H. G. Shirley Highway May Open September 6,” *Washington Post*, August 30, 1949, B1; “New Shirley Highway Closed to Allow Finishing Touches,” *Washington Post*, September 14, 1949, M6; “Shirley Road Saves Time, Test Reveals,” *Washington Post*, September 7, 1949, B1; “Shirley Highway Gets You There in a Breeze,” *Washington Post*, October 13, 1949, C2.

16 "Senators Plan for DC Belt Highway," *Washington Post*, March 8, 1951, 2; "Debate Set for Tuesday on Federal Dispersal," *Washington Post*, April 15, 1951, M17.

17 "Springfield, VA, Is One-Year, 385 Houses Old Today," *Washington Post*, February 15, 1953, R2.

18 "Need of Belt Highway Shown with DC Hub," *Washington Post*, June 14, 1951, B4; Netherton, Fairfax County, 595–596.

19 "Sen. Case to Seek DC Radial Route," *Washington Post*, January 21, 1952, 2; "Beall Seeks $36 Million Ring Highway in Area," *Washington Post*, February 15, 1952, 14.

20 Susan E. Jones, *Reston, Virginia: A New Town* (Reston, VA: Reston Historic Trust, 2010).

PHOTO CREDITS

CHAPTER 1

p. 3: Warner, John, Active, and Thomas Fairfax. *A survey of the northern neck of Virginia, being the lands belonging to the Rt. Honourable Thomas Lord Fairfax Baron Cameron, bounded by & within the Bay of Chesapoyocke and between the rivers Rappahannock and Potowmack: With the courses of the rivers Rappahannock and Potowmack, in Virginia, as surveyed according to order in the years& 1737.* [N.P., 1747] Map. https://www.loc.gov/item/99446122/.

p. 5: Courtesy of Shirley Plantation.

p. 6: Lord Fairfax Horydczak, Theodor, Approximately, photographer. *Paintings. Lord Fairfax VI, Masonic Lodge, Alexandria II.* United States Alexandria Virginia, None. ca. 1920-ca. 1950. Photograph. https://www.loc.gov/item/2019683094/.

CHAPTER 2

p. 8: *Tobacco Processing; Curing, Storing, Barreling and Selling.* 1800. Photograph. https://www.loc.gov/item/2002723409/.

p. 10: "*An Historical and Practical Essay on the Culture and Commerce of Tobacco.*" William Tatham. http://hdl.loc.gov/loc.pnp/cph.3a15205.

CHAPTER 3

p. 14: Washington, George. *A plan of Alexandria, now Belhaven.* [1749] Map. https://www.loc.gov/item/98687108/.

p. 16: Historic American Buildings Survey, Creator. *John Carlyle House, 123 North Fairfax Street, Alexandria, Independent City, VA.* Alexandria Virginia Independent City, 1933.

p. 17. Fairfax County Record of Surveys 1742-1856. Fairfax Circuit Court Historic Records.

p. 19: Parkyns, George Isham, Approximately 1820, Artist. *View of the suburbs of the city of Washington.* Washington D.C. Georgetown, ca. 1795. Photograph. https://www.loc.gov/item/2002695106/.

CHAPTER 4

p. 22: Historic American Buildings Survey, Creator, and John Wise. *Mason's Ordinary Coffee House, 128 North Royal Street, Alexandria, Independent City, VA.* Alexandria Virginia Independent City, 1933. Documentation Compiled After. Photograph. https://www.loc.gov/item/va0163/.

p. 30: Historic American Buildings Survey, Creator, and John Davis. *Colchester Inn, 2 Old Colchester Road, Lorton, Fairfax County, VA.* Lorton Virginia Fairfax County, 1933. Documentation Compiled After. Photograph. https://www.loc.gov/item/va0432/.

CHAPTER 5

p. 32: Virginia Room, Fairfax County Public Library.

p. 38: Carlyle House, NOVA Parks.

p. 41: Washington, George. *A map of General Washington's farm of Mount Vernon from a drawing transmitted by the General.* [S.l, 1801] Map. https://www.loc.gov/item/99466780/.

CHAPTER 6

p. 50: L'Enfant, Pierre Charles, and Thackara & Vallance. *Plan of the city of Washington.* [Philadelphia: s.n, 1792] Map. https://www.loc.gov/item/88694159/.

CHAPTER 7

p. 55: Canal Lock, LOC-pnp habshaer-va-va1400-va1445-photos-161528pv.jpg

p. 61: Great Falls Historical Society, Virginia Room, Fairfax County Library.

CHAPTER 8

p. 64: J. Harry Shannon, "The Rambler." Virginia Room, Fairfax County Public Library.

p. 69: Dranesville Tavern, Great Falls Historical Society, Virginia Room, Fairfax County Library.

CHAPTER 9

p. 74: Colvin Run Mill, Great Falls Historical Society, Virginia Room, Fairfax County Library.

p. 78: Alexandria, Virginia. Slave pen. Price, Birch & Co. dealers in slaves. United States, None. [Between 1861 and 1869] Photograph. https://www.loc.gov/item/2018670631/.

p. 83: Smith, William Morris, photographer. *Washington, D.C. The Aqueduct bridge and Georgetown from the Virginia bank*. Washington D.C. United States District of Columbia Washington D.C, None. [Between 1860 and 1865] Photograph. https://www.loc.gov/item/2018667024/.

CHAPTER 10

p. 88: Sharon Plantation Plan, Southern Claims Commission Case File #21622 1877, National Archives.

p. 89: *Bailey's Cross Roads, Va*. United States Bailey's Crossroads Virginia, None. [Photographed between 1861 and 1865, printed between 1880 and 1889] Photograph. https://www.loc.gov/item/2013651895/.

p. 91: J. Harry Shannon, "The Rambler." Virginia Room, Fairfax County Public Library.

CHAPTER 11

p. 95: Barnard & Gibson, Copyright Claimant, Barnard, George N, photographer. *Departure from the old homestead, Centreville "And trembling, shrinking from the spoilers hand, far, far away, thy children leave the land."* United States, Centreville Virginia, 1862. [New York: E. & H.T. Anthony, 501 Broadway] Photograph. https://www.loc.gov/item/2016651687/.

p. 96 (top): Brady's National Photographic Portrait Galleries, photographer. *Chain Bridge/Brady's National Photographic Portrait Galleries, Broadway & Tenth Street, New York & No. 352 Pennsylvania Ave., Washington, D.C.* Washington D.C. Arlington Virginia United States, None. [New York; Washington, D.C.: Brady's National Photographic Portrait Galleries, Broadway & Tenth Street; no. 352, Pennsylvania Ave., between 1861 and 1865] Photograph. https://www.loc.gov/item/2016651685/.

p. 96 (bottom): *Mansion House, Alexandria, Va.* United States Alexandria Virginia, None. [Photographed between 1861 and 1865, printed between 1880 and 1889] Photograph. https://www.loc.gov/item/2014645767/.

p. 97: Library of Congress, Matthew Brady.

p. 98: Civil War photographs, 1861-1865, Library of Congress, Prints and Photographs Division.

p. 100: J. Harry Shannon, "The Rambler." Virginia Room, Fairfax County Public Library.

p. 102: Civil War photographs, 1861-1865, Library of Congress, Prints and Photographs.

CHAPTER 12

p. 106: Civil War photographs, 1861-1865, Library of Congress, Prints and Photographs Division.

p. 108: Orange and Alexandria Railroad Repair at Devereaux Station, Andrew J. Russell, photographer, Library of Congress Prints and Photographs Division Washington, D.C. 20540 USA. http://hdl.loc.gov/loc.pnp/pp.print

p. 110: Fairfax County Board of Supervisors. *Industrial and historical sketch of Fairfax County, Virginia.* [Falls Church, Va., Newell, 1907] Pdf. https://www.loc.gov/item/07038074/.

p. 111: Virginia Room, Fairfax County Public Library.

CHAPTER 13

p. 116: Andrew J Russell, photographer. Library of Congress Prints and Photographs Division Washington, D.C. 20540 USA.

p. 117: Fairfax County Board of Supervisors. *Industrial and historical sketch of Fairfax County, Virginia.* [Falls Church, Va., Newell, 1907] pdf. https://www.loc.gov/item/07038074/.

p. 118: Hopkins, Griffith Morgan, Jr. *Atlas of fifteen miles around Washington, including the counties of Fairfax and Alexandria, Virginia.* Philadelphia: G.M. Hopkins, 1879, 1879. Map. https://www.loc.gov/item/map53000779/.

p. 119: Hopkins, Griffith Morgan, Jr. *Atlas of fifteen miles around Washington, including the counties of Fairfax and Alexandria, Virginia.* Philadelphia: G.M. Hopkins, 1879, 1879. Map. https://www.loc.gov/item/map53000779/.

p. 120: Library of Congress Prints and Photographs Division Washington, D.C. 20540 USA http://hdl.loc.gov/loc.pnp/pp.print.

CHAPTER 14

p. 125: Library of Congress, HABS VA,30-MCLA.V,1–2.

p. 126: Virginia Room, Fairfax County Public Library.

p. 128: Fairfax County Board of Supervisors. *Industrial and historical sketch of Fairfax County, Virginia.* [Falls Church, Va., Newell, 1907] pdf. https://www.loc.gov/item/07038074/.

p. 129: Detroit Publishing Co., Copyright Claimant, and Publisher Detroit Publishing Co. *Trolley station, Mt. Vernon, Va.* United States Mount Vernon Estate Mount Vernon Estate Virginia, None. [between 1910 and 1920] Photograph. https://www.loc.gov/item/2016812316/.

CHAPTER 15

p. 136: Great Falls Historical Society, Virginia Room, Fairfax County Public Library.

p. 138: Author's personal collection.

p. 139: J. Berkley Green Collection, Herndon Historical Society.

p. 140: Frank Lyon, Courtesy of Steve Jones.

p. 142: Arlington County Public Library.

CHAPTER 16

p. 146: Falls Church RR Station Virginia Room, Fairfax County Public Library.

p. 148: Gasch Collection, Virginia Room, Fairfax County Public Library.

p. 150: Rosslyn Trolley Station, c. 1908, Library of Congress.

p. 152: Virginia Department of Highways.

CHAPTER 17

p. 156: *The Evening Star,* April 5, 1915, Library of Congress.

p. 158: Courtesy of Carolyn Cornwell Miller.

CHAPTER 18

p. 163: Harris & Ewing, photographer. *FORT MYER OFFICERS TRAINING CAMP.* United States, Virginia, Fort Myer, 1917. Photograph. https://www.loc.gov/item/2016867852/.

p. 164: United States Army. Quartermaster Corps, Hoffman & Lane, photographer. *Virginia Shipbuilding Corporation's fleet of heavy duty White trucks which aided in making a record for shipyard construction/ Hoffman & Lane, commercial photography, Cleveland.* Alexandria Virginia, 1918. Photograph. https://www.loc.gov/item/2002697560/.

p. 166: Paus, Herbert Andrew, Artist. *The Woman's Land Army of America—Training school, University of Virginia—Apply Woman's*

Land Army, U.S. Employment Service, Richmond, Va./Herbert Paus. United States, ca. 1918. Photograph. https://www.loc.gov/item/97520484/.

CHAPTER 19

p. 170: J. Harry Shannon, "The Rambler." Virginia Room, Fairfax County Public Library.

p. 171: Harris & Ewing, photographer. *FORT HUMPHRIES. ARMY POST IN VIRGINIA. NARROW GAUGE ROAD ON RIVER BANK.* United States Fort Humphries Virginia, 1917. Photograph. https://www.loc.gov/item/2016869298/.

p. 172: Harris & Ewing, photographer. *FORT HUMPHRIES. ARMY POST IN VIRGINIA. WORKING IN THE CAMP.* United States Fort Humphries Virginia, 1917. Photograph. https://www.loc.gov/item/2016869301/.

p. 173: Harris & Ewing, photographer. *FORT HUMPHRIES. ARMY POST IN VIRGINIA. TENT ENCAMPMENT.* United States Fort Humphries Virginia, 1917. Photograph. https://www.loc.gov/item/2016869302/.

CHAPTER 20

p. 178: *Market, Wash. D.C., World War I period.* United States Washington D.C. District of Columbia Washington D.C, None. [Between 1910 and 1920] Photograph. https://www.loc.gov/item/2016824435/.

p. 181: Leyendecker, J. C., Artist, and Funder/Sponsor United States Fuel Administration. *Order coal now/J.C. Leyendecker.* United States, 1918. [Chicago: Edwards & Deutsch Litho] Photograph. https://www.loc.gov/item/95500966/.

p. 182: Hine, Lewis Wickes, photographer. Library of Congress.

p. 183: Hine, Lewis Wickes, photographer, Library of Congress.

CHAPTER 21

p. 186: *Demonstration at the Red Cross Emergency Ambulance Station in Washington, D.C., during the influenza pandemic of.* United States Washington D.C. District of Columbia Washington D.C, 1918. Photograph. https://www.loc.gov/item/2016844534/.

p. 190 (top): Jesse Smith, courtesy of Karen Grasso.

p. 190 (bottom): J. Berkley, Green Collection of the Herndon Historical Society.

p. 191: Great Falls Historical Society collection, Virginia Room, Fairfax County Library.

CHAPTER 22

p. 195: Fairfax Police Historic Association.

p. 196: Author's personal collection.

p. 198: *Lyon Park, Va.* United States Arlington Virginia, None. [Between 1921 and 1922] Photograph. https://www.loc.gov/item/2016823810/.

p. 199: *Cherrydale house, Arlington, Virginia.* United States Arlington Virginia, None. [Between 1920 and 1921] Photograph. https://www.loc.gov/item/2016823446/.

CHAPTER 23

p. 202: *The Sunday Star,* April 25, 1920, Library of Congress.

p. 203: Harris & Ewing, photographer. *LINCOLN MEMORIAL BRIDGE. UNDER CONSTRUCTION.* Washington D.C. Washington D.C. District of Columbia United States, None. [Between 1905 and 1945] Photograph. https://www.loc.gov/item/2016861895/.

p. 204: *The Evening Star,* Washington D.C., August 7, 1926, Library of Congress.

p. 206: *The Evening Star,* June 19, 1927, Library of Congress.

CHAPTER 24

p. 211: Library of Congress, https://www.loc.gov/pictures/item/2016825057/.

p. 213: Author's personal collection.

p. 216: Library of Congress, https://www.loc.gov/pictures/item/2016862575.

CHAPTER 25

p. 219: Virginia Room, Fairfax County Public Library.

CHAPTER 26

p. 226: Courtesy of Carolyn Cornwell Miller.

p. 229: *The Evening Star,* Washington, D.C. August 22, 1931.

p. 231: *The Evening Star,* May 18, 1929, May 18, 1929.

p. 233: Library of Congress, http://hdl.loc.gov/loc.pnp/pp.fsaowi.

p. 234: Fairfax Hunt, Author's personal collection.

p. 236: Copyright, Wolf Trap Foundation for the Performing Arts.

CHAPTER 27

p. 243: *The Evening Star*, September 24, 1932.

p. 245: Fairfax Police Historic Association.

CHAPTER 28

p. 250: Library of Congress.

p. 256: Fairfax Police Historic Association.

CHAPTER 29

p. 264: J. Harry Shannon, "The Rambler."Virginia Room, Fairfax County Public Library.

p. 265: Author's personal collection.

CHAPTER 30

p. 273: Library of Congress, https://www.loc.gov/pictures/item/2010650603/.

p. 274: Library of Congress, https://www.loc.gov/pictures/item/97520475/.

CHAPTER 31

p. 278: *The Evening Star,* March 16, 1936, Library of Congress.

p. 282: Leiter Mansion Virginia Room, Fairfax County Library.

p. 283: *The Evening Star*, October 31, 1936, Library of Congress.

CHAPTER 32

p. 292: Library of Congress Historic American Buildings Survey, Creator. *Buckingham Apartment Complex, Building No. 12, 4009, 4011 Fifth Street North, Arlington, Arlington County, VA*. Arlington Virginia Arlington County, 1933. Documentation Compiled After. Photograph. https://www.loc.gov/item/va1717/.

p. 293: Library of Congress Historic American Buildings Survey, Creator, Henry Wright, and Sponsor Arlington Heritage Alliance. *Buckingham Apartment Complex, Bounded by George Mason Drive, Henderson, Glebe, & Pershing Roads, Arlington, Arlington County, VA*. Arlington Virginia, Arlington County, 1933. translated by Price, Virginia B. Mitter Documentation Compiled After. Photograph. https://www.loc.gov/item/va1716/.

CHAPTER 33

p. 296: *The Evening Star*, October 22, 1938, Library of Congress.

p. 298: *The Evening Star*, September 14, 1940, Library of Congress.

p. 300: *The Evening Star* June 28, 1941, Library of Congress.

p. 302: Library of Congress, https://www.loc.gov/pictures/item/2017806921/.

CHAPTER 34

p. 306: Library of Congress, https://www.loc.gov/pictures/item/2021640398/.

p. 307: Library of Congress, https://www.loc.gov/pictures/item/2017822344/.

p. 308: Library of Congress, https://www.loc.gov/pictures/item/2018742551/.

p. 309: Library of Congress, https://www.loc.gov/pictures/item/2017765411/.

p. 310: Library of Congress, https://www.loc.gov/pictures/item/2017854117/.

p. 312: Library of Congress, https://www.loc.gov/pictures/item/2017822418/.

CHAPTER 35

p. 321: *The Evening Star,* May 24, 1952, Library of Congress.

p. 322: Virginia Department of Transportation.

INDEX

Note: Page numbers in italics indicate figures, **bold** *indicates tables in the text, and references following "n" refer to notes.*

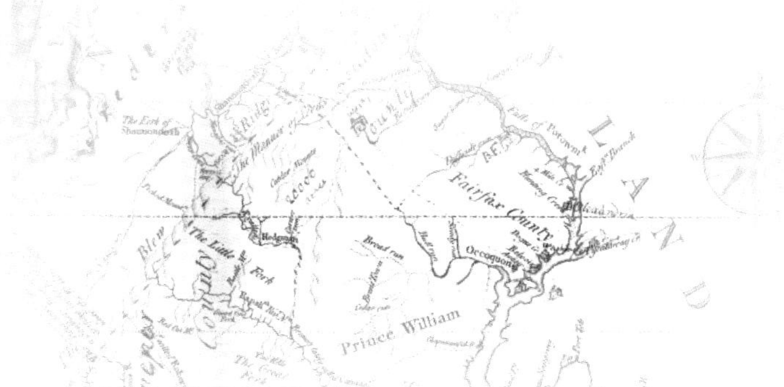

ABOUT THE AUTHOR

Karen Washburn has been researching and interpreting Northern Virginia history for forty years.

She is a Realtor and an independent historian and consultant for private individuals and projects funded by government grants. Her research has been part of multiple National Register nominations and she has negotiated multiple easements to protect historic buildings.

Washburn has served as president of the Great Falls Historical Society (1979-81), Fairfax County History Commissioner (1997-2005), and chair of the Fairfax County History Commission for two terms.

She wrote local history articles for *Elan* Magazine for twelve years, holds a degree in history from Roanoke College, and has received awards for Northern Virginia history preservation projects.